W9-DII-881

AUSTRALIAN CINEMA IN THE 1990s

Books of Related Interest

Australian Cinema in the 1990s

Editor

IAN CRAVEN

FRANK CASS
LONDON • PORTLAND, OR

First published in 2001 in Great Britain by
FRANK CASS PUBLISHERS
Newbury House, 900 Eastern Avenue, London IG2 7HH

and in the United States of America by
FRANK CASS PUBLISHERS
c/o ISBS, 5824 N.E. Hassalo Street
Portland, Oregon 97213-3644

Website www.frankcass.com

British Library Cataloguing in Publication Data

Australian cinema in the 1990s
1. Motion pictures – Australia 2. Motion pictures, Australian
I. Craven, Ian
791.4'3'0994'09049

ISBN 0 7146 4974 0 (cloth)
ISBN 0 7146 8034 6 (paper)

Library of Congress Cataloging-in-Publication Data:

Australian cinema in the 1990s / editor, Ian Craven.
p. cm.
Includes bibliographical references and index.
ISBN 0-7146-4974-0 (cloth) – ISBN 0-7146-8034-6 (pbk.)
1. Motion pictures–Australia–History. I. Craven, Ian.

PN1993.5.A8 A953 2001
791.43'0994–dc21

00-060177

This group of studies first appeared in a special issue of
Australian Studies, ISSN 0954-0954, Vol.14, Nos.1&2 (Summer/Winter, 1999)
published by Frank Cass and Co. Ltd.

Printed in Great Britain by Antony Rowe Ltd., Chippenham, Wiltshire

Contents

Australian Cinema Towards the Millennium

IAN CRAVEN

The history of the 'new' Australian Cinema's revival since the 1970s often now feels like a relatively settled one. A range of studies chart the political cultures which talked the 'renaissance' into being, the institutional frameworks which guided production or formulated policy,[1] and survey the eventual output of a growing number of state-backed and independent producers.[2] Significant contributions, of course, to the revision of the critical literatures continue to be made, recognising shifts of commercial and aesthetic direction in the 1980s, and locating the various 'hidden' histories overlooked in the critical project of constructing a 'national' Australian cinema.[3] Such work on the mainstream cinema has triggered research on more neglected areas such as the non-fiction film, the short film, and the experimental and avant-garde sectors. Scholarship across the board has helped stimulate a conspicuous intensification, since the 1980s, of attention to Australian television.[4]

The essays collected in this volume seek to extend this work with reference to the 1990s, by offering a series of overlapping but distinct perspectives on Australian cinema of the past decade, and sketching possible directions for its development beyond the coming Millennium. Attention is given to cinema at every stage of its movement from conception to consumption, and close readings of particular movies, or clusters of movies, are balanced by more contextual work on issues of industry, policy, criticism and reception. Taken together, the essays suggest something of the remarkable diversity of the feature output since 1990, and the challenges that this body of film poses to the critical and theoretical paradigms through which the work of Australian filmmakers has come to be understood both within and without the academy.

The sequencing of contributions aims to suggest the outlines of residual and emergent trends, and to clarify recurrent themes in the output. If the cinema of the 1970s has come to be understood broadly in terms of a national 'project' driven by intellectualist-managerialist impulses, and underwritten by a regime of formal regulation and public subsidy,[5] and the 1980s has been characterised as an era of de-regulation, encroachment by the market, and a new commercialism aesthetics,[6] the 1990s might well be viewed as a period marked by *re*-regulation at the levels of both text and context, and by structures and discourses fusing nostalgia for the heady days of the nationalist 'renaissance' with a futuristic open-ness to the possibilities of the global. Both impulses of course have their counter-tendencies; one need not look far through Australian cinema of the 1990s to identify evidences of scepticism around the once-confident articulation of cultural nationalism with political progressiveness, and of millennial anxiety generating more than a fair share of suitably apocalyptic narratives.

The conflicting trends are contextualised initially here by scrutiny of the film industry's performance and structure, which reveals dramatic shifts in fortune, and almost constantly changing patterns of ownership and control. The picture in terms of policy-making and implementation is equally dynamic. No national film industry on earth seems to have been subject to more constant surveillance, re-definition and re-direction than the Australian; reconstructions of the government film's instrumentality following consultancy reports, position papers and counter-manifestos became almost seasonal at times during the 1990s, and instabilities at these discursive levels played a crucial role in delineating the product eventually reaching movie theatres. Lisa French provides an informative account of the production sector since 1990, with reference to the key policy documents generated, the responses of filmmakers and financiers, and the performance of the industry which they helped to shape. As the hard statistical data indicates, Australian feature-filmmaking remained a fragile enterprise in the 1990s, and the conspicuousness of a small number of films at the international box office often concealed a production sector struggling to find a secure route through distribution to reach audiences still demonstrating a consumer preference for imported, usually American, movies.[7] The few 'breakthrough' pictures of the decade, around which the history of the Australian cinema seems certain to be extended, efface numerous other works whose significance awaits assessment.[8]

The picture of the industry in the 1990s which French delineates does much to explain the unevenness of the output, which often seems to exhibit little consistency beyond its insistence upon the idiosyncratic, despite sporadic critical attempts to detect a unifying sensibility, preoccupation or aesthetic.[9] Tom O'Regan however provides a useful starting-point for understanding this manifest diversity, when he suggests that: 'The history of Australian film is largely a history of the combinations of possible projects, and an indication of which of these are ascendant', and remarks that the conditions generating these 'combinations' include:

> the nature of state support offered, the policy framework for delivering it, the extent to which talented film workers concentrate in an area, the international opportunities available in commercial and critical terms through working in a film form, and the critical celebration of this or that film-making.[10]

In their various ways, the essays included here work to track such 'combinations', often in very localised contexts, and to indicate the relationship between such conjunctural forces and a wider socio-political culture unifiable at other levels.

Late-National Cinema?

By the late 1980s, a number of commentators were already speculating about the disintegration of the 'project' which had driven both national-cultural revivalism and national-commercial entrepreneurialism since the 1970s.[11] In their essay here on 'The Heterosexual Dynamic', Nigel Spence and Leah McGirr track some of the thematic shifts which have accompanied this re-definition of Australian filmmaking, and focus in particular on the rise of a personal-relations cinema occupying a somewhat marginal space in the earlier output. As the emblematic landscapes of the 1970s and 1980s have given way to the more banal locales of the 1990s, the authors see the preoccupations of Australian narratives contracting towards a closer concern with inter-personal, especially inter-gender relations. Both a recognition of absence in the earlier output, and a desire to match the narrative standards of the international marketplace are seen as triggering the 'turn' in the 1980s, which develops and becomes more complicated in the 1990s. Starting with higher-profile movies such as *The Year My Voice Broke* (1987), the impulse is seen as finding expression in later works such as *The Last Days of Chez Nous* (1992), *The Sum of Us* (1994), *Love Serenade* (1995) and many others. The significance of the analysis in this context is that it begins to chart a fresh history of Australian cinema in terms of genres, and more specifically, views an exploration of the heterosexual dynamic as cutting across the more teleological trajectories of the rites-of-passage sub-texts which have so often underpinned the exploration of character in Australian cinema, to encourage new structures, styles and definitions of Australian filmmaking. This unhinging of self-formation from national-formation is explored across a range of exemplary movies which chart wider movements from 'realist' to 'generic' filmmaking apparent in the 1990s output. If Spence and McGirr reach fairly pessimistic conclusions about the possibilities for creative relations between the sexes suggested by Australian cinema in the 1990s ('a relationship's deterioration [is] regarded as some kind of grim inevitability'), they also chart some fundamentally different preoccupations for a 'late' national cinema.

Creativity stands at the very centre of the works examined by Liz Ferrier in her essay on 'Vulnerable Bodies'. Noting the conspicuousness within the output of movies such as *Proof* (1991), *Bad Boy Bubby* (1994), and *Shine* (1995), centred on embattled artists or performers struggling for recognition and excellence, Ferrier develops an analysis of such films in relation to Australian cultural traditions, which offers a suggestive commentary on contemporary economic conditions. Her study stresses the protagonists' progression from isolation to recognition, and notes the generative axis constructed within the films between elements of the dysfunctional within the family, and their protagonists' subsequent creativity and acceptance. Understood in these terms, the films offer little resistance to a reading as discourses on Australian cinema's own imaginary, and are readily distilled as promises of reconciliation between industrial and aesthetic imperatives largely antagonistic in the 1980s. Ferrier's essay however re-locates such contradictions on new ground, and its attention to the body as a site of discursive conflict re-introduces a discussion of performance in Australian cinema often neglected by a concern with narrative structure and visual style shown in the recent scholarship. Most of the films under analysis here function as enabling contexts for virtuoso performances, narratively motivated as eccentricity, disability, or less specific indexes of a de-stabilising personal history, but also suggesting, amongst other things, a continuing intimacy between Australian cinema and theatrical traditions that has received surprisingly little attention within accounts of Australian movie-making.[12] Ferrier's attention to these performances is suggestive of the issues embedded within them, and of their sophisticated transcodings of socio-cultural concerns with market viability into discourses of aestheticism and creativity. Clearly her analysis of the *faux-naive* innocence seen as preoccupying Australian narrative in the 1990s, could be extended to incorporate a number of other movies not touched upon here, such as *Stan and George's New Life* (1992), *Hotel Sorrento* (1994) and *Mr Reliable* (1996).

Ferrier's characterisation of the 'soft' male body within 1990s cinema is clearly suggestive of profound re-definitions of male identity taking place in the output under consideration here. The stigmatisation of the male protagonist which she notes in *Proof* and *Shine* is also a common motif in the films examined by Philip Butterss' essay on constructions of masculinity in recent Australian cinema, where it is linked expressly to a diminishing 'will to power' associated with shifts characteristic of a post-industrial and post-feminist society. What is striking about his analyses of *The Big Steal* (1990), *Death in Brunswick* (1991), *Strictly Ballroom* (1992) and *The Heartbreak Kid* (1993), is their revelation of the movies' residual commitment to highly-mythologised gender definitions, alongside a tangible awareness of the social inter-texts which may compromise the effectivity of their representational preferences for actual cinema-goers. Butterss reveals suggestively the various ways in which the films work (via ludicrous comedy, an appeal to generic convention, narrative 'sleights of hand', or even an insistence on the very exceptionalism of their representations) to resolve these contradictions, and the aesthetic effects of such transcodings between the social and the textual. In the process the essay underlines the centrality of the oedipal trajectory noted elsewhere,[13] which unifies their narratives, and indeed the more specific project of 're-masculinisation' they develop in response to contemporary crises in gender identifies and roles. The framing of 'mateship' as a developmental stage necessarily renounced *en route* to adulthood perhaps suggests more specifically Australian 'accents' within narratives with clear counterparts in both British and American cinema of the same decade.[14]

Post-National Cinema?

Consensus seemed to exist amongst commentators on Australian cinema by the mid-1990s that even the residual elements of 1970s cultural nationalism had now finally dissolved. Charting a history of policy discourse which increasingly refuses to recognise the national as a basis for defence of the industry, or offer a justification for the subsidy of cultural-nationalist fiction-building, a growing body of writing constructed Australian cinema as distinctly post-national. Noting a tendency at more representational levels to address experience of the local or regional, rather than the national, this work suggested new divisions within constituencies once united in their polemic for national cinema. Some regretted the apparent dismissal of the national as a category and argued for its retention on the basis of its potential inclusiveness,[15] others welcomed the dissolution of the category, as heralding a new pluralism, in keeping with the increasingly diverse composition of Australian society, traditionally unrecognised by a national tradition overly concerned with the fabrication of a metonymic Australian masculinity, an ethnic and racial exclusiveness, and an account of progressive politics limited by the assumptions around radicalism as authenticity.[16]

Anxieties about the serviceability of the national category are explored by essays here which examine the narrativisation of Australian anxieties at a variety of often overlapping levels. One of the most problematical connections established for example, almost incidentally, in Butterss' essay is that between gender and ethnic identity made in movies such as *Death in Brunswick* or *The Heartbreak Kid*, which attribute particularly traditional definitions of masculinity to Hispano- and Graeco-Australian males, respectively. Patriarchal authority and sexual machismo often find their fullest embodiment in non-Anglo-Celtic characters on the Australian cinema screen. Whilst the tendency to conflate such definitions of ethnic and gender 'authenticity' is apparent on a wider scale across the 1990s output as a whole ('new' Australian men are often constructed as 'preserving' masculine behavioural conventions either discredited or under severe pressure in the wider culture), the films under specific scrutiny offer a particular distillation of ideological positions, which draws heavily upon their characterisations of ethnicity. *Nirvana Street Murder* (1991) and *Aya* (1991) offer just two of many other examinations of this 'overlapping' of differences which would repay exploration along these lines. In David Callahan's contribution here, a wider take is made on the cinema's figuring out of ethnic presence, in an essay which foregrounds a number of movies which have received very little critical attention, and triangulates between concerns with Aboriginality, whiteness and new 'migrant' ethnicities which rarely find connection.[17]

Callahan's essay provides a refreshingly functional analysis of ethnic presence in Australian film narrative, concentrating on questions of structural position rather then representational adequacy, and on presence as a an effective and simultaneous experience of activation/concealment, alluding to histories and memories, that maintains a principle of deniability crucial to the ideological management of Australian narratives of the nation in general, but with a particular pertinence to storytelling on film and television.[18] Rather than noting again the apparent reluctance the Australian cinema has shown in acknowledging ethnic diversity within the nation, Callahan argues for the necessity of such presences to the discourse of 'belonging' still central to the project of Australian cinema in the wake of the cultural-nationalist 'push' of the 1970s: 'non-Aboriginal ethnicities provide welcome material through which belonging can be dealt with as a theme' without engaging more problematical questions of entitlement raised by white-Aboriginal relations. At the same time he echoes Butterss' stress on the qualification of critique, in for example, noting *Strictly Ballroom*'s selection of the Spanish, rather than say, the Japanese, as its representatives of an alternative ethnicity to the Australian 'norm'. Signs of greater change are evident however: movies such as *Death in Brunswick* evidence a positional democracy, in which ethnicity itself is regarded as a universal condition of presence, and specific constituencies are detailed by gradations of class and the particularities of gender. Crucially, for Callahan, these ethnicities are experienced as much as liabilities as anchors to otherwise unstable senses of identity, lending support to framings of these works as at least 'yearning' for the post-national, whilst resisting the obliteration of all ethnic presence suggested by movies such as *The Custodian* (1993), or *Love and Other Catastrophes* (1996). As a counter, Callahan argues for the necessity of an attention within criticism to 'whiteness' as an ethnic identity constructed in relation to its significant others. One need look no further than a film such as *Romper Stomper* (1992) in order to recognise both the very real problems of attempting such a turn on celluloid, and of the necessity of doing so if the disabling and silencing 'postcolonial ethnic diffidence', of which Callahan writes, is to be avoided.

Several of the essays included here allow some force to environment in their accounts of emerging 'national' tendencies, alongside the more usual qualifying factors of class and gender, and a more cultural-geographical emphasis is intermittently visible in much recent writing on Australian cinema. According to the movies Callahan examines for example, it is in the city, apparently, that ethnic presence seems most tangible, as trigger to narrative conflict, or visual guarantor of cultural exactitude. This emphasis on place is developed further by Ben Goldsmith in his analysis of a suburban consciousness in 1990s cinema, which still demands further exploration.[19] Goldsmith allows suburbia a presence in the films under analysis that exceeds its more classical functions as location in mainstream filmmaking, ie. as narrative *mise-en-scène*, visual spectacle or guarantee of the reality of the events depicted. In the process, Callahan's characterisation of 1990s cinema as practising an 'enclave politics' whose 'principal moral centre consists in shoring up the enclave against the social, the individual against the public, the group against the wider polity', finds a spatial counterpart in Goldsmith's focus on the local, so often constructed as refuge from the bewildering topographies of the outback, the city or the wider world in recent Australian cinema.

For Goldsmith, a recognition of the local, and an emphasis on that specifically suburban version of that local in which so many Australian cinema-goers actually live out their lives, helped Australian movie-makers to re-connect with the domestic audience in the 1990s. Often taking its cue from the theatre, which had maintained a closer connection with the suburban scene, the cinema began to generate movies such as *Hotel Sorrento* (1994), *Blackrock* (1997), which spoke more directly to popular experience than the trans-Pacific fare often favoured by producers in the 1980s. Indexing the shifting policy expectations detailed earlier by Lisa French, Australian cinema began to address constituencies effaced in the drive towards the national representation, to propel micro-narratives set within micro-geographies, to relish eccentricity rather than the emblematic, and to refuse the whole burden of representativeness with which cinema had been saddled in the 1970s. Ironically, of course, in doing so, the invocation of suburbia, often seems to have touched upon a sense of national 'authenticity' which had functioned as something of a Holy Grail for the 'official' cinema of the 1970s.

Goldsmith identifies *Metal Skin* (1995), *Idiot Box* (1996) and *The Castle* (1997) as instances of 'noise' within the communications system of Australian national cinema, and generates analyses which are developed in later essays in this collection along rather different lines. Goldsmith's stress is on the 'disturbances' of these films, both formal and mythological, and their tendency towards the 'abjection' of their audiences, via a refusal of secure vantage points and narrative positions, dramatised as much at the level of sound as image. The acoustic dimensions of Australian film style have rarely been addressed in critical writing, and Goldsmith's essay makes a suggestive intervention in this area.[20] These are 'noisy' films in every sense, dramatic networks of tangled communications and half-established propositions, unresolved contradictions and highly ironised narrations. *Metal Skin* emerges as one of the bleakest texts of the 1990s output 'the wail of the repressed, patient, unloved finally demanding to be heard', whose aim is the absorption of its audiences into its own dystopian nightmare. *Idiot Box*, on the other hand, is at least modestly optimistic, 'the characters are at home in their environment, although this is not to say that they do not long to escape… ', whilst *The Castle* is unashamedly populist and nostalgic, 'In many ways the family stands for a core set of values more suited to the 1950s than the 1990s'. The range of different responses to tangibly common issues in the three films ('place and placelessness, home and homelessness

... ') is thus suggestive of suburbia's importance as a catalyst for the generation of 'noise' within the representational system as a whole.

No collection of writing on Australian cinema in the 1990s could claim coverage without offering attention to the three films which, more than any others, reacquainted audiences around the world with Australian production during the first half of the decade. For Emily Rustin, *Strictly Ballroom* (1992), *The Adventures of Priscilla, Queen of The Desert* (1994), and *Muriel's Wedding* (1994) suggested something of a stylistic trend, 'popularly termed the "glitter cycle" on account of their luminescent and colourful visual style', and a critique of national narrative traditions symptomatic of specifically millennial anxieties, and troubled senses of identity in general. All three films have attracted considerable critical attention,[21] which Rustin's essay surveys carefully before allowing her own account of the films to emerge. The stress here is on revisions of inherited narrative traditions, the apparent *limits* of those revisionary impulses, the regional dimensions of the narratives (in particular the presentation of Queensland as 'other' to preferred constructions of Australia, in *Muriel's Wedding*) and the exploration of aesthetic modes which transcend the respectable codes of 'official' realism. Her recognition of the necessity of fantasy underlined in these films, is clearly suggestive beyond their boundaries, and finds an echo in those accounts of Australian economics and politics which have also identified the new rhetorical force of fantasy in the wider Australian public culture.[22]

Of all the movies produced in recent years, perhaps *Babe: The Gallant Pig* (1995), represents the clearest distillation of the turn towards fantasy advocated in the 'glitter' pictures. In her study of the film, Tara Brabazon identifies the movie with a 'de-territorialisation' of Australian cinema, a term suggesting movement away from primitive preoccupations with the tracing of national roots in the soil, towards a fascination with more virtual geographies which deliberately frustrate attempts at specification; 'the New World Order relies on a landscape that is magical rather than national.' Since the time of Brabazon's writing, this has been a move developed further, in the film's sequel, *Babe: A Pig in The City* (1998) set in a collage-city of impossibly juxtaposed national landmarks, and emphatically studio-set locations, which blend filmic and extra-filmic reference in a manner calculated to cancel even the most provisional attempts at the formation of a recognisable geography. This is indeed a cinema of 'semiotic tourism', offering pleasurable lococentric distractions but little in the way of explanation for temporal change; the landscapes of *Babe* thus offer fantasies of a pastoral retro-world existing in parallel with that of modernity and industrialisation, a space out of time, or rather, a time out of history. More importantly, they eschew a specifically national reference, in favour of a 'heterotopic visuality, where multiple ideologies are collapsed and othered'. Whether or not Brabazon' assertion, on the evidence of *Babe*, that the Australian film industry 'no longer requires a national adjective to verify its importance' remains very much to be seen. It does however seem to suggest that this might appropriately now be so.

Directly or indirectly, several of the essays gathered here address the growing sense of connection evident between Australian cinema and television in the 1990s. It has indeed become a commonplace in economic accounts of both mediums to find combinatory reference to the 'audio-visual' or 'moving image' industries, rather than to cinema or television *per se*. Studies of policy frequently recognise a correspondence of concerns around questions of ownership and control, support for training, archival funding, and of course in areas such as the establishment of censorial standards. Stephen Crofts sees clear signs of aesthetic convergence between cinema and television in his analysis of *The Castle* (1997), which he discusses as a site for the drawing together of codes developed in small-screen political satire in the 1980s, and nostalgic film comedy of the 1930s. Contra-*Babe*, the film demands a nationalising 'adjective' at every turn, relishing its national origins, and celebrating the vernacular. For Crofts however, the return to such emphases does bespeak a new politics; *The Castle* is no *Adventures of Barry McKenzie* (1972) for the 1990s; the former's critique is affectionate rather than ridiculing, with its protagonists cherished by the narrative rather than rendered grotesque by the potential cruelties of its discourse. For all its differences of tone and visual style, *The Castle* is therefore perhaps closer in spirit to earlier comedies such as *Emoh Ruo* (1985) or *Spotswood* (1992), than to the acidities of its televisual antecedents. For Crofts, the movie still involves a certain cultural assertiveness however, but draws out a sense of identity rooted in the domestic, rather than the national, and displays a visual style that owes more to the adhoceries of 'reality television' (the video-diary, the home video, the 'blooper' show) and the academic naturalisms of much Australian cinema in the 1950s, than the award-seeking cinematography of the 'renaissance' pictures. Its centring on the 'battler' Kerrigan family, struggling to prevent the compulsory purchase and demolition of its home, is not without ambivalence of course: endorsement is regularly undercut with sarcasm, distanciation alternates with identification, but an overwhelming approval saturates the film. As such, *The Castle* suggests something of a pre-millennial nostalgia for mid-century securities at both formal and thematic levels. This is a nostalgia which Crofts links to the film's underlying anxieties around questions of race and gender, signalled as much as anything by its reliance upon an almost deliberately implausible 'deus ex machina', in the form of the retired QC who will argue the Kerrigans' case for free, as far as the High Court in Canberra. The very 'ordinariness' of the values that the Kerrigans supposedly embody (defined perversely through the stigmatisation of their expression in particular taste-preferences and lifestyle-choices) is thus secured thanks only to the intervention of fate, and the good offices of an exceptional individual prepared to 'side' with them against the largely abstracted logics of a marketplace, which refuses to recognise those values, let alone their supposedly 'essential' Australian-ness.

The ambivalent address of *The Castle* is a far from isolated phenomenon in Australian cinema as it approaches the Millennium. Kay Ferres' analysis of *Idiot Box* (1996) finds similar hesitations in her examination of that film's transcoding of the discourses surrounding discussions of television-effects in Australia. Highlighting the movie's blending of picaresque affection and bemused satire, she identifies ficto-critical variants of the generational backlashes against contemporary youth culture, which have been identified elsewhere, and with which the film sees television as crucially implicated.[23] Concerns around the effects of television on the social behaviour of young people are dramatised ambiguously in *Idiot Box,* specifically around the story of would-be desperadoes Kev (Ben Mendelsohn) and Mick (Jeremy Sims), who plan a bank-heist to demonstrate their superiority to the screen criminals they see brought to justice week after week on their television sets. When their skills as 'active' spectators, manipulating generic codes, producing subversive readings etc., prove only minimally transferable to the world outside the sitting room, backlash is demonstrated graphically, in the form of a sustained set-piece demonstration of police firepower, reminiscent of numerous earlier crime dramas. Appropriately enough, Ferres' analysis aims less to discuss *Idiot Box* as a representation of contemporary experience in the outer suburbs, than to locate points of contact between *Idiot Box* and surrounding debates about television's place within social relations, and its consequent role in the formation of class and gender identities. It is the maintenance of this insistently media-oriented and economic dimension which distinguishes *Idiot Box* from countless other youth-alienation pictures of the 1980s and 1990s. Here, 'alienation' is contingent and dynamic, a strategic response to a range of improvisatory situations; at the same time, the cultivation of a 'poetic disposition' is far from incompatible with a surfeit of video-watching, routine trips to the bottle shop, and cruising the local shopping mall.

One of the most conspicuous signs of development within any national cinema is the gradual displacement or supplementing of one cluster of screen performers by another. Just as the 'new wave' of the 1970s established the screen images of actors and actresses who would become national and international stars, so the 1990s witnessed the re-alignment of these screen presences in relation to newer arrivals. Over time, longer-standing performers assume iconic status: the fabrication of their star images, and their embellishment in screen narratives built around them, allows particular performers to come to embody sets of values, whose significance may certainly be 'national'. Performers such as Wendy Hughes, or Bill Hunter or Russell Crowe, become 'living proof' of an Australian reality, almost 'texts' on which the national context is inscribed. Despite occasional recognitions of such processes of inscription, studies of particular stars are rare in writing on Australian cinema, and Alan McKee's essay here on Ernie Dingo makes an original contribution to the field. His study of Australia's best-known Aboriginal screen performer emphasises Dingo's role in a mediasphere ceaselessly troubled by indigenous issues. Partly his significance is as 'auteur' (his industrial status is suggestive of a point of representational origin); partly it relates to Dingo's apparent 'realism' (his star image synchronises with the meanings attributed to his screen characterisations, underwriting their authenticity); partly it is a matter of his functioning as a site onto which cultural aspirations can be projected (Dingo provides an embodiment of the possibility of reconciliation); partly it is a matter of his seeming ability to live 'between' cultures, retaining a connected-ness with Aboriginal lineages, whilst functioning effectively within a non-indigenous 'mainstream' (Dingo is thus suggestive of fluidity and expediency, rather than any sense of identity as essence or fixity that is fundamentally non-negotiable). McKee's analysis is thus suggestive of the highly layered quality of Dingo's image, and its ability to sustain contradictory readings across distinct audience constituencies; crucial to this capacity is that image's parallel circulation in cinema *and* television: if cinema may be tempted to explore the exoticism of the Aboriginal performer, television insists upon its banality and availability. Concentrating, as the essay advances, on the television mini-series *Heartland*, McKee begins to suggest something of the crucial role played by his stardom in negotiating a 'nice politics' between indigenous and non-indigenous Australia; *Heartland*'s narration may be sceptical of his character's ability to live between two cultures, but Dingo and media constructions of his celebrity seem to be proof that this is possible. Above all, Dingo's image seems to stress its idiosyncrasy, and to refuse the burden of representativeness which his positioning seems to accrue. Like all the other essays collected in this volume, McKee's analysis of Dingo's image says much about the 'noise' of Australian cinema in the 1990s, struggling with its own histories, struggling with its own sense of possibility. As that cinema approaches the Millennium, it seems on the evidence of these essays that cinema in Australia as a whole, has at least begun to escape its 'burden of representativeness' too.

NOTES

1. Of the various invaluable histories, see in particular: Susan Dermody and Elizabeth Jacka, *The Screening of Australia Vol.I: Anatomy of a Film Industry*, and *The Screening of Australia, Vol. 2: Anatomy of a National Cinema* (Sydney: Currency Press, 1987 and 1988); Tom O'Regan, *Australian National Cinema* (London: Routledge, 1996) and James Sabine (ed.), *A Century of Australian Cinema* (Melbourne: Mandarin, Reed Books, 1995).

2. Brian Reis, *Australian Film: A Bibliography* (London and Washington: Mansell, 1997); Scott Murray, *Australian Film 1978–1994: A Survey of Theatrical Features* (Melbourne: Oxford University Press, 1995).

3. Jocelyn Robson and Beverley Zalcock, *Girls' Own Stories: Australian and New Zealand Women's Films* (London: Scarlet, 1997); Karen Jennings, *Sites of Difference: Cinematic Representations of Aboriginality and Gender* (Melbourne: Australian Film Institute, 1993).

4. See, for example; Albert Moran, *Projecting Australia: Government Film Since 1945* (Paddington, New South Wales: Currency Press, 1991); Peter Mudie, *Ubu Films: Sydney Underground Movies* (Kensington, New South Wales: University of New South Wales Press, 1997); Stuart Cunningham and Toby Miller, *Contemporary Australian Television* (Kensington, New South Wales: University of New South Wales Press, 1994).

5. Ben Goldsmith, 'Government, Film and the National Image: Reappraising the Australian Film Development Corporation', *Australian Studies*, Vol.12, No.1 (Summer 1997), pp.98–114.

6. Neil Rattigan, 'Film', in Philip Bell and Roger Bell (eds.), *Americanisation and Australia* (Kensington, New South Wales: University of New South Wales Press, 1998), pp.210–227.

7. For reliable statistical data on the industry, see Rosemary Curtis and Cathy Gray (eds.), *Get The Picture: Essential Data on Australian Film, Television, Video and New Media* (Sydney: Australian Film Commission, 1996), esp. pp.46–89, and 136–173.

8. Adrian Martin, 'More Than Muriel', *Sight and Sound*, Vol.5, No.6 (nos) (June 1995), pp.30–32.

9. The consistencies identified of course vary according to what is being demonstrated. See for example: (on aesthetic unity) Karl Quinn, 'Drag, Dags and The Suburban Surreal', *Metro*, No. 100 (Summer 1994–95), pp.23–26; (on linguistic unity) Tim Rowse, *Arguing The Arts* (Penguin: Ringwood, 1985), pp.70–72; (on institutional/industrial unity) Peat, Marwick, Mitchell Services, *Towards A More Effective Commission: The AFC in the 1980s* (Sydney: Peat, Marwick, Mitchell, 1979) and Australian Film Commission, *Film Assistance: Future Options* (Sydney: Allen & Unwin, 1986).

10. Tom O'Regan, *Australian National Cinema* (London: Routledge, 1996), p.175.

11. Susan Dermody and Elizabeth Jacka, 'Australian Cinema: An Anachronism in the 80s', in their *The Imaginary Industry: Australian Film in The Late 1980s* (Sydney: Australian Film, Television and Radio School, 1988), pp.117–131.

12. Notable contributions in this area include: Hal Porter, *Stars of Australian Stage and Screen* (Adelaide: Rigby, 1965); Adrian Martin, 'Nurturing the Next Wave: What is Cinema?', in Peter Broderick (ed.), *Back of Beyond: Discovering Australian Film and Television* (Sydney: Australian Film Commission, 1988), pp.90–101; a number of theatre histories identify points of significant contact between stage and screen, eg. John West, *Theatre in Australia*

(Stanmore, New South Wales: Cassell Australia, 1978); Philip Parsons with Victoria Chance (eds.), *Companion To Theatre in Australia* (Sydney: Currency Press, 1995).

13. See for example, Barbara Creed, 'Mothers and Lovers: Oedipal Transgressions in recent Australian Cinema', *Metro*, No.91 (Spring 1992), pp.14–22.

14. See Brian McFarlane and Geoff Mayer, *New Australian Cinema: Sources and Parallels in American and British Film* (Cambridge, New York and Oakleigh: Cambridge University Press, 1992) for an extended discussion of areas of overlap and distinction between Australian and other Anglophone cinemas in the 1990s.

15. Graeme Turner, 'The End of The National Project?: Australian Cinema in the 1990s', in Wimal Dissanayake (ed.), *Questions of Nationhood and History in Asian Cinema* (Bloomington: Indiana University Press, 1994), pp.202–16; James Walter, 'From *The Weird Mob* to *Strictly Ballroom*: Politics and Public Culture in Australia Since The Forties', *Australian Studies*, No. 10 (October 1996), pp.1–14.

16. John Docker, *Postmodernism and Popular Culture* (Cambridge: Cambridge University Press, 1994).

17. For a valuable recent contribution to the study of ethnic presence see Jon Stratton, 'National Identity, Film and the Narrativisation of Multiculturalism and "Asians"', in *Race Daze: Australia in Identity Crisis* (Annandale, New South Wales: Pluto Press, 1998), pp.134–168.

18. For a discussion of ethnic presence in Australian television soap opera, for example, see Ian Craven, 'Race and Ethnicity in the Drip-Dramas', in Werner Senn and Giovanna Capone (eds.), *The Making of a Pluralist Australia* (Berne: Peter Lang, 1992), pp.241–256; Lesleyanne Hawthorne, 'Soap Opera in Multicultural Australia: *Home and Away* Vs *Heartbreak High*', in Hilary Ericksen (ed.), *The Media's Australia* (Melbourne: The Australia Centre, University of Melbourne, 1996), pp.64–69.

19. See, for example, Ian Craven, 'Emoh Ruo: The Suburbanisation of Australian Cinema', *Antipodes*, Vol.11, No.1 (June 1997), pp.25–32; Rose Lucas: 'Round the Block: Back To the Suburb in *Return Home*', in Sarah Ferber et. al. (eds.), *Beasts of Suburbia: Reinterpreting Culture in Australian Suburbs* (Melbourne: Melbourne University Press, 1994), pp.111–126. An important contribution to cultural-geographical study in relation to Australian film is represented by: Rosalyn Haynes, *Seeking The Centre: The Australian Desert in Literature, Art and Film* (Cambridge: Cambridge University Press, 1998).

20. The majority of writing on acoustic style is concerned with film music, the aesthetic and technical conventions of film scoring etc.: see for example; Peter Beilby, 'Peter Fenton: Mixer', *Cinema Papers*, No. 3 (July 1974), pp.254–257; Andrea Gray (ed.), *Music For Film: Papers Delivered at the National Music for Film Symposium* (Sydney: Australian Film and Television School, 1985); Albie Thoms, 'The Sound of Film', *Filmnews*, Vol.10, Nos.1 & 2 (January–February 1980), pp.4–5.

21. See, for example: Mary Anne Reid, *Long Shots To Favourites* (Sydney: Australian Film Commission, 1993); Al Clark, *The Lavender Bus: How A Hit Movie Was Made and Sold* (Sydney: Currency Press, 1999); Susan Barber, '*The Adventures of Priscilla, Queen of The Desert*', *Film Quarterly*, Vol.50, No.2 (Winter 1996) pp 41–45; John Champagne, 'Dancing Queen? Feminist and Gay Male Spectatorship in Three Recent Films From Australia', *Film Criticism*, Vol.21, No.3 (Fall 1997) pp.66–88; Chris Berry, 'Not Necessarily the Sum of Us: Australia's Not-So-Queer Cinema', *Metro*, No.101 (Autumn 1995) pp.12–16; Pamela Robertson, 'The Adventures of Priscilla in Oz', *Media Information Australia*, No.78 (November 1995) pp.33–38; Alan McKee's forthcoming article, 'How To Tell the Difference Between a Stereotype and A Positive Image: Putting *Priscilla, Queen of The Desert* Into History', in the e-journal *Screening the Past*, (web address: http://www.latrobe.edu.au/ screeningthepast/) includes a detailed discussion of the reception and circulation of the film.

22. See, for example: Doug Cocks, *Future Makers, Future Takers: Life in Australia 2050* (Kensington, New South Wales: University of New South Wales Press, 1999), and Lindsay Tanner, *Open Australia* (Annandale, New South Wales: Pluto Press, 1999).

23. See, for example: Mark Davis, *Gangland: Cultural Elites and The New Generationalism* (Sydney: Allen & Unwin, 1997); Rob White and Christine Alder (eds.), *The Police and Young People in Australia* (Cambridge: Cambridge University Press, 1994).

2

Patterns of Production and Policy: The Australian Film Industry in the 1990s

LISA FRENCH

This paper offers an overview of the Australian film industry in the 1990s and attempts to track the shifts in policy that have affected patterns of film production. The primary focus of this article is on Australian feature films, although the associated television production industry is also discussed.

The Current Climate for Film Production in Australia

It could be said that currently the Australian film industry is enjoying a degree of maturity and success that compares favourably with other non-Hollywood film locuses of film production such as France, India, Canada and the UK. Internationally, the film industry is dominated by the Hollywood players, particularly in the US domestic market, but also throughout the world. One example of the Australian industry's accomplishments is the critical and commercial success of *Shine* (1995), a film which won a host of both national and international awards including an Academy Award for Best Actor, Geoffrey Rush. The film, which cost just over $6 million to produce, has grossed over $64 million Australian dollars (April 1997 figure) at the international box office. It was the subject of a fierce dispute to acquire US distribution rights at the 1996 Sundance Film Festival, and is now regarded internationally as a model of accomplishment.

The industry's success is perhaps the culmination of the experience gained since the industry's rebirth during the 1970s, and the steady development of all aspects of film production. Before *Shine*, the Australian film industry has enjoyed other notable successes, either at the box office, critically, or both, with such films as *Muriel's Wedding* (1994), *The Adventures of Priscilla, Queen of the Desert* (1994), *The Piano* (1993),

Strictly Ballroom (1992) *Babe* (1995), and *Green Card* (1991). The latter two films are particularly of note in the current context in view of the involvement of American studios. *Love and Other Catastrophes* (1996), directed by Emma-Kate Croghan, was also notable in securing a sale in the order of $1 million to Miramax for distribution in the US, virtually double its budget. By way of contrast, *Shine* is an example of a film which was produced with funding from the Australian Film Finance Corporation (AFFC) in conjunction with local funding, with international sales agent Pandora having rights to market the film throughout the world outside Australia, and Ronin Films, a local distributor, having domestic distribution rights. The film was developed with assistance from the Australian Film Commission (AFC), the South Australian Film Corporation and Film Victoria, and illustrates a successful partnership between private and public sectors.

Since the seventies, it has been consistently recognised that government has a crucial role to play in supporting the film industry. It has been repeatedly argued that some degree of subsidy is required if Australians wish to see Australian culture on their screens. Despite the domestic and international successes of some recent Australian films, this argument is as valid today as it was in 1970. The Howard Liberal Government, brought into office in 1996 ending thirteen years of Labor rule, presides over film policy at the national level. In line with the Howard government's general economic philosophy, federal policy on film can be characterised as encouraging the free play of market forces while reducing the involvement and size of government funding to the industry.

Shortly after taking office the federal government initiated a review of film policy which culminated in a report titled, 'Review of Commonwealth Assistance to the Film Industry', written by David Gonski (hereafter referred to as the Gonski report). One of the Gonski report's main recommendations, the development of FLICS (Film Licensed Investment Scheme) as a source of film funding, is yet to be implemented, although a revised version of the scheme is due to become a reality in 1999 (discussed later in this paper.) Despite this review, some sectors are still under the microscope; the Department of Communications and The Arts (DOCA) have just begun another review of screen culture. The Gonski report recommended that the AFC reallocate funds from screen culture to other core activities and to script development but the current government did not implement this, particularly due to lobbying by the group formed for this purpose, the Australian Screen Culture Industry Association (ASCIA).

In general, the Federal Government has not dismantled the policy set by its predecessor under Creative Nation in 1994, as was initially feared. However there has been a consistent reduction in funding allocations to film bodies, particularly the AFC. In the past the AFC has been a source of funding for low-budget features and script development but at present does not seem to have the resources to maintain this role (the effects of which will only become apparent in the years ahead.) The national broadcaster, the ABC, has also been cut and this has drastically reduced the amount of quality television drama being produced locally.

Overall, exhibition is currently doing well, with domestic box office grosses continuing at high levels, although many Australian releases do poorly – the most notable recent failure is the film *Oscar and Lucinda* (1997), which despite its $20 million budget and the support of Fox Searchlight, a subsidiary of Fox in the US, only took around $1 million domestically. This film also fared badly in the international market. All government-funded film bodies rely for part of their funding on returns from previous investments, and returns from *Shine* will top up the resources of the Australian Film Finance Corporation. However, the industry will perhaps soon require a break-out film like a *Shine* or a *Muriel's Wedding* to keep money flowing into the coffers of the AFFC and the state-funding bodies.

One development in the Australian industry over the past several years has been the gradual infiltration of overseas interest, particularly from the US. Several international distributors have offices in Australia and actively seek participation in new Australian films, including Miramax and Fox Searchlight. Fox Studios recently opened in Sydney, and Queensland continues to function as an offshore Hollywood backlot, with a number of films being shot at the Warner Brothers/Village Roadshow Movieworld studios.

To conclude, the current position of Australian film production is broadly market-driven, with a number of players in production, distribution and exhibition successfully surviving and thriving in the marketplace. Government policy appears to recognise that the economics of film production require significant government underpinning and support, and much of the infrastructure established by the previous Labor government, and earlier governments as well, remains in operation. But in many areas funding has been reduced, in some cases significantly. Competition for both government support and marketplace interest amongst new and established filmmakers has perhaps never been more intense. The influence of overseas involvement in film production is yet to be determined and the effect of cutbacks, particularly on film development, have yet to make themselves felt. And there are other significant issues troubling the industry looming on the horizon, including the decision by the High Court of Australia to allow New Zealand production to count as Australian production in television quotas, and the fight for Australian scriptwriters for their moral rights.

The Historical Context

The current situation of Australian film production must be viewed in the context of recent film history stemming from the renaissance of the industry in the 1970s, a history that has been well documented elsewhere. Although Australian film production began strongly at the turn of the century, it declined until there was little activity from the 1930s until the late 1960s. Throughout the 1960s lobby groups argued for government financial support until, in 1970, the federally-funded Australian Film Development Corporation (AFDC) was established by the Gorton government. This body was later re-established with wider powers as the Australian Film Commission (AFC) in 1975. Between 1972 and 1978, state-funded government agencies were established in every state. Although in several instances their scale and function was re-defined significantly in the 1990s, these instrumentalities (with the exception of Tasmanian Film Corporation), continue to function.[1]

From the 1970s there has been a recognition of the pivotal role of government in fostering and regulating the development of Australian film and television. Historically, the Australian film industry has been Federally-funded at both the 'commercial' and 'experimental' levels. As Tom O'Regan notes:

> In the 1970s there was the mainstream Australian Film Development Corporation and the minor stream Experimental Film Fund; from the mid-1970s to the mid-1980s there was the mainstream Industry Branch and the minor stream Creative Development Branch of the AFC; since 1988 the division has been represented by the Australian Film Finance Corporation and the AFC.[2]

Within the AFC there are various schemes which have particular targets, such as the Women's Film Fund, the Indigenous Film Branch and funding for New Media, documentary and short film production. As the Gonski report found, the Commonwealth currently plays a dominant role in support of the industry with state/territory funding being under 15 per cent of the Commonwealth total. However, state organisations have supported different levels of participation in collaboration with the local 'independent' sectors that have tended to grow up around them, through 'Young Filmmakers' or 'New Writers' funds, and through mentor programmes and 'Producer Support' packages. Sometimes this has led to their direct investment in film and television produced in these sectors.

The AFC in particular also supports the production of short films, experimental films and documentaries. This support has been reduced over the past few years as a result of a reduction in the AFC's budget. In 1997 a cap of $50,000 per short film project was established, in order to spread financial assistance as widely as possible. Short films are viewed as an important part of film production in their own right, as well as a means for recent film graduates and other filmmakers, writers, actors and crew members to hone their craft.

The AFC also supports development and production of documentaries. However, this area has also been reduced due to funding reductions and the Commission will now only fund projects which have received interest from a broadcaster (the state-funding bodies are generally more lenient in this regard). The number of documentaries that are made each year in Australia is declining as a result of budget reductions by the two main broadcasters that screen such films, the Australian Broadcasting Corporation (ABC) and the Special Broadcasting Service (SBS). The ABC has reduced the budget it will support for one-hour documentaries, and is now commissioning fewer films. One significant effect of these budgetary reductions is the number of documentaries that originate on 16mm film. Currently it is very difficult to justify the cost of shooting on film, unless the project is an international co-production. Correspondingly, the Australian Film Institute (AFI) has recently changed the rules regarding the eligibility of documentaries into its annual AFI Awards, allowing video-originated documentaries to be eligible for competition. The categories of 'Best Television Documentary' and 'Best Documentary Film' have been replaced by 'Best Documentary' and 'Best Achievement in Direction of a Documentary'.[3]

The establishment of the AFC and state-based funding agencies, coupled with the introduction of tax concessions later in the 1970s, caused major growth within the Australian film industry. In 1978 tax laws under section 10B of the Tax Assessment Act were re-drafted, to allow film investment to be written off over two years, allowing investors considerable savings on their tax bills. Initially the scheme attracted little attention; the provisions seemed insufficiently generous to attract the desired level of private investment, until a significantly more generous scheme was introduced in

1980, known subsequently as '10BA'. This move generated an expansion in film production, rising levels of employment in the industry, significant profits to mostly private financiers, and the proliferation of films, targeted at the 'exploitation' and 'direct to video' market. Under 10BA, investors in film and certain types of television programmes could claim a $150 tax deduction for every $100 spent, whilst every $50 earned on the investment was exempt from tax. However, these concessions were gradually wound back following criticism that they had created a finance-tax-driven industry, characterised by inflated budgets. Deductions were subsequently reduced from 120/20 to 100 per cent, with no tax shelter for returns.

The phasing out of tax concessions created considerable disturbance within the industry in the mid-1980s, and calls for alternative funding mechanisms echoed throughout the industry. In 1988, after much deliberation and consultation, the Australian Film Finance Corporation (AFFC) was established, with an annual grant from the Commonwealth for investment in features, tele-movies, mini-series and documentaries. The sums of money involved were, and remain, considerable: the 1997–98 budget was $48.01 million ($48.5 m in 1996–97 and $50 m in 1995–96.) This level of investment suggested something of the AFFC's intended role, namely to function as a sort of film bank, offering loans at preferential rates and enjoying the right of 'with profit' participation in the projects invested in. Applicants to the AFFC must demonstrate market potential: theoretically if a project's producers can demonstrate sufficient market interest – say a pre-sale of around 35 per cent for a feature film, depending on its budget, then the AFFC will provide the other 65 per cent of the necessary funds as a recoupable investment. Questions of national 'interest' and 'quality' are inscribed in the AFFC's brief: there are a number of requirements, including eligibility under 10BA, which places Australian content requirements on proposed projects. In the wake of the tax concession years, during which many more films were made, but during which fewer made money, it was intended that the AFFC would fund commercially viable films, and it was hoped that these films would return enough of their investment to become at least partly self-sustaining. By April 1997, the AFFC had funded 111 feature films, of which only five have gone into profit, namely; *Strictly Ballroom, Muriel's Wedding, Green Card, The Adventures of Priscilla-Queen of the Desert* and *Shine*. Unfortunately, other headline successes of the 1990s, such as *Babe* and *The Piano* did not utilise AFFC funds.

Clearly, the AFFC was set up with largely commercial aims, unlike earlier government bodies which had a more strongly cultural–nationalist inflection, and owed much to public service antecedents such as Film

Australia. Susan Dermody and Elizabeth Jacka have suggested of the AFFC that:

> The announcement of the Corporation was made purely in financial terms; there was little or no debate about the cultural and aesthetic consequence of the system it was replacing and no statement of what government subsidisation of a film and media industry is supposed to achieve.[4]

To many, the record of the AFFC since its introduction in 1988 confirms this commercial imperative only too clearly.

The Role of Governments

Successive governments have also supported the cultural importance of the portrayal of Australian stories, themes and culture on cinema and television screens. Cultural objectives as well as economic ones have frequently driven government support, and have sometimes seemed to gain a particular ascendancy. In the 1990s, intervention assumed a distinctly cultural 'gloss' in the form of the 'Creative Nation' initiative, as Jock Given noted in *Filmnews*:

> Every living Australian Prime Minister has run a government that did something for Australian film. Gorton's started federal assistance to the industry, Whitlam's increased it and reorganised it, Fraser's introduced 10BA, Hawke's established the Film Finance Corporation. Keating's government has delivered Creative Nation, an expansive, expensive statement of cultural policy announced in October, 1994.[5]

The significance of 'Creative Nation' was that it was a commitment to the importance of cultural policy from the top level of government (a recognition of culture as a political factor), and provided for continued direct funding to support the production of Australian films, and to help stabilise the industry, as part of a creative infrastructure deemed important to the definition of an Australian public media sphere. Keating's intervention had a distinctly symbolic air about it: the arts were represented at Cabinet level for the first time since the Whitlam government; a vision for the next ten years of national policy development was established; a joining of arts and communications in one federal government portfolio was achieved: and there was a focus on cultural mapping, cultural impact statements and attention to 'culture industries' in general.[6] A key focus of 'Creative Nation' was on the 'new' media, indicating a conceptual shift towards new forms of information-packaging and presentation, although this was done in addition to traditional forms of film support. The 'Creative Nation' investment in new media gave additional funding for this purpose (over four years) to the AFC ($5.25 million), Australian Film, Television and Radio School (AFTRS) ($950,0000), as well as investing $84 million in the Australian Multimedia Enterprise, Co-operative Multimedia Centres, a series of National Multimedia Forums and the 'Australia on CD' programme. This trend was also echoed by state governments, for example, in Victoria, where the Liberal Government headed by Jeff Kennett currently invests $13 million per year in supporting the development of new multimedia. Alan Stockdale became the first Minister for Multimedia establishing a new department called Multimedia Victoria, and the Multimedia 21 Fund which provides project development for, and investment in, multimedia.

More recent political developments may well have softened the financial and critical edge of the 'Creative Nation' initiative. The John Howard-led Liberal/National Coalition came to power in March 1996 with an agenda to cut government spending in almost all areas. This government, for example, appraised the ABC and reduced funding (by $65 million in 1996–98 budgets), and reviewed commonwealth assistance to the film industry. The ensuing 'Gonski Report' report recommended that current levels of assistance were adequate (and did not recommend any increase), but devised tax incentives (FLICs) intended to help close an anticipated gap between income and expenditure, which are discussed later in this paper. The Commercial Television Production Fund (CTPF) was another major casualty of the Federal Government's 1998 Budget which slashed its revenues, and created a storm of protest. In May 1998, the Australian Writers' Guild's executive director Sue McCreadie characterised the scale of the cuts in the following way:

> This CTPF cut contributes to a 25 per cent reduction in development and production funding to the industry since the Coalition came to power in March 1996.[7]

Reviews did help to provide a clearer statistical picture of the state of the industry in the later years of the decade. The Gonski report found that in 1994–95 only 20 per cent (i.e. four) of the films produced in that year were made without Federal funding, and that only one in ten feature films usually returned their original investment. In 1997, direct federal funding for Australia's film and television industry was set at the level of $115 million, and has scarcely risen subsequently. The only increases given by the current federal government have been to Film Australia; other areas have generally been maintained. In the 1997–98 Budget the Australian Film Finance Corporation (AFFC) funding was cut slightly to $48.01 million for 1997–98 to 2000/1; the AFC was cut, receiving $29.7 million (this figure included almost $15 million earmarked for the Australian Commercial Television Production Fund (ACTPF), which subsequently lost independent funding altogether in 1998), whilst the National Interest Program (NIP), managed by Film Australia was maintained at stable levels ($46.4 million for another two years until 1998–99). In November 1997, the government extended support for Film Australia to 2003, and extended support for the National Interest Program; the Australian Children's Television Foundation was maintained at current levels ($2.3 million) and levels of funding for The National Film and Sound Archive and The Australian, Film Television and Radio School were maintained. Support for SBS Independent was continued, and tax concessions for the industry were maintained pending possible replacements.[8]

In November 1997, Senator Richard Alston announced that provisions under Divisions 10B and 10BA of the *Income Tax Investment Act 1936* for investment in Australian film and television production would be retained but a new pilot scheme – the Film Licensed Investment Scheme (FLIC) would be introduced. It was envisaged that FLIC would provide a 100 per cent tax concession to investors in companies which are licensed to invest in a slate of film and television production. The scheme was expected to raise concession capital of up to $20 million a year.

Australia and the Global Film Industry

As in virtually all countries throughout the world, the Australian film distribution and exhibition industries are dominated by American product. To a lesser extent, American influences can also now be felt in the production and distribution sectors of Australian cinema as well. As the 1990s wore on, US film production companies appeared with greater frequency on Australian territory; Village Roadshow went into partnership with Warner Brothers some years ago to establish Movieworld in Queensland, a fun park and production studio. More recently, Fox Studios has opened its doors in Sydney. Many other US-based companies have representation in Australia now, notably Miramax (the distributors), Fox Icon and Fox Searchlight. Other companies seem set to follow their example.

The return of the Americans has come about for two main reasons. Firstly, whilst there has long been a recognition in Hollywood that while high-budget (i.e. $100 million or more) films are needed to win substantial box office grosses on opening, there has also been a growing recognition that there is also a market for smaller films, which may build their revenues more slowly. Films like the British hit *The Full Monty* (1997), are cited as examples of low-budget films with no recognisable American stars that have grossed over $200 million worldwide, making them more profitable than even the most successful blockbusters in terms of returns on investment. This recognition has caused US distributors to seek out low-budget films that have the potential to break out into big box office successes. Accordingly, Miramax paid $1 million for the rights to distribute *Love and Other Catastrophes*, a film made in Australia by Emma-Kate Croghan, and planned initially around a projected budget of just $40,000, before gaining support from the Australian Film Commission, top the tune of a reported additional $500,000.

The second reason for the American presence has undoubtedly been the globalisation of the film industry, manifest in this context by the recognition that there are film subsidies in non-US markets to be taken advantage of by productions which can qualify as 'domestic'. To access these subsidies, Hollywood studios have sought ways to form partnerships with 'offshore' producers and distributors, with a view to establishing an international base for motion picture financing. Some indication of why Hollywood might be interested in Australian projects as potential co-productions is suggested by Tino Balio when he notes that:

> Studios chose this option mostly with 'unusual material' – which is to say a picture that was not a sequel, that did not have a major international star, or that did not have an 'unflaggingly high-concept'.[9]

On the domestic front, Australian films continue to be generated by a large number of independent production houses and companies which have minimal profitability. In the 1990s, some re-organisation of this traditionally fragmented sector became evident. A number of the larger production companies such as Village Roadshow, Beyond Films and Southern Star attempted to pull together 'slates' of feature films, in the manner of some of the smaller Hollywood studios, and to market them as packages. It is noticeable that these production companies are either also distributors and/or exhibitors, such as Village Roadshow, or also producers of television such as Beyond and Southern Star. Such diversification allows these companies to fund the development of a number of speculative film projects. This tendency seems set to continue beyond the 1990s.

There is perhaps therefore some justification for the Gonski report's claim in 1997 that an air of confidence now surrounds Australia's film and television industry. Overall, the picture contrasts strongly with that of the fledgling industry of the 1970s, when for many years there was only one major Australian film distributor (Village Roadshow), and with the 1980s when rorts encouraged a plethora of films to be financed under Division 10BA as tax write-offs, many of which were never even screened. In the 1990s, there is clearly a more a stable and established atmosphere in the Australian film industry, and a more clearly defined mechanism via which government funding underpins the private sector, without leading to an over-inflation of production.

The industry continues to grow steadily. The Australian Bureau of statistics report, *Film and Video Production and Distribution* (1995–97), estimated the total audio-visual production in Australia as being worth $1.3 billion annually to the Australian economy. The Gonski report found that it employs more than 20,000 people and earns considerable revenue from export. The films themselves have altered considerably in quality and quantity since the 1970s. In the 1990s Australia's annual level of production was 20 to 35 films, mostly costing less than $4 million each. In the period 1988–96 Australia produced an average of 26 features, 15 mini-series, 9 tele-movies and 14 television series or serials per year.[10] Despite these successes, it is recognised that the Australian film industry is small. Government support is still necessary, and without it, production output would shrink to a handful of films per year.

Film Funding

Federal governments in Australia have used a range of policy instruments since the 1970s to ensure that a diverse slate of productions is maintained – including direct funding, tax incentives and regulating the broadcast of Australian content. The Australian Film Finance Corporation (AFFC) remains the principal source of funding for local films. The AFFC is primarily commercially orientated, and considers 'deal' elements such as cast, crew, distribution, marketing, budget and script in assessing proposals for possible support. To fund projects, the AFFC requires evidence of market interest (to a specified amount which varies depending on the budget of the film) in the form of either a pre-sale or distribution guarantee, although having these elements in place does not automatically gain funding. Not surprisingly, the AFFC's funding decisions have often proved controversial. Investment by Australian distributors and exhibitors rarely provides the full cost of production, and so very few Australian films are made without Government assistance. The Gonski report found that international pre-sales and distribution guarantees are therefore crucial to assist in raising funds for production and maximising the potential for the programme to return its costs to investors.

Support from non-AFFC sources has also become a significant force in the 1990s. In recent years, offshore companies including Miramax, PolyGram and Pandora, have been co-financing films as well as making advances against distribution. Offshore companies are, however, generally reluctant to invest in first-time directors, and much successful Australian talent was certainly lured away during the decade. Curtis and Gray have written that 'while Australia continues to lose its key talent to Hollywood, it is unlikely the industry will ever be self-funding', although it is questionable whether the industry could be self-funding, even if key talent stayed.[11] Many practitioners now divide their time between Australia, Europe and Hollywood: actors such as Russell Crowe, Toni Collette, Judy Davis, Nicole Kidman and Geoffrey Rush; cinematographers such as John Seale, Dean Semler and Don McAlpine; directors such as Gillian Armstrong, Bruce Beresford, Baz Lurhmann and George Miller and writers such as Laura Jones and Craig Pearce, all built significant careers outside Australia in the 1990s.

Achieving funding for a feature film in Australia has become increasingly complex and some films are made despite failing to attain money from the AFFC. An example is *The Boys* (1998) a low-budget feature which premiered recently in Australia. Five years ago, *The Boys* would probably have been fully financed by the AFC, but since the cuts in government funding noted above, the AFC has been unable to fully fund features.[12] The producers of *The Boys* applied to the AFFC but were refused support, and so had to pursue a very complicated financing package which involved investment from Axiom Films (an international sales agent), Footprint Films (a distribution company), The Globe Company (a local distributor), a private investor, Premium Movie Partnership (a pay TV investment company), the AFC, and SBS Independent, with the NSWFTVO providing the cash-flow facility. There is some evidence that such complex funding mechanisms have aesthetic implications. *The Boys* and other releases such as Ana Kokkino's *Head On* (1998) and Richard Flanagan's *The Sound of One Hand Clapping* (1997) have already been described as parts of 'a new wave of dark films ... taking over from "quirky" comedy',[13] a label which had previously characterised many Australian films of the 1990s.

Australian filmmakers are not just concerned with box office or television ratings to establish their credentials of course, as academic Tom O'Regan points out, cultural imperatives persist:

> The continuing survival of some forms of filmmaking can be, at times, due to successful lobbying of state agencies rather than any underlying economic characteristics of the film form or the overall political agenda of the government of the day[14]

and suggests that governments supporting national cinemas must still satisfy themselves that their support satisfies the potentially incompatible objectives of economic viability and cultural accreditation. This struggle clearly continued to face the Australian industry in the 1990s, and seems likely to remain a problem given that, in the foreseeable future, it is unlikely that the industry will be self funding – especially the more independent or experimental areas which are culturally important but attract small audiences.

Statistical evidence adds complicating detail to the picture sketched in the above sections, which suggests real polarisation in terms of the output. The AFC's *National Survey of Feature Film and Independent TV Drama Production 1996–97*, for example, revealed that, in terms of production budgets, there were more films with budgets in the $3–6 million range than in any other year since the first survey in 1988–89; in the years 1995–96, budgets increased by 12 per cent (an increase of $62m) on the previous year; the budgets of five Australia features made that year were greater than $6 million compared with only two in the previous year.[15] At the same time, the number of movies in the under $1 million range was the highest recorded since 1991–92. Clearly the boom in low-budget features was helped along by projects such as the AFC's 'Million Dollar Movies' initiative, aimed at stimulating innovative work by new practitioners.[16]

In terms of where funding came from, 87 projects (features and television drama) were produced by the independent sector (34 were Australian features.) Of these projects, 38 per cent were mainly financed by Australian government sources (a decline on the previous year), 26 per cent were mainly financed by overseas investors (the same as the previous year) and 36 per cent were mainly financed by Australian commercial broadcasters and private investors (mainly production and distribution companies). In regard to monies involved in the production during the

1996–97 period, 39 films were produced worth a total of $249m; the 34 Australian titles cost $130m, and the five foreign titles cost $119m.

Production: The Influence of Foreign Players

The Gonski report found that there has been a significant increase in the level of foreign investment in the film industry in Australia in the 1990s, and that this had occurred in three areas: production of foreign films in Australia, investment by foreign companies in infrastructure in Australia; and foreign investment in the production of Australian films. Interestingly, the penetration of foreign capital is largely viewed positively in the report. Overseas investment is seen as confirming Australia's international reputation as a supplier of reliable production infrastructures and talent. Examples of such investment are provided by *Dark City* (1996) and *Oscar and Lucinda* (both receiving money from Fox Searchlight), *The Piano* (funded largely by French money), and most conspicuously, *The Adventures of Priscilla-Queen of the Desert* (whose $2.7m production budget came mostly from PolyGram).[17] More concern is sometimes voiced over the growing control over Australian 'plant' facilities by Australian practitioners. The production of foreign films in Australia increased conspicuously in the 1990s, and several international companies, such as Twentieth Century Fox (at its Fox Studios) and Warner Bros. (at its Warner-Roadshow Movieworld Studios), began to invest themselves in infrastructure. Government, however, demonstrated little such discrimination. In November 1997, for example, Senator Richard Alston announced that the government recognised the growing importance of international partners in the developing the Australian industry, and the government stated that it would 'work to reduce the barriers of overseas production in Australia'.[18]

In fact, production surveys in the period suggested that contraction in the Hollywood industry back home was having some effect on the majors' offshore operations in countries such as Australia; during the later 1990s fewer foreign features were shot in Australia than in the mid-decade years, but because more co-productions were financed, there was a higher level of investment than in previous years.[19] Financing at this stage consisted of contributions from the private sector (mainly production and distribution companies) having increased from $16m (18 per cent) to $36m (28 per cent) in 1996–97. Of the 87 productions, 23 were majority-funded by overseas investors; there were 13 Australian productions worth $123m and 10 foreign productions shot in Australia worth $143m. In addition, six of the

Australian productions (worth $68m) were co-productions with foreign companies who contributed half the budget.

The increase in production by foreign companies in Australia is largely seen as attributable to operations at the Warner-Roadshow Movieworld Studios in Queensland. Although the facility is primarily geared towards producing programmes designed for the American market, its executive is keen to stress its value to the Australia industry. This has certainly given a significant boost to the level of production in that state, which now has the highest production output in Australia. It should be noted however that the production of foreign films in Australia provides very limited opportunities for Australian creative talent whose contributions are effectively controlled by overseas companies. As such, offshore productions have little impact on the Australian industry (except perhaps in some technical areas), or on those areas of output associated with concepts of 'national' cinema. In real terms, production is predominantly located in New South Wales and Victoria, and not surprisingly, the Gonski report found that 90 per cent of income was earned in these two states.

New South Wales in particular competes seriously for overseas revenues with Queensland, and has also recently welcomed overseas investment in plant facilities. On 2 May 1998 the Fox Studios opened in Sydney at an estimated cost of $200m, providing the city with state-of-the-art production, and post-production facilities. Although the studios may be used by offshore producers, they have been established primarily to house Australian productions, and management anticipate two or three features will pass through the premises per year. Aesthetic implications are anticipated in the Gonski report: 'it may lead to a wider genre of studio-based productions',[20] and interest in the facilities is high across the industry. Fox Studios chief executive Kim Williams told *Encore* on 6 May that they had 'pencil bookings until the year 2001'.[21]

The next ten years promises considerable shifts in the present production sector, which seems poised for a new stage of development. A new production and exhibition centre in Victoria is set to go, with VIACOM Themed Entertainment Group (the parent company of Paramount Pictures) as the tipped preferred developer of a $350 million theme park, film complex and megaplex cinema, due to be completed in late 2000 or early 2001. Local Victorian company, Crawford Productions, it is believed, will manage the production studios. In March 1998, Village Roadshow Pictures and Hoyts announced the formation of a joint company, the Village Roadshow-Hoyts Film Production Partnership, through which they will produce one or two films a year for at least the next three years. Like other

new players in the sector, the group announced an intention to produce
'mainly' Australian films, although the first film to be produced would be
Disturbing Behaviour (1998), in association with MGM Pictures: 'mainly'
Australian is a category apparently compatible within their discourse with a
focus on 'commercial movies for a world wide audience'.[22]

One of the most striking features of the production sector in the 1990s
was its tendency to seek partnerships globally, and to lobby for legislation
enabling internal co-productions. A number of production 'treaties' were
signed in the decade, and collaborations with countries other than America
became more and more conspicuous. In February 1998, for example, a
government treaty to co-produce Irish/Australian films was signed, leading
to the production of Barron Films' *Kings In Grass Castles*. In March 1998,
a six million dollar Indian musical, *Prem Aggan (Heat of Love)*, was shot in
Sydney and Victoria using a 35 per cent Australian crew.

Distribution

In general, Australian films are not produced in conjunction with large
distribution and exhibition companies, as they are, for example, in the
American industry. Where such an 'integrated' system, such as the
American one, might allow producers to share the risk of production costs
across a slate of productions, the Australian system does not have this
advantage, and 'relies on complex financial arrangements involving equity
investment, the provision of pre-sales and distribution guarantees, and
Government funding to raise financing for program production'.[23]

Marketing and distribution are heavily concentrated between three
dominant distributors (Roadshow Film Distributors, Fox Columbia TriStar
and United International Pictures) who have either ownership or contractual
links to major US studios. Between 1989 and 1993, films distributed by
these companies (in general American product) earned more than 96 per
cent of the Australian box office. All of the Australian product was also
handled by these companies. In terms of exhibition, these three companies
accounted for 46 per cent of all screens in Australia in 1995. Television also
of course provides a crucial distribution outlet for Australian cinema.
Commercial television is dominated by three commercial broadcasters
(Channels Seven, Nine and Ten) and two national broadcasters (ABC and
SBS). Cable television was introduced in 1995 with Galaxy satellite/MDS
Services, Foxtel and Optus Vision, but only a minority of Australians
subscribe; in 'September 1996 the proportion of households connected to
pay TV was around six per cent'.[24] Pay television may become a useful

source of new financing, although there is still no effective quota legislation governing Australian content on these channels, although 10 per cent of programme expenditure for predominantly drama channels must be on new Australian drama.

The distribution and exhibition sector is soon to set up a voluntary code of conduct and a dispute-settling system following an inquiry into the industry by the Australian Competition and Consumer Commission (ACCC). During 1998, the commission investigated the industry, following complaints regarding pricing and release policies from independent exhibitors. The ensuing report, 'The Cinema Industry', which documented the commission's investigation found that:

> although there was no hard evidence of anti-competitive behaviour under Australia's Trade Practices Act, there was little doubt that independent exhibitors could be damaged by policies of distributors, which favoured the larger exhibitors.[25]

Overseas distributors have had an increasing role to play in the 1990s in foreign investment in Australian independent films. The Gonski report found that this could be seen as a direct result of the success of Australia's niche product and:

> The increased presence of overseas distributors in Australia (including Miramax) and their willingness to distribute and, in some cases, increase investment in Australian productions augers well for the long-term exposure and profitability of Australian productions.[26]

One area not frequently discussed but which is performing well is video business. Video distributors earned $153m wholesale revenue from sell-through titles, and $228m from rental titles in 1995. It was estimated by the Australian Video Retailers Association (AVRA) that the video rental market was worth $705m in 1995.

Exhibition

The exhibition sector in Australia demonstrated consistent growth throughout the 1990s. The Australian Bureau of Statistics found that from 1979 to 1987 the motion picture industry had experienced a major decline in terms of box office returns for exhibition, but that by 1993–94 there had been a recovery from this, which has continued on an upward trend through the 1990s.[27] Curtis and Gray found that:

Australians paid out over a billion dollars to go to the movies in 1995; this represented 69 million admissions (a rise of two million, or 5 per cent over 1994) ... The theatrical business has had eight consecutive years of growth and there's no sign of its abating. ... Good product, high-quality cinemas and affordability all contributed to growth, as did the increasing numbers of screens.[28]

In 1995 The Village Roadshow/Greater Union/Warner Brothers joint venture announced it would spend $350m to more than double its screen count to 525, in 1998. Hoyts also doubled its screens, and the US-based Reading Corporation announced they would add 150–200 screens to the Australian landscape over the next ten years. Conspicuous in the 1990s was the new visibilty of the 'alternative' sector': arthouse or independent boutique cinemas were in fact so successful in Australia during the decade that mainstream interests began to bid for a corner of their markets. In 1994, Palace Pictures, a distributor and emerging cinema chain, went into partnership with Village (enabling it to get the pick of the product distributed through Village's distribution arm): the resulting company, Palace-Village, then expanded into several states of Australia.

The Future

The global environment for moving image products is changing rapidly at the end of the 1990s, and film production will undoubtedly be affected by increasing levels of international trade, and global strategies designed to liberalise/regulate that trade. The development of new technologies and the convergence of existing ones will also certainly play a part in shaping the future of Australian cinema production. Current industry orthodoxy's seem to suggest that the future of Australian filmmaking lies in the contact zone between commercial formula and the idiosyncrasies of the indigenous. Policy discourse continues to insist that Australian film producers will never be able to compete with dominant producers, such as the USA, and that the way forward lies in the production of niche product – which is 'unusual' and of palpably 'high-quality'. The Gonski report found that:

> The commercial distribution and exhibition of product will be increasingly decided by a small number of global information and entertainment companies, whose economic power and inter-relationships has the potential to 'squeeze out' product for a small, independent Australian industry.[29]

Tom O'Regan has argued that regulatory, commercial and technological changes within Australian media have fundamentally reconstructed the social and cultural agenda, encouraging corridors of information and a 'high communications policy' in which 'a logic of spreading messages further in space and reducing costs of transmission dominates'.[30] In recent times, the threats to cultural sovereignty which may come out of this climate have become more apparent. Project 'Blue Sky' has, for example, been received in Australia as a significant threat. In mid-1998 the decision by the High Court of Australia to allow New Zealand television programmes to qualify as part of Australian local content rules was received by the Australian film and television industry with dismay. Under this legislation, an Australian content quota effectively supports the New Zealand Television (and film) industry. Industry lobbies have argued that this was against the spirit and intention of Australian content requirements and are lobbying for the reversal of the High Court decision, and raising money for a fighting fund, described by the trade paper *Encore*, as a 'war council'.[31] Such rhetoric found numerous echoes in the 1990s, as globalised debate over the regulation/de-regulation of world trade impacted on nationally-based industries of all kinds in Australia.

In 1990, for example, Australia and other signatories to the General Agreement on Tariffs and Trade (GATT) began negotiating fifteen separate multilateral trade agreements. A key area for negotiation was 'trade-in-services' which includes film and television. Australia's limits on foreign ownership of broadcasting, Australian content, government financial support for production and marketing, and limitations on foreign content in television commercials all represent barriers to free trade, to those arguing for a de-regulation of 'restrictive' practices. To those concerned with the preservation/development of national screen practice, on the other hand, they represent crucial 'enabling' mechanisms, which protect fragile systems of cultural difference.

The culturalists' argument, pitched for exemptions on culture, has been made for decades, and is based in a fear of cultural imperialism from America and Britain. Those arguing in the 1990s against cultural protection claimed that the maturation of audiences now meant that consumers wanted the widest choice of audio-visual materials possible, and insisted that 'the least regulated cultural economy can best deliver this plethora of choice'.[32] As Cunningham explains, the maturation of audiences led in the 1990s to the:

> erosion of the idea that they need protection; globalising trends in
> carriage and content; microeconomic reform to encourage more

competition and allocative efficiency, leading to the withdrawal of government from unnecessary, intrusive or irrational regulatory activity; and the ascendancy in theory of political, economic and cultural models that support and render these trends.[33]

The economic attack on the cultural mandate model is further evidenced by current trade liberalisation discussions. In Paris, on 16 February 1998, the future of the Australian production industry was debated at the Organisation for Economic Co-operation and Development (OECD), in discussions on the Multilateral Agreement on Investment (MAI). The MAI is designed to free restrictions on the international flow of investment capital, making it easier for global economic interests to challenge national control of finance and investment. What is of concern to the film and television industries in Australia, and other countries, is that 'barriers' to trade are being defined as including cultural and environmental laws which protect the cultural integrity of member countries. Unless Australia obtains an exemption for its cultural and broadcasting policies, it could be forced to open all its cultural assistance measures and media ownership laws to complete access by all other OECD members. At an extreme, this could this mean that the AFC or AFFC could have to fund all those who are OECD members. Industry groups in Australia have, in the absence of government debate on the cultural impact of the treaty, lobbied extensively for cultural sovereignty, and sent representatives to the GATT meetings. In the shadow of the 'Blue Sky' finding, this is seen by the industry as the most significant threat (industrially and culturally) to the Australian film and television industry to date.

Conclusion

In conclusion, although the film industry appears relatively buoyant, it still relies heavily on government support, and is likely to do so for the foreseeable future. Whilst state subsidy has effectively been shrinking, and the sources of film funding have been changing since the 1970s, when the AFC and state agencies invested in 90 per cent of the films, and contributed 60 per cent of the funds, it remains fundamental. Australian filmmakers have demonstrated their resourcefulness in seeking out new ways to fund film production, whilst overseas players have sought Australia out as both location and co-venturer, increasing capital turnover in the industry considerably in the 1990s. Perhaps the most significant feature of the decade was the maturation of distributors, who came to play a much more significant role, and proved crucial in finessing some of the decade's most imaginative production deals. Yet despite new cinemas apparently opening everywhere, and Australians flocking to them in droves,[34] the future could be bleak for Australian productions if exemptions for culture are not made by OEDC members signing the Multilateral Agreement on Investment. Undoubtedly, 'landmark' successes will determine production levels in the future, given that government bodies like the AFFC will increasingly need returns on their investments, in order to support new projects. As the 1990s drew towards their close, there were at least some signs that such successes were still possible; there was at least still some real sense that the Australian film industry had a future.

NOTES

1. The current state funding agencies for film and television in Australia consist of: Cinemedia (Film Victoria and the State Film Centre of Victoria merged to become Cinemedia in 1997); New South Wales Film and Television Office (NSWFTO), Northern Territory Department of Asian Relations, Trade and Industry (mainly promotes the Territory as a location); Pacific Film and TV Commission (PFTC is now an amalgamation of Film Queensland, and Film Events Queensland); Screen West (formerly The Western Australian Film Council), and the South Australian Film Corporation (SAFC). At the time of writing, Tasmania has no 'Film Office', although Arts Tasmania (AT) facilitates film development in the state. Information on Australian screen organisations is now networked on the internet at 'Screen Network Australia', address: www.sna.net.au.
2. Tom O'Regan, *Australian National Cinema* (London and New York: Routledge, 1996), p.15.
3. The Australian Film Institute now also allows features and shorts originating on videotape, although features still must be made for theatrical release and submitted on film. This is a recognition of the shifts towards the cheaper new digital format in production generally.
4. Susan Dermody and Elizabeth Jacka, *The Imaginary Industry; Australian Film in the Late '80s* (Australia: Australian Film, Television and Radio School, 1988), p.20.
5. Jock Given, 'Creating the Nation – Is This A Film Policy?', *Filmnews*, Vol.25, No.1 (1995), p.6.
6. For detail see: Stuart Cunningham, 'Willing Wonkers at the Policy Factories', *Media Information Australia*, No.73 (1994), p.4.
7. Sue McCreadie, quoted in Tracey Prisk, 'Budget scraps CTPF', *Encore*, Vol.16. No 7 (1998), p.1.
8. The AFC received federal funding of (not counting the Commercial Television Fund) $15.53 million in 1997–98, $16.71 million in 1996–97 and $20.5 million in 1995–96.
9. Tino Balio, 'Adjusting To The New Global Economy: Hollywood in the 1990s', in Albert Moran (ed.), *Film Policy: International, National and Regional Perspectives* (London: Routledge, 1996), pp.33–34.
10. Source: AFC website: http://www.afc.gov.au/resources/online/general/ overview/afto1.html.
11. Rosemary Curtis and Cathy Gray (eds.), *Get The Picture: Essential Data on Australian Film, Television, Video and New Media*, 4th edition (Sydney: Australian Film Commission, 1996), p.7.
12. The *Newsletter of the Australian Writer's Guild* (2 March 1998) reported that there was currently a crisis in development funding at the AFC, with the Commission having only 1.2 million dollars in that financial year (most of which was committed by March 1998).
13. Sandy George, 'Producers Question Genre Debate', *Encore*, Vol.16, No.2 (1998), p.12.
14. O'Regan, *Australian National Cinema*, p.15.
15. The AFC's *National Survey of Feature Film and Independent TV Drama Production 1996–97*, published with the *AFC Information Update Newsletter*, No.165 (October 1997), pp.2–3.

16. A good example of a movie funded under this initiative is *Tangle* (written by John O'Brien, directed by Scot Patterson and produced by Nikki Roller); the movie went into production at the end of 1998, with investment from SBS Independent and the Premium Movie Partnership.Beyond International is the Australian sales agent, although the film still awaits release.

17. For an instructive account of the complexities of deal-making see Al Clark's, *The Lavender Bus: How A Hit Movie Was Made and Sold* (Sydney: Currency Press, 1999).

18. Senator Richard Alston, *Media Release*, Ministry for Communications and the Arts (15 November, 1997), p.2.

19. See the Australian Film Commission's *National Survey of Feature Film and Independent TV Drama Production 1996–97*, published with the *AFC Information Update Newsletter*, No.165 (October 1997), pp.2–3.

20. David Gonski, *Review of Commonwealth Assistance to the Film Industry* (Australia: Australian Government, 1997), p.18.

21. Tracey Prisk, 'Fox Site Opens Its Doors', *Encore*, Vol.16, No.6 (1998), p.1.

22. Tracey Prisk, 'Village and Hoyts for Joint Venture', *Encore*, Vol.16, No.6 (1998), p.3.

23. Gonski, p.19.

24. Rosemary Curtis and Cathy Gray (eds.), *Get The Picture: Essential Data on Australian Film, Television, Video and New Media*, 4th edition (Sydney: Australian Film Commission, 1996), p.2.

25. Tina Kaufman, 'High Court Decision Opens Door to NZ Television Programs', *Metro*, No.115 (1998), p.4.

26. Gonski, p.19.

27. Source: Australian Council, *The Australian Council's Compendium of Arts Statistics* (Australia: Australia Council, 1996), p.72.

28. Curtis and Gray, p.8.

29. Gonski, p.16.

30. Tom O'Regan, 'Towards a High Communications Policy, Assessing Recent Changes', *Media Information Australia*, No.58 (1990), p.123.

31. Tracey Prisk, 'War Over Blue Sky', *Encore*, Vol.16, No.9 (1998), p.3.

32. Stuart Cunningham, *Media Information Australia*, No.63 (1992), p.35.

33. Ibid., p.34.

34. Australians are still amongst the most frequent cinema-goers in the world. The AFC web site reports that in 1997 cinema admissions increased for the tenth consecutive year with 76 million paid admissions recorded at the box office. In 1997 the national box office was $584 million which accounts for an estimated 76 million admissions at a total of 1422 screens.

3

Unhappy Endings:
The Heterosexual Dynamic in Australian Film

NIGEL SPENCE and LEAH McGIRR

> But falling in love ... was not the same as loving. It was in an imagination that one fell in love, and what one fell in love with was only an abstraction.[1]

Many critics have commented on the fact that in very few early Australian films, and in disproportionately few made before the 1980s, do realistic/naturalistic depictions of romantic love and relationships stand out. Brian McFarlane notes that 'rather than make a relationship the central issue of the narrative, many Australian films have chosen to place it either in a recognisable generic framework or subsume it in a more comprehensive social discourse'.[2] Sandra Hall, writing in 1985, reinforces his point in making the observation that 'there are few convincing Australian films which treat the subjects of love, sex, marriage and divorce among the urban middle-class'.[3]

The principal areas of thematic concern evidenced by Australian cinema over its broader historical span are fairly easily identified. Bruce Molloy, for example, notes that 'bush life, family life and class structures have been shown to be consistent components of feature films made in Australia', since the silent period.[4] Concomitantly, analyses of Australian film, aware of its prime modalities and preferred narrative and visual tropes, have focused more on the individual and his/her relationship with land/landscape, and groups or trends in Australian society, than on the individual's relationship with other individuals.

Is one not entitled to find this shying away from stories about individuals relating in the personal and private arena surprising, given that the romantic comedy and romantic drama have long been staples of English-language, particularly American, cinema? Are specific local contexts a factor here? One might propose, as does McFarlane, that a characteristically Australian 'reticence in expressing feeling' is at work here,[5] and perhaps even that this can be attributed to a general disinterest amongst Australian filmmakers in broaching the topic, demonstrating not only a social disinclination for the public expression of deep personal and private emotions, but also supporting Meaghan Morris's stressing of an alternative 'fascination with group behaviour and with relationships seen in the context of social institutions'.[6]

However, by the 1980s, commercial considerations and Australian films' general movement towards the themes and aesthetic standards of the international marketplace, saw Australian filmmakers overcoming their reluctance to position the heterosexual relationship centrally in relation to their narratives.[7] Susan Dermody and Elizabeth Jacka, charting the loss of dominance in the 1980s of what they term the 'AFC-genre and social-realist strands of Australian filmmaking',[8] and the displacement of the 'emphasis on the oppressed or the marginal that was evident in at least the social-realist films of an earlier period with a more middle-class strand of filmmaking',[9] make reference to the rise of what they call the 'personal relations' film.[10] Dermody and Jacka regard such movies, depicting intimate relationships between individuals as 'the most interesting and complex of the recent period', arguing that they attest to the depth of characterisation and narrative intricacy of a number of films featuring heterosexual relationships at their very core.[11]

A rapid survey of the relevant filmographies reveals that there has been an ever-increasing awareness of the complexity of the heterosexual dynamic across the even more recent output, and the list that Dermody and Jacka present as belonging to the category 'Films about Personal Relations/Sexual Mores, 1984–87' is easily extended into the 1990s.[12] Their list includes *My First Wife* (1984), *The Still Point* (1985), *Travelling North* (1986), *Jilted* (1987) and *The Year My Voice Broke* (1987), films which in retrospect offer templates for a longer sequence of later films such as *The Crossing* (1990), *Proof* (1991), *The Last Days of Chez Nous* (1992), *The Nostradamus Kid* (1993), *The Heartbreak Kid* (1993), *The Sum of Us* (1994), *All Men Are Liars* (1995), *Love and Other Catastrophes* (1996), *Angel Baby* (1996), *Dating the Enemy* (1996), *Love Serenade* (1996), and *Hotel de Love* (1996), which alongside their own more localised concerns, can also be viewed as films about personal relations and Australian sexual mores. The analysis presented here focuses on the 'heterosexual dynamic' in these, and some related texts.

The heterosexual dynamic can be defined as the relationship which exists between a male and a female person engaged in an ongoing relationship based on mutual sexual attraction (usually involving cohabitation), and the 'forces, physical or moral, at work'[13] within that relationship. One might extend the application of the term to include those physical, emotional, psychological and behavioural forces which operate within a relationship, conditioning the way in which people view each other and their interaction through the lens of expectations and pre-existing beliefs about the nature of relationships. These forces change over time and could be viewed as possessing an energy and intensity that is not static, hence the use of the term 'dynamic'. Because of the interactive nature of heterosexual relationships, it is difficult to make highly specific statements and observations about the often subtle and variegated forces at work within filmic heterosexual relationships.

Addicted to Love: *Monkey Grip*

A number of films of the 1980s and 1990s have continued to explore and expand the articulation of the themes of the 'personal relations' film, employing one or more heterosexual relationship(s) as the principal means of narrative and thematic development. In looking at such films, one might initially be interested in the way in which Australian cinema constructs and depicts romance and heterosexual interaction, and consider the ways in which these representations could be considered distinctive. Such attention quickly raises related questions: in what ways is representation of the heterosexual dynamic conditioned by earlier modalities of filmmaking, and earlier thematic preoccupations? Put even more simply, one might ask: what do recent examples of films tell us about the way heterosexual Australian men and women relate to one another? How do Aussies love? What significant aspects of the dynamic between Australian men and women emerge from an examination of recent Australian films in which heterosexual dynamic is the central subject?

Films which feature the heterosexual dynamic to a significant degree often display complexities of narration in which the relationship between a man and a woman must reach a point of conflict (usually the climax point of the film) before the relationship can either succeed, or fail. This point of conflict, and occasional subsequent resolution, is a result of emotional, psychological, physical and behavioural factors creating a barrier between men and women in Australian filmic heterosexual relationships. This point of conflict and the issues which are raised in its resolution, engage issues at the heart of the divide between men and women in contemporary Australia.

One might look at a film from the 1980s to provide a brief illustration of the issues involved, before proceeding to more recent films: Ken Cameron's *Monkey Grip* (1982) is both a typical example of a personal relations film of the 1980s, and an early precursor of the more distinctive, more 'muted' approach which Australian filmmakers would bring to this subject matter in the following decade. Set in a contemporary, grimy, hedonistic urban inner-city culture, *Monkey Grip* exemplifies the desire of Australian film producers at the start of the 1980s to depict 'current' issues and a real, 'happening' Australian culture.[14] The film considers 'relationship[s] in socially significant contexts',[15] in this case, the heterosexual dynamic between the central film's narrator, Nora (Noni Hazlehurst), and her lover, Javo (Colin Friels). According to Graeme Turner, the 'realist visual style'[16] of *Monkey Grip* portrays the 'obsessive' relationship between Nora and Javo as fraught with complex physical and emotional burdens and broken by friction and conflict;[17] Nora's addiction to highly emotionalised identification, and Javo's physical addiction to heroin delineates the relationship's form, and colours the couple's interaction at every turn.

As the film begins, Nora reflects on her past experiences; her voice-over commentary, a reminiscence from an unspecified point after the events, recurs regularly throughout the film, revealing her most private thoughts and feelings. This feature is a successful adaptation of the original novel by Helen Garner; as McFarlane writes of director Ken Cameron: 'by retaining a good deal of the novel's 'metalanguage' in Nora's voice-over, he achieves an often startling replication of the feel and tone of the novel'.[18] Describing the start of the relationship as an outgrowth of a rather listlessly – and passionlessly – conducted affair defined mostly by its casualness, Nora's voice-over implies she is already emotionally involved with Javo: 'I think I already knew that this one was going to be trouble'. For three days and nights Javo and Nora have been constantly in each other's company. Nora's voice-over states that for her, 'three nights is enough to make it too late', inextricably linking questions of physical and emotional gratification, which the film will explore further. She does not crave sex purely for pleasure, but is attracted to the associated stimulations of the feelings which accompany the sexual act; she craves the thrill of limerance and the excitement of exploring a new relationship with a new person. As Sandra Hall states in her review of the film:

sexual love is not just part of the psychological scenery – an interesting occupation contemplated or indulged in on the way to manhood or womanhood or war or gaol. It's like a bolt from the blue – arbitrary and destructive. It brings out unscrupulousness in otherwise reasonable people and so makes lovers out of those least likely to be happy together.[19]

Nora understands that Javo's attitude to casual sex is just that, but 'it becomes clear that she would like something more dependable' than her previous liaisons.[20] Despite her modern attitudes, Nora seems to view love as if it is some kind of universal panacea; Javo however, having taken his gratification, sees the affair complicated by Nora's romantic notions of love – especially those which relate to commitment, fidelity, openness and a shared dream of the future. Nora's friend and housemate gives the clue that it is the thrill of new love, rather than any specific person, that Nora seeks. As if recognising the signs of relapse in a junkie, Nora's housemate asks: 'You're not doing it again are you? … You know what you're doing? You're looking at every new one and going, is this the one? There's no future in it'.

The audience gains a sense of the real complexity of the inter-personal dynamic between Nora and Javo as the film's narrative follows them on a 'merry-go-round of parties, drugs and sexual manoeuvres'[21] Narrative and character discourses gradually converge: eventually Nora recognises that she is caught in what she describes as a 'dance' of unrealised, and perhaps unrealistic, dreams of life and love with the shiftless junkie Javo. However, Nora is as addicted to the intense emotional experience of 'love' as Javo is physically addicted to heroin, and as his is a selfish, unsharable 'high', their demands are mutually exclusive. It is some time before either can see this: ironically, it is Javo who eventually acknowledges the problem: 'You only like me when I'm off dope and I only like myself when I'm on it and that's something you won't accept'.

Both characters are morally irresponsible, and in thrall to hedonistic imperatives which they pursue recklessly. It is their very characters, their selfish pursuit of their individual desires, which threatens the relationship's survival. Nora's emotionally self-destructive personal 'roller-coaster' has much in common with the dishonest, unreliable and selfish behaviour Javo exhibits as part of his addiction. She is, it seems, bent on seeking a strong, stable male figure in a milieu comprising persons as emotionally fragile, and as uncertain, as she is. Experiencing cycles of attraction, lust, sex and then boredom, hoping to find 'true love', Nora has spent her adult life drifting from one sensation to another, one friend to another, and one bed to another in what she describes as 'fits of wandering heart'. Nora blames Javo's increasing heroin addiction for the eventual failure of their relationship, but it is their shared dynamic of attraction, their complementary weaknesses and strengths, and resultant interdependence, that condemns them both to the emotional instabilities that the film dramatises.

In *Monkey Grip,* the Australian relationship is shown as existing between two beings barely capable of relating to themselves, let alone to even one other person. Modern life, modern morals, the aimlessness of a society for which leisure time is a burden, these seem to be as much a peril as any physical dangers the film might depict. Nora and Javo have no time to relate to each other; and when they do, they do not seem to have the language. Each relates to a vision of the other, and between them there seems to be an unbridgeable gulf.

Cultures of Blame: *The Last Days of Chez Nous*

The Last Days of Chez Nous is a film concerned with 'how interpersonal relationships develop and change', and examines the heterosexual dynamic in detail while investigating at the same time the nature of the forces which destroy such relationships.[22] The film provides an interesting illustration of the variety of pernicious elements, apparently pervasive, characterising heterosexual relationships in recent Australian film, and has been described as an 'art cinema tale of a marriage break-up'.[23] While *Last Days* manifests some attributes of the personal relations film, certain aspects of the movie might seem to limit its value within a study of a 'typically' Australian heterosexual dynamics, since the notion of 'typicality' undergoes considerable qualification here. The film has mostly been understood in rather different terms, valued for its recognition of a multicultural Australia, and the need to speak to this experience. Positive readings construe the film as reflecting the new and diverse nature of Australian society, and the relationships it produces. Certainly *Last Days* understands that Australian society, its mode and definition of interpersonal relationships are increasingly conditioned by many different ethnicities and cultures.

Beth (Lisa Harrow) is the matriarch of an inner-city Sydney home. With skill and tact she manages her family, not least by remaining dominant in the stormy relationship she enjoys with JP (Bruno Ganz), her husband, a romantic, emotionally powerful Gaelic male, at once practical and passionate, strong (sometimes) and altogether thoroughly unconventional. As the title of the film suggests, the viewer is to witness 'the last days' of their relationship and the fragile ideal of domestic life which has been constructed in the house around this unlikely couple. As the two characters struggle to save their marriage, caught as they are between their conflicting desires and ambitions, the intimate unity they once enjoyed wanes, and their commitment and shared history are set aside in favour of the pursuit of individuation and individual desires.

Both characters are caught in a complex network of drives. Beth desires to resolve the tumultuous relationship she has experienced since childhood with her father; she also wishes to pursue her professional writing career, without surrendering her capacity (and her right) to 'manage' the lives of those around her. JP craves the love and passion which has faded, over time, from his relationship with Beth. He sees this as symptomatic of Beth's assertion of her 'selfish' imperatives, rather than as being a function of his own refusal to compromise, and to abandon his demanding, patriarchal ways.

Beth is further delineated by her interaction with her sister Vicki (Kerry Fox), her daughter Annie (Miranda Otto), boarder Tim (Kiri Paramore) and her parents (Bill Hunter and Lynne Murphy). Beth's natural tendencies towards matriarchal behaviour are exemplified by her agreement with her friend Sally's maxim 'Rosemary only grows where a woman is in control'. Beth is a woman who demands order (and seeks control) not only in her own life but also in her relationships with others. Although she seeks the resolution of family conflict when it occurs, and sees herself as a peacemaker and facilitator, she conspicuously fails to either address or resolve the problems she is experiencing in her relationship with JP. Beth is eventually able to come to terms with, and clarify aspects of, her relationship with her father and maintain the close connection she enjoys with her daughter; however, the emotional turmoil and subsequent division in the marriage that results from both her and JP engaging in extra-marital affairs creates an irretrievable rift in the couple's relationship. JP's later affair with Beth's sister finally completes the destruction of the relationship; his betrayal is compounded by the loss of the strong sororial bond Beth and Vicki once shared.

The nature and history of the stormy relationship between Beth and JP is illustrated early in the film. Their troubled rapport is traced through the diction and tone of a series of idle carpings Beth directs toward JP while he works in the kitchen: 'You always hmm when you sing ... Your sauce is burning ... Put the plate on the mat ... You're worse than my father ...

You'll have to get changed', and so on. JP is, in turn, forthright in his criticism of domestic arrangements as they concern Beth's family and their behaviour: 'She never lifts a finger, your sister ... Your bloody sister. She is still hopeless, spoilt like a baby. This girl will have to break one day from you'. Beth, however, defends her 'baby' sister, claiming that her presence in the house is a comfort to Beth ('I missed her'). JP, however, sees more in this, believing that Vicki serves as some kind of alter-ego to his wife: 'You missed your mirror', he replies. JP's insinuation points to a truth regarding Beth's influence upon Vicki, and Vicki's unconscious desire to be like Beth. Vicki only exacerbates a situation which sees Beth and JP criticise and blame each other for their continued frustration and dissatisfaction, venting submerged feelings of growing resentment upon each other while not focusing on its causes.

The first public articulation of discontent between JP and Beth occurs when JP, Vicki and Annie return from the beach. JP discovers that Beth has eaten some of the French brie that he had placed aside to mature. Reacting with frustration and fury, he berates Beth; 'You are so greedy. You're family is the same; greedy and selfish!'. Such aggression expresses the distaste he feels in response to Beth's actions, but his anger traps him into a vehement display of his deeper resentments toward her family. Caputo is struck by:

> the strong sensation of barriers being slowing erected through the emotional cracks put under pressure by the tug and tow of minute details. *Chez Nous* gets into niggly and prickly areas of interpersonal relationships.[24]

As JP gives vent to his anger; Beth too gradually loses her temper. She slams pots down, sarcastically addressing a 'Sorry!' to her husband in her confusion, as she tries to understand JP's outburst. She accepts that she has made an error; but, as she explains simply, 'I was hungry'. That her husband takes the opportunity to raise long-buried issues is clear to her. The atmosphere of conflict grows, and JP's failure to come to terms with a minor act of lack of consideration is soon amplified into the expression of concern over what he sees as deep-seated 'problems' with his wife (and her family). The brie was, as he points out more than once, 'high up on the cupboard', a sign that it was not to be touched. This careful placement, he feels, no reasonable person could have misconstrued. JP reiterates his feeling that Beth should have read this signal to mean that the cheese was 'out of bounds'. As the audience is becoming aware, there is a great deal more to JP's anger than his frustration with purloined dairy products. His Gaelic temperament is rendered more explosive by recurring feelings of home-sickness ('For two years I have been searching for this kind of cheese'), and his continuing frustration over his deteriorating relationship with Beth. His often volatile emotional state is all hyper-sensitivity, macho-bluster and easily-wounded pride. From this moment on, the pace of the relationship's decline accelerates: the incident with the brie acts as the catalyst for a series of subsequent events, marked by bitter verbal warfare as the final demise of their marriage, which ends in the midst of their escalating mutual disregard for each other.

The marriage between Beth and JP has, one deduces, always been open to unusual strains. The 'practicalities' behind the union are not specified, and a number of crucial questions are left unanswered. Marriage to an Australian citizen had solved JP's residency problems, but what, if any, was Beth's motive in entering into the union? She is revealed as a successful writer, dedicated to her career, endlessly responding to phone calls, all of which seem particularly 'important'; but she desires it both ways, as retaining close control over domestic matters is equally necessary to her. The implication is that 'something has got to give', and in the end it does so. In the end, it is the relationship with JP which she, perhaps unconsciously, releases.

In contrast with the complicated Beth, JP's characterisation shows him to be an honest, forthright, but patriarchal French male. This impression is counterbalanced by his romantic notions of love and life. He feels ignored by Beth, shunted aside as she pursues experiences or attainments she feels she has missed. His response, however, is to ignore the imperilled marriage and simply seek to satisfy his own needs. The degree of deterioration in his marriage is signalled explicitly when he takes Beth's sister, Vicki, as a lover. Although both he and his wife have been guilty of infidelity in the past, there is a vengeful, dangerous edge to this almost 'incestuous' adultery. JP is attracted to Vicki's youthfulness, her vitality and her need to be protected, traits manifestly absent in the independent, feminist-minded Beth. Perhaps he hopes to shock his wife; perhaps Vicki promises a less threatening, but similar, 'replacement': whichever, the contradictions within JP's character and attitudes rise to the surface, just as they do within Beth.

The French-born JP adheres to a belief in traditional gender roles and family structures. However, he and his wife discuss their infidelities openly and honestly, although it is moot whether or not this helps old wounds heal; for Beth the openness doubles as a kind of torture, exacerbating her bitterness and sense of failure. There is no doubt that she feels JP's liaison with her sister is a betrayal, as much for Beth as on her husband's part. JP's rationalisations of the situation are more complicated: he simultaneously entertains the notion that Vicki will provide him with the offspring he has not had with Beth, and articulates the self-serving notion that by having a wife and her sister for mistress, he could come to 'love Beth more'.

Positioned by the narrative as the central character, we are biased towards Beth's point of view, and often share her experience of events as they unfold around her. Much of what we come to learn of the state of the marital relationship, and the relationship between the other members of the family, we witness from her perspective. For example, Beth's daughter and her sister are always contextualised through the lens of her interaction with them. When Beth goes away on a trip in order to attempt to resolve her relationship with her father, we witness the home for the first time without Beth: the extent to which she has dominated the house – and perhaps repressed others through her assumption of control – is revealed in a number of ways. Vicki's doubts about her decision to have an abortion resurface, and she begins to reassess her reliance on Beth, and er previous valorisation of her sister's attitudes. With JP's help, Vicki learns a measure of independence that had been less possible in Beth's company.

Shared moments lead to the emergence of romantic and sexual feelings when JP sees that Vicki is upset. He offers her solace (and more) saying to her: 'You could have given me this baby'. Beth's absence allows a re-alignment of a whole network of interpersonal axes: Tim's blossoming romance with Annie seems only to occur once Beth is removed from the scene, leaving him to 'look after her'. Everyone seems alive to new possibilities, new modes of expression. It is as if the household experiences a flood of energy; as if the stifling force which governed the thoughts, actions and liberties of the group have now lifted. These same people are now free: free to dance around with colanders on their heads, free to dress up, free to sing and be 'wild' – and free (however unprepared) to explore individuality and pursue emotional fulfilment. Gradually however, familiar roles begin to be re-enacted: an intriguing development occurs in Vicki's character in particular. The pupil is seen to be eager to displace her teacher, as Vicki gradually usurps Beth's position. This succession is symbolised in a number of scenes: Vicki and Annie's 'dress-up' in Beth's room in Beth's clothes; Vicki's rejection of Beth's feminist ideology; and by statements of individualism and rebellion, such as her comment to JP: 'That's Beth's opinion. I'm not Beth you know'; and, most importantly, by her decision to acquiesce to an affair with her sister's husband. The message for those affected by these events is that Beth symbolises the forces which prevent people (including JP) from experiencing their true potential, from reaching heights, from making mistakes, from loving unwisely but passionately: in short, from living.

Later, a mood of rebellion is evident. While JP and Beth are having lunch, Beth's friend Angelo (Lex Marinos) indicates his disapproval of feminism as Beth's negativity and insensitivity concerning her marriage and her true feeling towards JP are revealed. 'Look at what you women have done to yourselves. You're like husks', Angelo asserts. The implication is that Beth's strong feminist ideals and the insensitivity she displays by openly belittling JP in front of their friends, show how her ideological stance has warped her instincts, leaving her 'unnatural', dry, embittered and unfulfilled. Additionally, Beth's adherence to a culture of blame seems to have played a considerable part in her disintegrating relationship with JP. Beth is convinced that feminism has the answers to her sense of emptiness, but instead of being disillusioned by feminism's failure to deliver happiness, Beth follows the intellectual non-sequitur of deciding that her sterile emotional state, too, is a function of patriarchy in general and of JP in particular. JP and Beth, so full of promise as individuals and as a couple, lack patience, and have been unable to allow their relationship to find its own level, its own path, and its own dynamic. Both have fixed, rather inflexible views of acceptable gender role behaviours. JP is stuck in a traditional, male-focused sexism; Beth seems hidebound by a modern view of history which seeks to blame men's sexism for all the ills of the world (as pregnant Sally relates: 'I'm not supposed to tell, but it's a boy'; Beth responds 'Oh well, better luck next time'). Neither view is real or realistic, and both ignore the extent to which a successful relationship must be based on giving and sacrifice, and on sometimes putting another's desires ahead of one's own.

Does *Chez Nous* have anything more agreeable to say about relations between men and women in 1990s Australia? While the film is pessimistic about the relationship between JP and Beth, it does employ a positive ongoing motif, in the piano duet of Annie and Tim, which does suggest some future for love and potentially creative partnerships between the sexes. The duo grows in proficiency as they practise their musical piece, and their relationship progresses along parallel lines. By contrast with Beth and JP, the pair displays patience and mutual concern. Rather than seeking individual happiness, each takes pleasure in making their partnership stronger, and in smoothing their teamwork and harmony as performers. Annie and Tim are content to take one step at a time, steadily improving; the duet becoming a symbol of the work required for a successful relationship as, indeed, 'practice makes perfect'. The strong implications of the narrative are that their relationship is the only one not doomed to failure: Tim teaches Annie (and learns from her) as she learns to play the piano piece and to participate in the relationship, in a vital heterosexual dynamic.

By the end of *The Last Days of Chez Nous* Beth has taken a lesson in life from the break-up of her marriage. At the film's conclusion she sets off with renewed ambition and purpose, intending to visit another distant (and symbolic) goal. She intends to travel to the base of the church spire she often views from 'Chez Nous', but which has hitherto remained a tantalising, distant signpost. As Beth and JP finally part, it is as if a veil softly settles over the house they shared and its previous occupants, along with a muted tone sounding failure, rejection and betrayal.

Generic Inspirations: *Love Serenade*

Recent examples of the personal relations film such as *Love Serenade*, *Hotel de Love*, *Love and Other Catastrophes* and *All Men are Liars*, reveal other aspects of the way Australian men and an Australian women relate, whilst, at formal levels, employing rather different aesthetic and stylistic strategies. These films qualify the avowedly 'realist' approaches represented by both *Monkey Grip* and *The Last Days of Chez Nous*, and owe more to the motifs and clichés of romantic narrative, and the love story genre, than to social-realist aspirations or the intensities of stage naturalism. Their importance in this context is perhaps that they deal with the heterosexual dynamic as their absolutely central subject matter.

Love Serenade, for example, poses a number of questions as it relates the quirky, surreally-edged tale of a bizarre love triangle in a town on the Murray River in Victoria: why do we choose to love someone? How much do factors like proximity weigh on the development of relationships? Do we love a person as an individual as much as we love being in love with someone? How often do we attribute characteristics to an object of desire, and insist on the attribution long after evidence might have lead us to change our minds? How much of love is illusion, in a final analysis, a tawdry cloth over which we drape the naked facts of the urge to reproduce?

In *Love Serenade* sisters Vicki-Ann (Rebecca Frith) and Dimity (Miranda Otto) Hurley are trapped in their hometown, the tiny, decaying agricultural community of Sunray. Vicki-Ann, as she is fond of reminding her sister, has taken their parents' place in the life of the young Dimity. With few marital prospects among the local men (Vicki-Ann's one-and-only love having perished years before in an accident involving a chainsaw), the siblings have been left to rely on each other for company and diversion, watching dreams of glamour and excitement fade like curtains in the sun as they move back and forth between their non-descript house and workplace, share lunch every day on the same seat at the local Rotary Park, and pass their time away, with sluggish habit becoming slow ritual as the years are eaten away by frustrated hopes.

However, great excitement is about to enter Sunray, and the sisters' lives, in the person of once-famous radio personality Ken Sherry (George Shevstov) , the newly-appointed disc jockey at the local radio station. At the film's opening, as Vicki-Ann and Dimity share an afternoon's fishing, we see the celebrated announcer's arrival in the town. Everything from his antiquated vehicle, to his hairstyle, to his choice of music, tells us that Sherry is caught in a time-warp, reflecting a world which is at least a decade and a half-vanished, except in places like Sunray, and for people like Ken Sherry.

Sherry's turn-off from the highway, over the bridge and into the town marks a significant, symbolic step for him. The outside world falls away, and we join him in a slow descent into a deceptive world, in which the sanest figure we meet is an enigmatic, Australian–Chinese cook with a penchant for nudism, a love of country and western music, and a fondness for bursting into song while mouthing dryly-phrased pop-Confuscian wisdom. Sunray is a town in which people might or might not be capable of turning into fish, and in which sisters, 'bewitched' by the Barry White records Sherry plays, see a prince in a garrulous, pretentious, has-been disc-jockey.

Long a fan of the moody, deep-voiced announcer, Vicki-Ann's thrill turns to ecstasy when the man around whom she has already constructed elaborate romantic fantasies moves in next door. Hoping against hope that she will be able to form a relationship with her suave-sounding idol, the love-starved Vicki-Ann is quick to allow wishful-thinking to turn into fact. She leaves Sherry meals about which he is off-hand, but which she deceptively describes to her employee at Vicki-Ann's 'Unisex Hairport' as being received with exceptional gratitude. Later she will allow herself to become convinced that a dinner-date and a one-off sexual encounter equate to a proposal of marriage. However, it is the unlikely figure of the dowdy Dimity who first finds her way into Ken Sherry's bed.

The merest hint of kindness and interest is enough to render Dimity vulnerable to Sherry's eventual seduction. Actress Miranda Otto conveys the emotional vicissitudes of the almost impossibly awkward and self-conscious Dimity through a repertoire of shuffling, evasive body languages: through her performance we discover a person of emotional intensity lacking the confidence, social skills, and vocabulary to articulate the feelings which besiege her as the film's events unfold. Life is lived second-hand through a network of inherited codes: as she undresses for Sherry, we can see her straining to recall the expressions and movements of actresses she has seen in films. There is both pathos and comedy in the scene in which she ambushes Sherry outside the radio station with a helium balloon bearing the saccharine legend 'I Wuv You'.

The unconscious competition which has arisen between the sisters escalates; Vicki-Ann, as one might imagine, turns angry and disconsolate when she learns of the liaison ('Having sex with someone doesn't mean they are your boyfriend, Dimity'). Not surprisingly, the sisters are temporarily estranged, and equally predictably, Dimity's limitations soon become obvious to Sherry who quickly turns his attention to her elder sister. Sherry's selfish drive to satisfy his desires triggers a series of events which dramatically illustrate the divide between male and female expectations of relationships and fulfilment.

Insensitivity seems to be Sherry's long suit; the audience has several times been shown how little the disc jockey cares for the feelings of others, but when he takes Vicki-Ann to Albert's Chinese restaurant for a meal (where, of course, they will be served by Dimity) we question his common sense. The potentially explosive situation is complicated by the fact that Albert (John Alansu) has always had strong feelings for Vicki-Ann. As the evening progresses, Albert favours Sherry with a critique of his programme (too many songs about the act of 'procreation', what's needed is more Charlie Pride), but Sherry responds with relaxed arrogance; 'It seems to me, that song ('Behind Closed Doors') is about, as you put it, the act procreation'. Albert's counter is telling; 'Maybe so, but at least Charlie Rich seems to base his acts of procreation on a foundation of love and mutual respect'. What comment might be being made on the loveless sexual shenanigans depicted in the movie is not clear; however, when Vicki-Ann and Sherry return to his house she, like her sister, offers little resistance to his blatant, sleazy, seduction. The resultant encounter occurs with deserted Dimity lying on Sherry's couch, the repetitive pounding in the adjacent bedroom causing the mounted marlin trophy to shake and fall from the wall.

Next afternoon, convinced that long-denied connubial bliss is now imminent, and all eager, gormless joy, Vicki-Ann arrives on Sherry's doorstep to model for him her carefully-preserved bridal dress. Sherry's immediate rejection of this notion precipitates the film's tragi-comic climax. Vicki-Ann flees to the top of a nearby grain silo and Dimity, fearing her sister will commit suicide, manages to persuade Sherry to follow her. With the three perched atop the giant structure, Sherry repeats a cliché-laden homily he has earlier delivered to Dimity: its gist is that the essence of love is like a bird which should never be constrained. 'Now I've set you free', he intones with an oily smile to Vicki-Ann, placing the best possible construction on his refusal to take responsibility for his callous exploitation of the sisters, 'as I've set Dimity free. Now, all I ask is that you set me free'.

Literally elevated perspectives seem to encourage insight. Dimity now seems to understand the true nature of that from which Sherry needs to be freed; it is his ego and his desires from which he needs to be liberated. She recognises that he is as trapped in the past, in the persona and in the music of his period of fame, as the sisters are trapped in stultifying Sunray. Recognition produces a rare moment of decisive action. Dimity gives Ken Sherry a sudden, brisk push, and he drops from the silo to his death. 'Well. Looks like I certainly won't be getting married to him now', notes a suddenly calm Vicki-Ann. That night the sisters dispose of Sherry's body in the Murray River. Dimity, her face suffused with spiritual awareness, reads a butchered fragment of a poem popular during the early 1970s, 'Desiderata', whose mock-antique theological vapidity Ken Sherry has recently introduced to the citizens of Sunray. 'Amen' echoes Vicki-Ann reverently, as they push Ken's body over the side of their boat. For a moment it seems their crime may be exposed. Dimity's 'wuv' balloon, still attached to the body, and then the body itself, bubble back to the surface. Fate is at hand however. As the sisters flee in their boat, screaming, what must be a giant carp takes the body of Ken Sherry. The irony is unmissable: in the last shot of the film the fish the DJ would not eat, and the fish to which he has been likened, even deliberately compared, drags Sherry down river, with the helium-filled 'I Wuv You' balloon, incongruously marking the body's course out of the narrative.

Love Serenade's black humour relies on revealing a culture which harbours some strange notions about what constitutes 'natural' activity, and the film works hard to 'estrange' its protagonists. In a culture of naive, sentimental romance people are seen as others would have them be; cliché passes for passion, and, in romance and relationships, appearance is revealed as being more acceptable than substance. Love is not a mutually fulfilling dynamic but a mechanism for gaining personal satisfaction. The division between the two women and Ken Sherry arises from the contradiction between Sherry's sexual desires and Vicky-Ann's attraction to emotional melodrama. Ken 'permits' the women to intrude on his time, a gesture which is reciprocated with the 'price' of sexual gratification. The unbalanced, almost black nature of the sisters' bewitched infatuation with Ken provides an example of an environment in which the murky waters of the Murray River and the 'atmosphere of yearning and desire and longing'[25] created by the music of Barry White combines to create a serenade that is 'beautiful on one level', but 'sinister' underneath.[26]

Conclusions

An analysis of heterosexual relationships, as they are presented in Australian films of the late 1980s and 1990s, reveals a number of common factors. Chief among these is a palpable 'separateness' or division which is assumed to exist between Australian men and women, and which allows the films to connect with the imagined experience of their audiences. For all the development and investment in the 'personal relations' film since the later 1980s, in the antipodean version of the war between the sexes, mutual incomprehension and a belief in the inevitability of mutual incomprehension is still particularly marked. The resultant uneasiness which often accompanies the workings of the heterosexual dynamic seems to derive from these assumed divisions between the sexes in Australia, which exist in terms both of sex-role stereotypes ('those beliefs concerning the general appropriateness of various roles and activities for men and for women')[27] and sex-trait stereotypes ('those psychological characteristics or behavioural traits that are believed to characterise men with much greater or lesser frequency than they characterise women').[28]

In the films under discussion, incompatibilities, misunderstandings and misconstructions in these areas result in conflicting expectations of relationships, as partners see each other simultaneously as an answer to life's problems and the very enemy of personal fulfilment. In these films, partners are unknown and unknowable quantities, only to be trusted conditionally, usually to be exposed dramatically. Beliefs about the insincerity and untrustworthiness of the partner in a heterosexual relationship are found to be illustrated regularly in these and other

Australian films of the 1990s. Parties regularly enter into Australian heterosexual relationships uncertain about the commitment and genuineness of the other. Even where the depiction of 'good' relationships occurs, it is as if there is a standing cultural order that men and women must act as if some compromising mutuality is to be avoided. A relationship's deterioration is regarded as some kind of grim inevitability in numerous films. What is more concerning perhaps is the frequent acceptance that mutual antagonism is a natural, even desirable, feature of the choreography of the attraction. The structure of feelings involved is perhaps best summarised in *Dating the Enemy* (1996), a macabre treatment of the themes in which a couple on the verge of breaking up wake up to find themselves inhabiting each other's bodies.

Certainly these emphases are not new to Australian cinema in the 1990s. As noted above, films of the early-to-mid-1980s portrayed the interaction between men and women as fundamentally problematic. Films such as *My First Wife, Jilted, My Brilliant Career* (1979), *Careful He Might Hear You* (1982), and *Travelling North*, all depicted the heterosexual dynamic as a multifaceted and dramatic interaction, characterised by repulsion as often as by attraction, and governed by economies of desire operative at a range of practical, emotional and discursive levels. The dramatic and antagonistic nature of the relationships presented in such films seems to justify descriptions of the heterosexual encounter as a 'symbolic battleground'.[29] Brian McFarlane rightly observes that:

> No one lives happily ever after in these films: if couples are together at the end, they can look forward either to bored frustration or further rancorous exchanges.[30]

Changes are evident however in the 1990s. One notes the development of various strategies in movies by contemporary filmmakers, designed to explore the heterosexual dynamic as something more positive, and to overcome the limitations imposed by inherited stereotypes and other culturally conditioned views. In the films discussed here, and in others such as *Country Life* (1994), *Waiting* (1991), *All Men are Liars, Love and Other Catastrophes*, and *Hotel de Love*, the heterosexual relationship is depicted with a greater sense of the 'real' – the relationships seem more genuine, as if there is a firmer desire to understand what men and women really think, and how men and women actually behave. Rather than expending energy on attempting idealised constructions, or in presenting appealing but misleading stereotypes as if they were a whole truth, these films work with more localised 'case studies'. Rather than emphasising the view of the often 'disturbingly dysfunctional' nature of Australian heterosexual relation-ships, these films work with possibilities, rather than (usually unrealised) expectations.[31] If these films offer little direct comfort, presenting Australian men and women in film retreating to silence (*All Men are Liars*), or relinquishing relationships amidst misunderstanding, mutual suspicion and fear (*Hotel de Love*), they also show diagrammatically that a loss of faith in the heterosexual dynamic creates a force that distances, disconnects and sunders individuals in ways which restricts the possibilities of real growth.

The effects of this division can be seen in operation in many Australian films of the 1990s. From the love-addicted and mutually destructive relationships in *Monkey Grip*, to the modern Australian feminist at odds with her passionate French husband in *The Last Days of Chez Nous*, to the frustrated spinster sisters and their unsuitable paramour in *Love Serenade*. Each of these films displays relationships that are as complex as they are inherently different; yet the same factors emerge from these films.

Many recent films provide evidence for a belief about heterosexual interpersonal relationships which seems to be widely held by Australian filmmakers (if not also by many Australians): a view that even the best relationships are characterised by dysfunctionality because there is some kind of unbridgeable gulf, some essential incomprehension, some incurable enmity, between Australian men and women. This feature is a bar, or barrier, an obstruction whose outline only becomes visible through the richness, complexity and honesty of depiction which has developed in Australian filmmaking during recent decades. The bar between men and women that can be seen in the analysis of recent Australian films demonstrates the 'recurring stress on the frustrations, inequalities, and destructive patterns at work in relationships',[32] suggesting that Australian heterosexual relationships are inherently flawed. Mutuality is viewed with suspicion, and relationships are therefore often unsuccessful, ineffectual and condemned to failure. The reasons for this separateness are complex. In the Australian films viewed, factors such as poor communication, sexual malfunction, emotional stagnation, adultery, drug dependency, insensitivity, high alcohol consumption, unrealistic expectations, obsession, frigidity, lying, ethnic and cultural differences, unfulfilled expectations, male camaraderie, psychosis, old age, death, and sexual aggression have been observed and found to contribute to the notion of separateness between Australian men and women.

However, the greatest problem might well be the negative view which individuals bring to their relationships from the very beginning. Once the first rush of hormones and the 'high' of initial joy has subsided, a culturally-conditioned pessimism and an almost ritual antagonism sets in, and the results can be observed in the progressive estrangement which characterises the relationships depicted in recent Australian films. 'Familiarity breeds contempt', as the proverb says, and when there was only mistrust to begin with, perhaps the best that Australian partners can say to each other as they leave the cinema, after witnessing yet another example of how poorly Australian men and women deal with the heterosexual dynamic, is: 'At least we're not that bad. Yet'.

NOTES

1. Aldous Huxley, *The Devils of Loudun* (London: Chatto & Windus, 1952), p.16.
2. Brian McFarlane, *Words and Images: Australian Novels into Film* (Richmond: Heinemann, 1983), p.117.
3. Sandra Hall, *Critical Business: The New Australian Cinema in Review* (Adelaide: Rigby, 1985), p.3.
4. Bruce Molloy, *Before the Interval: Australian Mythology and Feature Films, 1930–1960* (St Lucia: University of Queensland Press, 1990), p.209.
5. McFarlane, *Words and Images*, p.111.
6. Meaghan Morris, 'Personal Relationships and Sexuality', in Scott Murray (ed.), *The New Australian Cinema* (Melbourne: Thomas Nelson, 1980), p.135.
7. John Nicholl, 'Review: *The Year My Voice Broke*', *Cinema Papers*, No.67 (Jan. 1988), p.43.
8. Susan Dermody and Elizabeth Jacka, *The Imaginary Industry: Australian Film in the Late '80s* (North Ryde: Australian Film, Television and Radio School, 1988), p.111.
9. Ibid.
10. Ibid.
11. Dermody and Jacka, p.112.
12. Ibid., p.111.
13. Definition adapted from 'Dynamics', in Delbridge *et al.*, *Macquarie Dictionary* (North Ryde: The Macquarie Library, 1991), p.548.
14. Peter Lawrance, '*Monkey Grip*', in Scott Murray (ed.), *Australian Film 1978–1994: A Survey of Theatrical Features* (Melbourne: Oxford University Press, 1995), p.104.
15. McFarlane, *Words and Images*, p.120.
16. Graeme Turner, *National Fictions: Literature, Film and The Construction of Australian Narrative* (Sydney: Allen & Unwin, 1986), p.133.
17. Ibid.
18. McFarlane, *Words and Images*, p.138.
19. Hall, p.94.
20. Brian McFarlane, 'Review: *Monkey Grip*', *Cinema Papers*, No.39 (Aug. 1982), p.366.
21. McFarlane, *Words and Images*, p.120.
22. Raffaele Caputo, '*The Last Days of Chez Nous*', in Scott Murray (ed.), *Australian Film 1978–1994: A Survey of Theatrical Features* (Melbourne: Oxford University Press, 1995), p.343.
23. Tom O'Regan, *Australian National Cinema* (New York: Routledge, 1996), p.195.
24. Raffaele Caputo, 'Review: *The Last Days of Chez Nous*', *Cinema Papers*, No.90 (Oct. 1992), p.53.

25. Andrew L. Urban, 'Writer-Director Shirley Barrett interviewed by Andrew L. Urban', *Cinema Papers*, No.110 (June 1996), p.13.
26. Ibid., p.12.
27. John Williams and Deborah Best, *Measuring Sex Stereotypes: A Thirty Nation Study* (Beverly Hills: Sage, 1982), p.16.
28. Ibid.
29. Morris, p.137.
30. McFarlane, 'Review: *Monkey Grip*', p.112.
31. O'Regan, p.21.
32. McFarlane, 'Review: *Monkey Grip*', p.112.

4

Vulnerable Bodies:
Creative Disabilities in Contemporary
Australian Film

LIZ FERRIER

> In a post-industrial society, in which cultural services have replaced
> material goods at the core of production, it is the defence of the
> subject, in its personality and in its culture, against the logic of
> apparatuses and markets, that replaces the idea of class struggle.[1]

The internationally-acclaimed film *Shine* is one of a number of
contemporary Australian movies which portray embattled artists or
performers. Reminiscent of earlier works such as *Starstruck* (1982), *Man
of Flowers* (1983), *Malcolm* (1986) and *Sweetie* (1989), and several more
recent productions – *Proof* (1991), *Strictly Ballroom* (1992), *Bad Boy
Bubby* (1994), *The Adventures of Priscilla, Queen of The Desert* (1994),
Muriel's Wedding (1994), *Cosi* (1996), *Lilian's Story* (1996), and Jane
Campion's New Zealand/Australian films, *An Angel at My Table* (1990)
and *The Piano* (1993)[2] – it depicts a disadvantaged individual overcoming
setbacks through the passionate and eccentric expression of his creativity.
The film and the cycle to which it belongs offers a peculiar vantage point
from which to examine the problems and possibilities of Australian cinema
in the 1990s.

Express Yourself

Placing a particular strand of Australian cinema in the 1990s within the
overall output is difficult, given the apparent weakening of the 'aesthetic
force fields' which seemed to form production into recognisable groupings
in previous decades. Graeme Turner remarks on the heterogeneity of more
recent Australian cinema, and notes the 'fresh and unpredictable' quality of

many films produced since the 1980s.[3] Tom O'Regan echoes his observation, asserting that contemporary Australian cinema resists simple categorisation and is characterised by diversity.[4] Whilst it is doubtful that as varied and interesting a selection of films as those listed above can be reduced to the same formula, or even constructed as representing an organic series, it is useful to explore common ground between them, since they do exhibit remarkably similar narrative elements, and deploy distinctive combinations of those elements towards comparable ends. Judging by the popularity of many of these films, it would appear that this combination of elements has appeal for audiences, nationally and internationally.[5] It may be that the success of some of these films owes a lot to the repetition of popular myths about creative expression in the 1990s, repetitions which present creative, and compulsive, self-expression as a legitimate expression of the competitive performance ethos of the late twentieth century – sitting somewhere between Madonna's mantra 'Express yourself' and Nike's performance slogan 'Just do it'.

The films under discussion might be thought of as constituting a sub-genre or tropic-genre, which has meaning for contemporary Australian audiences for particular reasons. The immediate aim is to explore these reasons, and historically situate this quite distinctive Australian narrative pattern, suggesting ways of understanding it in terms of cultural traditions and current economic conditions. The pattern can be fairly easily delineated in schematic form: an embattled artistic individual, suffering from a disability or difference which isolates him or her socially, manages to find solace and ultimately social recognition, through creative performance and self-expression. It is a particularly Romantic conception of the artist, combined with a Modern interest in the psychological development of the individual. In most of the films, the individual's disability or difference is linked to their creativity and bad parenting.

The pattern runs close to the surface through several of the films already mentioned. In *Malcolm* for example, the protagonist (Colin Friels) is intellectually disabled, yet creative, and 'succeeds' through his ingenuity and skilful construction of gadgetry necessary to pull off a series of daring bank raids. In *Proof*, the blind central character, Martin (Hugo Weaving), still psychologically damaged from bad parenting, takes 'unseen' photographs of the world around him as his 'aesthetic' solution to that condition. In *Cosi*, patients in a psychiatric hospital successfully perform an opera. Both *Bad Boy Bubby* and *Shine* feature characters shown to be the disturbed products of extreme psychological and physical abuse (very bad parents), who both become exceptional artistic performers. *Strictly*

Ballroom shows two unconventional, isolated young people, Scott (Paul Mercurio) and Fran (Tara Morice), misunderstood by the dancing fraternity and their families (more bad parenting), get together and express themselves through dance, and succeed in a major competition. By contrast: Scott's father (Barry Otto) connotes disablement and emasculation; his creativity is shown to have been thwarted by the conventional dancing fraternity. In the sub-plot about Fran's emergence, plainness and physical clumsiness are presented as her disabilities, which are overcome through creative self-expression.

Muriel's Wedding extends the pattern further: the film's eponymous heroine (Toni Colette) is an oddball (bad parenting again), a social misfit rather than literally disabled, although as with Fran in *Strictly Ballroom*, her physical plainness is presented very much as a disability which is eventually overcome through performance. Disability is figuratively apparent elsewhere in the narrative about Muriel's family, and literally evident in the subplot concerning her best friend, Rhonda (Rachel Griffiths), who is affected by a spinal tumour and confined to a wheelchair. Muriel herself emerges as a complete (and physically beautiful) character only when she begins to express herself creatively. She dresses up (first as one of the ABBA stars, and later as a bride) and acts out wedding fantasies. Although Muriel, like Malcolm, is not portrayed so much as an 'artist' as a 'con-artist', her redemption is expressly linked with creative self-expression, and affinities with the 'disabled artist' cycle are particularly strong.

In *The Adventures of Priscilla, Queen of the Desert*, the transvestites also express themselves creatively through performance. *An Angel at My Table* shows a young woman, disadvantaged because of her sensitive artistic temperament, misdiagnosed and incarcerated as schizophrenic, who subsequently expresses herself, and wins acclaim through creative writing. The heroine of *Lilian's Story* is labelled as mad, and becomes a social outcast (her disability), and expresses herself through the reciting of poetry and Shakespeare. While she does not succeed or redeem herself through this, she acquires legendary status, and in this sense reaches a wide audience. *The Piano*'s Ada (Holly Hunter) is mute, and offers perhaps the limit case of the disabled-artist figure so prominent in the cycle; she expresses herself compulsively and finds redemption through the playing of her piano, tapping the keys with a silver false finger. Although the effect may seem grotesque in its description, like many of the films under discussion here, The *Piano* steers away from the grotesque by aestheticising it in depictions of the disability, emphasising the character's sympathetic vulnerability. As Campion herself stresses:

> There is no sense of her as a handicapped person, however. It is almost as though she treats the world as if it were handicapped. At the same time there is a great deal of suffering from this position.[6]

Even a brief outline of the cycle suggests several significant and recurrent features, worth noting before deepening an analysis:

- the motif of disablement and vulnerability;

- the related motif of isolation and incarceration;

- the emphasis on poor parenting (usually hopeless fathers – either repressive, or ineffectual); – the relatively 'passive' nature of the protagonists in the face of conflict, retreating into compulsive creative pursuits rather than external action (consistent with the disavowal of the agency of the individual identified by Turner in Australian narrative traditions[7]);

- the outstanding creativity of the protagonists, and their sensitive 'artistic' temperaments;

- the emphasis on performance and self-expression as solution or redemption, and

- the desirability of reaching large audiences. The latter suggests an 'art-as-therapy' solution in the narratives, which can become an 'art-as-meal-ticket' resolution. Success, when achieved, is the product of impractical, passionate self-expression, rather than pragmatism;

- the character's success has 'pure' rather than commercial origins.

There is much to be said about these various recurrent features, which seem amenable to explication in both industrial and cultural terms. Certainly, these films appear to reconcile, often at a narrative level, and sometimes in the marketplace itself, the culture/industry opposition that critics including Susan Dermody and Elizabeth Jacka claim has dominated the Australian film industry since the 1970s.[8] Many of these films find ways for 'passive' Australian characters (usually constructed as acted upon rather than acting) to participate in triumphant, and marketable, narratives about individual success. The characters are presented as vulnerable artists (dedicated to culture), who manage to succeed and find wider audiences (i.e. they succeed in the industry). Whilst the films announce an awareness of the potentially commercial and popular nature of aestheticism, a recognition of the commodification of culture, they remain outside of (and often lack the resources necessary for) mainstream commercialism. The non-generic, artistic, anti-commercial films of the 1980s (variously identified by Cunningham, Dermody and Jacka and Turner[9]), which differentiated themselves from the commercial industry and American cinema through their aestheticism (among other things), are thus effectively replaced in the 1990s, by more commercially viable films which celebrate in their narratives those values upheld by the 'Industry 1' (Culture) films of the 1980s.

The term 'commercial' is not used in a pejorative sense here, nor is it suggested that the movies in question are similar to Hollywood films in style and/or narrative form. By comparison with even average-budget Hollywood filmmaking, these recent Australian pictures are 'low-concept' and low-budget; their narratives follow the relatively loose or 'naturalistic' structure of their characters' lives, rather than the strongly-profiled trajectories of the usually unilateral Hollywood narrative. Driven by character rather than plot, they demonstrate a spatial rather than temporal logic, and attend to quirky details which particularise character and place, rather than opting for emblematic locales less likely to distract from the onward progression of narrative. In many ways the films thus develop distinctively Australian narrative traditions, even when working with Hollywood genres. As Turner puts it, many do not 'fit comfortably into already established genres', and even those that do work with commercial genres, offer a 'highly detailed representation of the local'.[10] Turner understands this new condition in terms of hybridity:

> The contradictions which have for so long dominated understandings of Australian films and genre films, between mainstream style and the cultural nationalist remit of the local industry, are reprocessed into a convincing, unselfconscious hybridity of structure and content.[11]

Precedents for this new fusion have been identified before. Stuart Cunningham, in his discussion of the musical *Starstruck*, highlighted its transcendence of genre, and its reconciliation of past oppositions between the art film and the overtly commercial film, in a now much-quoted article.[12] His comments remain suggestive for an understanding of the way these more recent Australian films have further challenged those culture/industry oppositions and reworked Australian narrative traditions to suit market conditions in the 1990s.[13] The films under discussion here are certainly more commercial in narrative structure than many earlier (and other contemporary) Australian films, particularly in the way that they work towards closure and resolution. The characters are often redeemed through personal success, rather than 'stranded at the point of conflict', although one might argue that their triumphant resolutions are far from complete.[14]

It is important to acknowledge that there are many recent Australian films which do not follow this narrative pattern, and do not work towards 'personal success' as resolution. *The Well* (1997), for example, a film which has many of the elements discussed above (a disabled, vulnerable, isolated, piano-playing individual, interested in culture, confronts a changed world of commodification and hybridised cultural forms) does not end with its protagonist's fulfilment. Hester (Miranda Otto) is 'stranded at the point of conflict' as the film concludes, and its central enigma is never fully resolved. In the current climate however, the film stands out for its refusal of the 'up-ending', signalling general industry unease about the viability of the less-than-optimistic narrative, or at least a recognition of the film's difference from mainstream commercial cinema.

Many of the films discussed here not only lack 'up-endings' demonstrated by fantastic personal achievement in performance, but are also identifiable in terms of commercial genres, and combine elements of genres, exhibiting the 'hybridity' identified by Turner.[15] Typically, they draw together elements of the musical with romantic comedy (*Strictly Ballroom*), or melodrama (*Shine*). 'The trappings of genre' are indeed 'put to quite varied uses' in these films.[16] The point to be made here is that these are (mostly) commercially viable films about eccentric, non-commercial, artistic characters. Without reducing a complex shifting field through simplistic periodisation, this could be thought of as marking a transition from the 'eccentric' movies of the 1980s (identified by Dermody)[17] to a series of more mainstream films *about* eccentrics in the 1990s. One could perhaps thus identify a sub-genre of 'eccentric artist films', which has its origins in those unusual films of the preceding decade. This is not just a matter of the (once marginal) eccentric/quirky film coming to occupy a more central position in the industry as it has grown in popularity, but of the actual structure of the eccentric/quirky film changing in response to industry and market forces. Many Australian films of the 1990s, made for international markets, are plainly conscious of the way that aestheticism can be commercialised; just as the characters often find wider audiences for their initially 'privatised' creative art/performance, so the films seem to find wider audiences, beyond both international niche markets and the art-house cinemas in which they might once have played in relatively splendid isolation.

The pattern identified in contemporary Australian film suggests a great deal about popular conceptions of creative practice in Australia, and the ways in which they answer the prevailing market conditions of the 1990s. The popularity of this pattern over the past decade in Australian cinema, and the particular inflection it has assumed, can be understood in terms of global economic restructuring, and the impact that this has had on Australia's culture industries. From this perspective, it can be argued that, the popular figure of the disadvantaged creative individual in Australian film is less an expression of a growing collective concern for the socially disadvantaged, than an articulation of anxieties and mythologies about the viability of local cultural industries in the context of deregulated international markets. Certainly, romantic portraits of the 'artist' as a young person, affirm individualism, trace the emergence of personality (indeed, endorse the cult of personality) and invest value in the notion of distinctive identity. Such portraits may also appear to confirm Touraine's observation, quoted at the beginning of this analysis, that class struggle is replaced in a post-industrial society, by the defence of the subject, in its personality and its culture, against the logic of apparatuses and markets.[18]

The image of the vulnerable body conveys anxiety about the shifting ground within and without Australia's culture industries, and a sense of loss of control over cultural boundaries. Uncertainty about boundaries is linked with uncertainty about audiences – local, national and international. Repeated scenes of artists performing in geographic isolation are emblematic of the sense of isolation haunting Australian culture industries seeking global markets and distribution. Scenes showing the playing of the trumpet in the outback, in *Dingo* (1992); Ada playing her piano on an isolated beach in *The Piano*; performances and displays in the desert in *The Adventures of Priscilla, Queen of the Desert* and so on, all offer powerful images of the artist confronting spaces devoid of audiences. In suburban contexts, Helfgott (*Shine*) performs brilliantly in the privacy of his home or room; Fran and Scott in *Strictly Ballroom* dance on a secluded rooftop; Muriel (in *Muriel's Wedding*) rehearses ABBA numbers and wedding processions in her bedroom. Such scenes of isolated performance play on the juxtaposition of culture in remote and unusual locations. They perpetuate the romantic myth of the antipodean landscape giving rise to strange yet creative expressions, and suggest that isolation is a prerequisite for romantic genius, as much as it is a torment. These scenes also serve as a narrative device, building hope and expectation that the protagonist's talent will be discovered by a wider audience. In many of the narratives this yearning is satisfied, in fairy-tale fashion, as we are presented with counter-point scenes depicting appreciative reception by a large audience.

Performing Vulnerability

> Naivety is an attribute of the other: there is no more blatant claim to cunning than the confession 'I am naive'.[19]

One could argue that the embattled artist pattern is not unique to Australian film narratives, and that it is common in post-colonial narratives (dealing with questions of identity, marginalisation and alterity) and in many women's narratives. Indeed, some of the films discussed here owe a great deal to melodrama (in both its literary and filmic traditions), and draw to a lesser extent from Gothic narratives, both particularly 'feminine' genres, which frequently centre women characters. Melodramas and Gothic narratives commonly feature the figure of disablement; characters are regularly crippled, paralysed, or disfigured. These genres inform many contemporary Australian novels and films, even though the latter might be categorised more variously (for example, as 'art-house', 'romantic comedy' and so on). At the same time, one might say that the Australian variants also conform to the Hollywood formula, in which a hero faces a problem (inner and external), strives to achieve some goal, but has to overcome obstacles and undergo inner transformation before eventually succeeding. The narrative pattern under discussion here could be seen as a more particular version of that formula.

Most of the films under consideration here do conform largely to the Hollywood 'three-act' narrative formula; through this they emphasise democratic values, individual freedom, freedom of speech (creative expression as manifestation of this – the US First Amendment), and they enact the capitalist dream of the individual rising above circumstances, succeeding in spite of disadvantage. In these senses they might be seen as 'American'. While Australian narratives (literary and filmic) have been characterised as depicting individuals shown to be powerless in the face of natural or social forces, even 'losers' who die or must accept defeat, many of these more recent Australian films show characters who succeed beyond their wildest dreams.[20] Australian films may have tended to resist narrative closure or to conclude with uneasy and ambiguous resolutions, yet most of these films conclude with measurable success. It appears that some Australian narratives have well and truly adapted to contemporary 'open-market' conditions. They do so, however, in ways which are different from their American film counterparts, and involve very different sorts of heroes. Rather than breaking with Australian narrative traditions, these films re-work those traditions in ways which enable them to reach wider audiences. The protagonists are still relatively passive, compared with American action heroes, and are presented as powerless against the forces of nature and society, but they succeed in their own way, sometimes becoming marketable commodities themselves.

Susan Jeffords, in her book on Hollywood masculinity in the Reagan era, notes the 'hard bodies' which are characteristic of the 1980s, the exaggerated masculine, tough, super-strong heroes of the time; she reads the heroes of movies such as *Rambo: First Blood* (1982), *Robocop* (1987), *The Terminator* (1984), and *Die Hard* (1988) as popular images of Reaganism.[21] Australian films of the 1990s are certainly, by contrast, characterised by vulnerable bodies; bodies which struggle with disabilities, physical or mental, that render them prone. At the same time, Australian protagonists, not always heroes, are feminised. They are often women – crazy women, old women, daggy women – or they are queers and queens, or emasculated, half-witted or eccentric men, none of whom embody hegemonic masculinity.

The Hollywood hero's 'toughness' of attitude, which matches his physical hardness, is replaced in the Australian protagonist by mental instability or acute sensitivity. If Reagan embodied toughness, Australia's leader of the 1980s, Bob Hawke, who occasionally wept on television for his nation, performed vulnerability, and embodied a slightly 'challenged' or reformed masculinity, which foreshadowed the emergent 'soft' body of the mid-1990s. Even the popular Australian celebrity 'entrepreneurs' of the 1980s, such as Bond, Skase, Holmes à Court and Packer, once renowned for their toughness and invulnerability, have become vulnerable bodies in more recent times (and, as Holmes à Court's fate reminds us, mortal bodies). Facing public scrutiny and criminal charges, Skase and Bond performed vulnerability (just as Queensland politicians Bjelke-Petersen and Hinze had done when held accountable) and media coverage attended in detail to physical ailments, disabilities and mental anguish, amnesia and loss of acuity.

As I have argued, contemporary Australian films repeatedly depict the sensitive, vulnerable artistic individual, expressing him/herself with a distinctive aesthetic. These vulnerable protagonists of Australian films are not only very different to the hard-bodied heroes of Hollywood's action films of the 1980s, but they are also different to the intellectually challenged stars of Hollywood's sub-genre of 'Dumb' movies; *Forrest Gump* (1994), *Clueless* (1995), *Dumb and Dumber* (1994), and the other Jim Carrey films. The Australian films under consideration invite us to take the disadvantaged status of the protagonists seriously, whereas many of Hollywood's 'dumb' films treat the hero as comic or cute, and show that the disability does not matter – they get by anyway, and transcend any handicap. *Babe* is more like a Hollywood film in this sense, as the narrative depicts the disadvantaged hero as cute, and concludes with a form of transcendence. By contrast to his/her American inter-texts, the 'vulnerable' Australian protagonists, such as Robert Helfgott (Geoffrey Rush) in *Shine*, remain firmly bound within the conditions which set them apart. The disability is linked with their creativity, and so they succeed because of it, rather than in spite of it. There is no transcendence, but there may be success through persistence, endurance, and acceptance. This is reminiscent of the early Australian novel by Louis Stone, *Jonah* (1911) which depicts a hunchback who succeeds as a businessman and entrepreneur.[22] As Cranston says 'Jonah's deformity becomes a positive factor. Jonah does not succeed in spite of his deformity but because of it'.[23] In every sense his deformity reforms him.[24]

It is productive to examine the motif of disability here, and to question the way disability permeates such a remarkable number of Australian films. Its recurrence in film can be partly understood in terms of Australian narrative traditions, since disablement, madness and eccentricity have been prevalent in Australian narratives, particularly in literature, since the nineteenth century. Barbara Baynton's *Bush Stories* repeatedly depicted insane, grotesque or disabled characters (for example, the characters in 'The Chosen Vessel', 'Scrammy And', 'Squeaker's Mate', 'Billy Skywonkie') as did the stories of Henry Lawson.[25] Madness and disability recur in the novels of Marcus Clarke, Henry Kingsley, Joseph Furphy, Henry Handel Richardson, and Louis Stone, among many others. In the nineteenth century, scientific theories (such as those of Henry Thomas Buckle in the 1850s,[26] linking racial development and environment) reinforced popular beliefs that the harsh and strange Australian landscape fostered madness and racial degeneration (Marcus Clarke parodied these theories in his essay 'The Future Australian Race'[27]). The Australian bush was frequently depicted by Henry Lawson as the 'nurse and tutor of eccentric minds'.[28] Graeme Turner takes up the link long recognised between representations of Australian landscape and national character, noting the irony that 'it is just these most harsh and bizarre aspects of the land which we perversely enshrine in our own image of national character'.[29] The emphasis on grotesque, bizarre and disabled characters has continued through twentieth-century Australian literature (an emphasis particularly noticeable in the works of Patrick White, Barbara Hanrahan, Elizabeth Jolley, David Foster, to name but a few). Given this rich national narrative tradition, the recurrence of bizarre, eccentric characters in contemporary Australian films is not surprising. 'Oddballs' have not just emerged in Australian narratives in the 1980s and 1990s, but the successful 'oddball' (oddball artist as commodity) does seem to be a product of more recent times.

Even though the eccentrics may eventually succeed in contemporary Australian films, disablement and vulnerability are focused on a great deal more in the narratives than the successes with which they often conclude. The films highlight disabilities of three main kinds. Firstly, protagonists are often physically disabled, like blind Martin in *Proof*; or mute Ada in *The Piano*; club-footed Hester in *The Well*, physical infirmities defined further in the decrepit ageing, ailing bodies of Rose (*Spider and Rose*) and the father in *The Sum of Us*. More often though, central characters suffer from mental illness or psychological disabilities. The characters in *Tim* (1979), *Malcolm, Phobia* (1990), *Sweetie, An Angel at My Table, Vincent* (1987), *Struck by Lightning, Angel Baby* (1995), *Lilian's Story, Cosi, Bad Boy Bubby*, and *Shine* mark the central tendency. In these movies, psychological disabilities create 'vulnerable bodies'. A third kind of disablement can be identified in a host of other recent films whose main characters, while not technically physically or psychologically disabled, are disadvantaged, because they are social outcasts. These characters are stigmatised because of their eccentricity or difference from the norm; thought of as 'mad': Fran and Scott trying to express themselves in *Strictly Ballroom*, the queens in *Priscilla* taking their performance to homophobic outback Australia, the oddball heroines of *Muriel's Wedding* and *Love Serenade* pursuing eccentric fantasies in very constrained social worlds.

The breaking of rules in these narratives may not be as radical as would first appear, as the characters often manage to succeed in fairly conventional ways, and sometimes seem to embody a free-enterprise spirit which reminds us more of the Australian corporate heroes of the 1980s,[30] than the anti-establishment anti-heroes of Australian folklore and narrative traditions, such as Ned Kelly.[31] It's hard to imagine characters of these recent Australian films declaring 'Unemployed at last!', as does Tom Collins in Furphy's *Such is Life*.[32] They are hard-working and productive, at times frenzied in their application to their work/art.[33] *Babe*'s radical and successful approach to working the sheep could be seen as representing the 'warm fuzzy' corporate spirit of the 1990s, a new style of management which does away with top-down, hierarchical management practices (the sheep-dog's way) and strives to achieve more efficient and productive team work based on consultation and co-operation, and the devolution of responsibility to workers. This could be seen as enterprise bargaining at work; after all, the sweet-talking Babe is still a sheep-dog in pig's clothing, a diplomatic manager getting the job done faster with the sheep's co-operation.

While not all of the films mentioned here with disabled or disadvantaged characters conform in the same way to the embattled artist motif, the disability has a similar narrative function in most of them. The disability or stigma of the subject is focused on and made central to the narrative; it is made essential to the story's meaning and to the identity of the protagonist, rather than remaining something incidental. So, for example, while in many Hollywood melodramas disablement is the tragic consequence of external forces, a plot device which underscores the horror of ruined lives, in the films under discussion here disablement is often ontological, central to the protagonist's being. Furthermore, stigma is fetishised, made a spectacle within the film. The narratives show us what it is like to live with this condition which makes the character different, say mental illness or blindness, and take us through other people's reactions to it. The stigmatised difference often moves towards moments of cathartic excess: Helfgott's breakdown in the midst of performance (*Shine*), Ada's mute collapse as her finger is axed (*The Piano*), Dawn's naked revelries in the tree house (in *Sweetie*), before she falls to her death. Such moments of excess are not always so grim; they may also be celebratory, as in the performances in *Priscilla*, *Strictly Ballroom*, and *Cosi*. The point here is that the rise and fall of the protagonist is linked to the stigma. The disability or stigma is far more than a device to evoke fear, horror, dread, or sympathy, which is its function in Gothic narratives.[34] Another difference here, from the way disablement functions as a device in Gothic narratives and in Hollywood melodramas, is that the Australian character's talents and creativity are linked to the stigma or disability.

Creativity is a burden which the character must learn to live with, both the problem and the solution, since creative expression is shown to be the way to cope with life, to gain personal fulfilment and social recognition. Yet the creative expression is less a conscious, pragmatic honing of skills, than an obsessive-compulsive activity. Great emphasis is placed on the irrational, and the deformed or disabled body comes to function very much as what

Cranston has described as 'a semiotic system of the irrational'.[35] Thus, we have a Romantic portrait of creative expression as passionate and irrational, pursued for its own sake, with any social recognition and success presented as largely incidental rewards. The stories may show that creativity can pay – an important outcome for the culture industries in the 1990s – but they deny the motivations of materialism in the creative process. Characters who strive to rationalise creative practice and exploit the protagonists' creativity are presented as villains. The father in *Shine* illustrates this, as does Stewart in *The Piano*, who attempts to 'sell' his wife Ada's musical ability for some of Baines's land. It is particularly noticeable in recent Australian films that these art-for-art's-sake narratives affirm an independent creative rhetoric echoed elsewhere. As Rolf de Heer, creator of *Bad Boy Bubby* and *The Quiet Room* (1996) comments: 'I guess for me the concept of going to Hollywood is fairly meaningless, it's not the way I think about things',[36] or Steve Jodrell, director of *Shame* remarks, on the value of staying in Western Australia: 'It's just that it's important to be in charge of one's own creative destiny'.[37]

Such film narratives (*The Piano, Shine, Cosi, Angel at my Table*) retrieve artistic production from the taint of commercialism, particularly important in the Australian film industry, haunted by the culture/industry opposition. The films show artists expressing themselves at any cost (not for financial gain); it is never the cynical attempt to reach wider audiences, to get rich and famous or to get Hollywood offers. The protagonists' limited intellect or vision, their naivety, or faux-naivety, preserves their innocence, and guarantees integrity. These most 'knowing' of subjects are depicted as unaware, caught up in their passion, and certainly not calculating. This does mark a departure from the pragmatic anti-romantic protagonist of earlier Australian fiction. It is particularly important in Australia that someone like Helfgott can be seen as a 'pure' artist, as non-pragmatic as imaginable. Such a fantasy of non-commercial artistic impulse is of course far removed from the reality of cultural production in Australia in the 1990s. This shift in heroic qualities occurs across genres, and is again clarified by trans-Pacific comparison. In the 1960s and 1970s a new style of hero emerged in Hollywood Westerns, the mercenary, a pragmatic calculating hero who set things straight for society while pursuing his own interests as well. The contemporary Australian films under discussion here, enact a transformation in the other direction, away from the pragmatist, towards an innocent or naive hero. It is important in the contemporary climate for the Australasian hero to achieve performance success through tireless application to a worthy activity, such as art, or sport. The pursuit of money and success in business may have been admirable and even heroic in the 1980s in Australia, but in the 1990s such mercenary figures are less popular; the struggling but successful artist seems to be a popular hero of the day.

The corporate/commercial appropriation of the embattled artist narrative affirms its popular status. Recently the National Australia Bank adopted such a narrative for one of its 'Many Rivers to Cross' advertisements. The advertisement depicts a young woman from a migrant family background (disadvantaged), wanting to be a fashion designer (creative ambitions), misunderstood by her father (bad parenting), continuing to apply herself to her art despite opposition. The advertisement closes with the suggestion of future success, as she shows her work to a fashion house with favourable response. NAB addresses the audience directly, along with this parable, telling us never to lose sight of the goals we set ourselves. Here, as in the ads which depict successful sporting heroes, capitalist mythologies are naturalised and legitimised, in this case through the figure of the vulnerable but tenacious artist.

Irrationality plays an interesting role in all of the film narratives under discussion here, and meaning is often organised around an opposition between irrational and rational. Usually the irrational is celebrated, is associated with a redemptive lyric impulse. In *Babe*, the pig continues to work as a sheep-dog, the patients strive to perform an opera, the blind man takes photos as his form of 'proof'; in *Sweetie* Kay (Karen Kolston) responds to superstitions and omens, Fran's (Tara Morice) Spanish family in *Strictly Ballroom* teach the young dancers to go beyond ballroom conventions and to embrace the irrational in their choreography; Helfgott in *Shine* lives and performs the irrational, especially in his rendition of Rachmaninov. Interestingly, the Maoris in *The Piano* are seen to represent an altogether more 'irrational' mode of living heavily coded as authentic in the movie, some of whose ways the romantic hero Baines has adopted. Ada's muteness can be understood as irrational response to the rational-oppressive law of the father. More explicitly, the rational is presented economic rationalism of the commercial world, and its irrational counter as the creative artistic world. Here we have the articulation of some very familiar oppositions (art – commercial) yet with some different results. Art often triumphs over the commercial. Regulations and social controls are presented in such a negative light, that the films might appear to articulate a response to the New Right's hostility towards State regulation and funding of the arts. Such a contextualisation assumes significance when considered alongside a sampling of commentary from Australian filmmakers. Mel Gibson remarks:

they brought those tax concession things in, that kind of screwed it up. And the fact that they haven't got those concessions now and people still were able to get stuff through that will work is a good sign ... (it's just because they have) a lot of talent and the ability to get something done despite the obstacles.[38]

Australian director (of *Pure Shit* fame) Bert Deling comments in much the same vein:

There's a lot of politically correct nonsense ... . Australian producers and Government bureaucrats are (unwilling) ... to take risks on serious films, especially those touching on issues that might offend elements of the public, especially Australia's native aborigines and other ethnic groups ... the young filmmakers are just not being allowed to go out and be crazy any more... he said of the government subsidy system.[39]

Steve Jodrell says something very similar:

I'm very, very anti-institutional. I'm against any institutionalised activity which tends to diminish personal responsibility – anything that favours a group ethic and negates individuality.[40]

Sally Bongers (cinematographer on *Sweetie*) believes the repressive influence of the education system stifles natural creativity and individuality, singling out the Australian Film, Television and Radio School as an institution which she believes attempts to control and mould its students:

We are all entitled to it and have it when we're born but it's beaten out of us along the way. I find individuality sadly lacking today ... . It was disappointing our work was not more appreciated.[41]

Comments such as these underline the fact that the films under discussion seem to present a fantasy of creative activity taking place independently, among isolated individuals, at a remove from paternalistic policy-formation, and certainly beyond cultural protectionism. In these fictions, protectionism is presented as stultifying, as a kind of slow death: Bubby's isolation from the outside world and his suffocating relationship with his mother appals the audience (the theme of suffocation is reinforced by his 'clingwrap' killings of oppressive parent figures); Ada is isolated, locked away by Stewart; Frame is incarcerated; Helfgott is sheltered by his father, forbidden to take up an opportunity to study overseas. While there may be anxieties about the removal of protection (Babe losing his mum, Bubby emerging into the real world after his isolated early years, the films' very nomenclature reminding us of their characters' vulnerability) the narratives seem to insist on the individuals' abilities to survive and succeed. Bubby's killing of his and Angel's parents is presented as a necessary step towards achieving independence. At one level the line, 'There's no one out there Bubby, there's no God' echoes the anxieties of a post-10BA, deregulated film industry, moving slowly away from its safety-net vision of creative existence. Yet at the same time, these 'independent' Australian films owe a great deal to the protectionist policies of successive Australian governments,[42] just as many successful actors, directors, cinematographers, are indebted, whether they acknowledge it or not, to the Australian government's support of the industry since the 1970s, in the form of subsidies, tax incentives, the establishment of AFTRS, the AFC, and so on. Perhaps the culture industries, in the current climate, need to perform 'independence' and demonstrate a resistance to regulation, along with a stress on their own vulnerability and their worthiness for support. Meaghan Morris's comments on the necessity are certainly apposite:

> Film is an industry in a Western mega-culture, and Australia is simply a part of it; ideals of originality, independence and authenticity are sentimental anachronisms, inappropriate to the combinatoire of industrial cinema: performance, in film, is all, and performance is by nature 'inauthentic'.[43]

The vulnerable, naive, yet independent artist figure appears to embody, at a mythic level, the reconciliation of this impossible dilemma; the naive artist performs 'authenticity', gives us an authentic performance. The immense popularity of Helfgott in his performance tours of the United States and Australia, despite reviews which seriously questioned his musical ability, indicates the mythic importance of this paradoxical figure of the 'authentic' performer. His embodiment of 'authenticity' in artistic self-expression (and he does appear to embody this for audiences, even in the context of tours which are organised to cash in on the success of the film, *Shine*) matters more to audiences, it seems, than artistic ability.[44]

Filmmaker As Embattled Artist

Throughout the foregoing analysis, allusion has been made to the way that a mythic pattern – that of the disabled or disadvantaged artist finding success – resonates beyond the films. Even a cursory reading of interviews with Australian directors, actors, producers and so on, and agreed histories concerning the 'renaissance' of Australia's film industry over the past few years, will soon reveal echoes of the emphases of these fictions. Why is this so? One could argue that this narrative is best understood allegorically, as a statement of the way many Australian filmmakers and actors (and perhaps other artists) have perceived themselves in the late 1980s and 1990s, in a deregulated economic climate, competing in global markets. It is, at least, a popular Australian narrative which informs media stories about our entertainment artists and filmmakers, and other creative individuals. The myth under discussion here is most noticeable in film narratives, but it also evident in meta-narratives about the Australian film industry and its recent successes. Interviews and articles about successful Australian directors, actors and producers, often tell similar stories; of embattled creative individuals, acutely aware of being disadvantaged – geographically and economically – striving to express themselves in a tough competitive world, without recognition (misunderstood, persecuted), until at last they succeed and achieve acclaim. I am not asserting this is the only (or even the dominant) narrative that circulates in relation to Australian artists and filmmakers, but it is a popular one, which sits comfortably with romantic conceptions of artistic practice and auteurism.

The narrative pattern is most evident in articles and interviews with filmmakers. Note for instance, Mary Colbert writing about cinematographer Sally Bongers; she highlights the awards and nominations Bongers' work has received (understandably) and then goes on to deliver a romantic portrait of the embattled artist:

> In an area where females experience great difficulties getting a job, a nomination is a bonus ... Art has played a significant role in moulding her approach and was an integral part of family life, her mother working as a potter. The only subjects Bongers enjoyed at school were art and its components, including stills photography and the super-8 club ... Without those I would never have survived school; they were its only redeeming features. The inspiration to become an artist was my central impulse; it is directly related to my filmmaking. I saw film as a way of incorporating art with earning a living ... I have always had a way of looking at things that was different. I need to be passionate about what I'm doing.[45]

International recognition is an important feature of the narratives about creative success in the Australian film industry – invitations to compete at international festivals, nominations for awards, the winning of international awards and prizes – these are important signs of success, more than signs, since they facilitate the business of securing international and local markets. As Quinn says 'the laurel of approval from foreign film festivals has become an indispensable marketing tool for Australian movies.[46]

The significance of winning international recognition is also apparent in the film narratives themselves; the gifted protagonists often win major awards or attain notoriety or legendary status. In *Shine*, it is crucial to the narrative resolution that Helfgott receives international acclaim, just as it is important for the climax and resolution of *Strictly Ballroom*, that the young dancers win the Pan Pacific competition. The narrative in *Babe* is only complete when Babe wins a major sheep dog trial and receives wide recognition (his performance is televised). Bubby (*Bad Boy Bubby*) eventually has something of a cult following in his musical-poetic performances. The Janet Frame character in *An Angel at My Table*, wins awards for her writing and acquires an international reputation – she is literally saved by her writing and international recognition, as it is the publication of her book that earns her freedom from the asylum.

The narratives place great emphasis on performance, inviting audiences to evaluate the characters' performances, as well as showing characters going through external evaluation. The films demonstrate the viability of the local cultural product (the performance) through a kind of bench-marking process, ensuring that the performance is successful by international standards. While the motif of performance and the winning of awards are conventional and popular narrative devices for signalling personal progress and triumph, they assume particular significance in the context of late capitalist economic conditions, in a culture of performance indicators and benchmarks. They take on heightened significance in an entertainment industry undergoing rapid change in response to the opening up of new markets. Participation and success in international film festivals are of great importance to the marketing of Australian films. The films under discussion here enact fantasies of successful performance; they literally show performers, who are vulnerable soft bodies facing a too-tough world, succeed and reach wider audiences. The stories serve to legitimate and dispel anxieties about performance in an era of performance evaluation.

The stories of the creative success of the characters in these films blur with stories about the success of the films and the filmmakers. *An Angel at My Table* won the Jury Prize at the Venice Film Festival, Most Popular Film at the Sydney Film Festival, Best Film at the New Zealand Film Festival. Interviews and stories about the actor Kerry Fox, about Janet Frame, the book's author (subject of the film), Laura Jones the scriptwriter, Bridget Ikin the producer, Jane Campion the director, and Campion's mother, actor Edith Campion, who played a role in the film (and whose struggle with mental illness – depression – was also subject of public discussion at about this time, inviting comparisons and contrasts with Janet Frame's psychiatric history) – at times they all seem to merge and become a composite. We hear and see versions of this same story about a creative individual facing obstacles and overcoming disadvantages to succeed.

Geoffrey Rush, the actor who played pianist Helfgott in *Shine*, succinctly conveyed the embattled artist narrative when awarded Best Actor at the Academy Awards, saying that this victory was for all those people who would only back the film if he was not in it. This remark contains all the elements for a compelling antipodean success story – the talented underdog artist, disadvantaged because he is Australian (unknown in the States), manages to succeed in spite of opposition. Reiterating the pattern, and highlighting the notion of disability, are the many feature articles, programmes and stories about the pianist, David Helfgott – his life, his talent, his mental collapse, his musical comeback – and about his recent controversial performances in the United States (receiving damning reviews from music critics, then widespread praise from popular audiences).

Interviews with the artists' proud mothers – David's, Geoffrey's – reinforce our sense of the vulnerability of these artists, their child status, their need of nurturing, and more generally, the vulnerability of creative individuals in a society affected by economic rationalism. Such interviews overlap with narratives about the creative process of filmmaking, inviting parallels with mothering; patient, devoted parents, enduring long gestation periods, coaxing the films into being. There is a moral to the on-screen and off-screen narratives; it is about the need to nurture creativity, and about demonstrating, through the fairytale successes, that creativity *can* pay its way. Creative Babe, the little pig sheep-dog, not only overcomes his disadvantaged status, but he can indeed earn his keep (or as many news stories suggest 'bring home the bacon'). These are stories which may be comforting to small players in a deregulated economic climate. This certainly has been the case for several Australian independent filmmakers, who have found international markets with low-budget Australian films, and have become international players from these Australian successes.

Australian nationalist discourses have been characterised by efforts to differentiate the national culture from British or American cultures. One might expect that narrative traditions would be radically transformed in the current economic climate, and that Australia's cultural products would become more generic, emphasising cultural similarity rather than difference from the 'imperial' culture in order to secure international markets. Popular discussions about Australia's film industry repeatedly raise concerns about the blurring of boundaries between American (Hollywood) and Australian film cultures, questioning the impact these conditions have on our cultural industries – concerns about the influences of global markets, and about the siphoning-off of Australian talent to Hollywood. Australian narrative traditions have undergone transformation in response to shifting market forces – for example, the move towards genre – but the transformation defies expectations. In a post-Fordist era of product differentiation and niche markets (as opposed to the standardisation associated with mass production) Australian films can emphasise cultural difference and capitalise on it. Cultural difference is marketable. Australian films are marketed as 'original', 'quirky', 'off-beat', and these are qualities which are repeatedly mythologised and symbolically enshrined – through eccentric artist characters – in film narratives.

NOTES

1. Alain Touraine, *Qu'est-ce que La Democratie?* (Paris: Fayard, 1994), quoted in Manuel Castells, *The Rise of the Network Society* (Oxford: Blackwell, 1996), p.23.
2. The Australian residency of the filmmakers does not position these as Australian films, yet the films have many narrative elements which invite comparison with the Australian 'artistic expression' films. *The Piano* was an Australian/New Zealand co-production, with Australian, New Zealand and French funding; many of the production team were Australians. *Angel at My Table* was more clearly a New Zealand production (with an Australian scriptwriter, Laura Jones), yet the director Jane Campion and producers Bridget Ikin and John Maynard have been long-term Australian residents.
3. Graeme Turner, 'Whatever Happened to National Identity? Film and the Nation in the 1990s', *Metro*, No.100 (Summer 1994–95), pp.32–35.
4. Tom O'Regan, *Australian National Cinema* (London: Routledge, 1996).
5. The 'success' of these films varies. Films such as *Babe* and *Strictly Ballroom*, *The Piano*, *Muriel's Wedding*, and *Shine*, were commercially successful, as well as critically acclaimed, and successful in terms of nominations and awards, while others such as *Cosi* received critical acclaim but were not so successful at the box office.
6. Jane Campion, 'Interview with Miro Bilbrough', *Cinema Papers*, No.93 (May 1993), pp.4–11.
7. Graeme Turner, *Making It National: Nationalism and Australian Popular Culture* (Sydney: Allen & Unwin, 1994).
8. Susan Dermody and Elizabeth Jacka (eds.), *The Imaginary Industry: Australian Film in the Late 1980s* (Sydney: Australian Film, Television and Radio School, 1988).
9. Stuart Cunningham, 'Hollywood Genres, Australian Movies', in Albert Moran and Tom O' Regan (eds.), *An Australian Film Reader* (Sydney: Currency Press, 1985), pp.235–41. Elizabeth Jacka and Susan Dermody (eds.), *The Imaginary Industry*; Graeme Turner, 'The

Genres are American: Australian Narrative, Australian Film and the Problems of Genre', *Literature/Film Quarterly*, Vol.21, No.2 (1993), pp.113–21.

10. Turner, *Making it National*, p.32.

11. Ibid., p.33.

12. Stuart Cunningham, 'Hollywood Genres, Australian Movies', pp.237–41.

13. It is interesting to note that Cunningham proposed that the musical 'may well be the preeminent genre though which reconciliation' (p.237) of past oppositions is possible, through the Australianisation of a Hollywood genre. Two of the most successful recent Australian films under discussion here are musicals – *Priscilla*, and *Strictly Ballroom* – and many others are very much like musicals, placing great emphasis on musical performance – eg. *Shine*, *The Piano*, *Cosi*, *True Love and Chaos*. The other genre which seems to be frequently adopted in the 1990s, occupying the middle ground between commercial and art-house cinema, is the Road Movie.

14. Graeme Turner, 'The Genres Are American: Australian Narrative, Australian Film and the Problems of Genre', *Literature/Film Quarterly*, Vol.21, No.2 (1993), pp.113–21.

15. Turner, 'Whatever Happened to National Identity?', p.33.

16. Ibid.

17. Susan Dermody, 'The Company of Eccentrics', in *The Imaginary Industry: Australian Film in The Late 80s* (Sydney: Australian Film, Television and Radio School, 1988), pp.131–54.

18. Touraine, p.23.

19. Meaghan Morris, 'Tooth and Claw: Tales of Survival and *Crocodile Dundee*', *Art and Text*, No.25 (June–August 1987), pp.36–38.

20. Graeme Turner, *National Fictions* (Sydney: Allen & Unwin, 1986).

21. Susan Jeffords, *Hard Bodies: Hollywood Masculinity in the Reagan Era* (New Brunswick, NJ: Rutgers University Press, 1994).

22. Louis Stone, *Jonah*, with an introduction by Ronald McCuaig (Sydney: Allen & Unwin, 1981).

23. C. A. Cranston, 'Sentimental Jonah's Heart of Stone', *Australian Literary Studies*, Vol.14, No.2 (1989), pp.216–28.

24. Ibid., p.218.

25. Barbara Baynton, *Bush Studies* (1902) in Sally Krimmer and Alan Lawson (eds.), *Barbara Baynton 1857–1929* (Sydney: Angus and Robertson, 1972); Brian Kiernan (ed.), *Henry Lawson* (St Lucia: University of Queensland Press, 1976).

26. J. M. Robertson, *Buckle and His Critics: A Study in Sociology* (London: Swan, Sonnenschein, 1895).

27. Marcus Clarke, 'The Future Australian Race', in Bill Wannan (ed.), *A Marcus Clarke Reader* (Melbourne: Lansdowns, 1963).

28. Henry Lawson, 'The Bush Undertaker' in Krimmer and Lawson (eds.), p.111.

29. Turner, *National Fictions*, p.36.

30. Turner, *Making it National*, p.32.

31. G. O'Ryan and Brian Shoesmith, 'Speculation, Promise and Performance: Businessmen as Stars', *Australian Journal of Cultural Studies*, Vol.4, No.2 (1987).

32. Joseph Furphy, *Such is Life* (1901), edited with an introduction by John Barnes (St Lucia: University of Queensland Press, 1981).

33. One might claim that Tom Collins' declaration is precisely that, an articulation of a desire to dedicate himself completely to his writing.

34. Lenora Ledwon, 'Twin Peaks and TV Gothic', *Literature/Film Quarterly*, Vol.21, No.1 (Winter 1993), pp.260–70.

35. C. A. Cranston, 'Sentimental Jonah's Heart of Stone', *Australian Literary Studies*, Vol.14, No.2 (1989), pp.216–28.

36. Lyndon Barber, 'Right Direction, Wrong Destination', *The Weekend Australian*, 3–4 August 1996.

37. Bron Sibree, 'Steve Jodrell After *Shame*', *Cinema Papers*, No.70 (Nov. 1988), p.32.

38. Mel Gibson interview, in Peter Galvin, Ben Holgate, '100 Years of Film: A Maturing Industry Embraces the Present and the Personal', *Sydney Morning Herald*, 5 June 1995.

39. Bert Deling, 'Australian Cinema', *New York Times*, 15 Oct. 1995.

40. Sibree, p.32.
41. Mary Colbert, 'Sally Bongers: Cinematographer Particulaire', *Cinema Papers*, No.75 (Sept. 1989). pp.5–8.
42. Turner, *Making it National*, p.105.
43. Morris, pp.36–38.
44. For a discussion of Helfgott's reception by critics and popular audiences see Alan Saunders, 'Helfgott', *24 Hours* (June 1997).
45. Mary Colbert, p.7.
46. Karl Quinn, 'Drag, Dags and the Suburban Surreal', *Metro*, No.100 (Summer 1994–95), pp.23–26.

5

Becoming a Man in Australian Film in the Early 1990s: *The Big Steal, Death in Brunswick, Strictly Ballroom* and *The Heartbreak Kid*

PHILIP BUTTERSS

For a cinema whose heroic male leads had been figures like Bryan Brown, Jack Thompson, and Paul Hogan, the films of the early 1990s represented a radical shift in its image of Australian masculinity. A new generation of actors was emerging, playing roles which, whilst they shared some continuities with earlier representations of masculinity, broke away from established stereotypes in several important ways. As Graeme Turner noted in 1994, 'the semiotics of Australian ethnicities and masculinities would seem to have changed'.[1] Much more than a change of personnel marked the new decade however; not only was there a shift in the image of Australian masculinity embodied in particular performers, film narratives themselves seemed newly preoccupied with questions of gender identity, and the construction of the masculine subject. A crop of films, including many of the most successful Australian productions, were now consciously exploring the process of becoming a heterosexual man in contemporary Australian society. Ben Mendelsohn in *The Big Steal* (1990), Noah Taylor in *Flirting* (1991), Sam Neill in *Death in Brunswick* (1991), Hugo Weaving in *Proof* (1991), Paul Mercurio in *Strictly Ballroom* (1992), and Alex Dimitriades in *The Heartbreak Kid* (1993) offered fresh constructions of male identity, within films whose narratives turned openly on the issue of masculinity. This contribution examines four of these films in detail – *The Big Steal* (1990), *Death in Brunswick* (1991), *Strictly Ballroom* (1992) and *The Heartbreak Kid* (1993) – suggesting that they reveal a tension between the conventional narratives which are at their core, and changing patterns of masculinity in contemporary Australia.

In a couple of chapters in *Fathers, Sons and Lovers*, a recent study carried out in the Penrith area of Sydney, Peter West has set out what he believes to be the chief elements of 'being a boy' and 'being a man' in Australian culture. It is worth briefly summarising his conclusions so that they can be set against what early 1990s film has to say about the growth to adult masculinity.[2] West finds that boys must be tough, must be stronger than girls, must prove their masculinity, and must not show emotion. He suggests that the first rule for becoming a man is that a boy must develop his body in size and strength. Having sex with a woman 'helps a man establish himself in the eyes of his peers'. Becoming a man 'means being successful in sport', and 'often means preparing for war'. Finally, a man 'still feels the responsibility to provide shelter and protection for his loved ones'.[3]

By the early 1990s, however, the prescriptions identified by West were becoming increasingly inappropriate within a world in which what it meant to be a man was being substantially redefined. It was clear that Australia was moving from the status of an industrial to a post-industrial society, and that this change was having a serious impact on patterns of gender in employment. Changes in the workplace were being accompanied by changes in the home as men and women living together were forced to re-negotiate the division of domestic labour and power within the household.[4] Many of the arguments of feminism, of course, were having an impact on the relations between men and women in a variety of public and private arenas. In addition, the increasing public prominence of gay men, indigenous men, and men from non English-speaking backgrounds were contributing to a fragmentation of what masculinity meant.

Certainly some of the elements identified by West occur in *The Big Steal*, *Death in Brunswick*, *Strictly Ballroom* and *The Heartbreak Kid*, but what is striking is how much the films deviate from his conclusions. They are products of a period of substantial flux, and they reveal a complex mix of contradictory forces. In spite of their essentially conventional structures, these four films make profound criticisms of hegemonic masculinity, demonstrate that unitary notions of masculinity are inadequate, and offer ways of behaving that are outside the patterns proposed by West.

Passages to Manhood

The Big Steal begins with a voice-over stating that the two things its main character, Danny Clark, wants in this life are a Jaguar and Joanna Johnson (Claudia Karvan) (in that order). With an opening like this, it's not surprising that the film propels a largely traditional narrative of the adolescent male's growth to heterosexual manhood. What drives most of the narrative is the desire on the part of various would-be men not to lose face, or not to be bettered by other men. By the end of *The Big Steal* Danny has emerged from his parents' world; he has defeated the sleazy used-car salesman, Gordon Farkas (Steve Bisley), in a sequence of events that culminates in a car chase; and he is about to receive his birthday present from Joanna – sex for the first time.

One indication that the old certainties are not so sure, however, is the fact that the twin goals of car and girl are both open to question early in the film. At the beginning of the narrative, Mark (Damon Herriman), one of Danny's mates tries to convince Joanna to go out on a date with Danny. 'Danny Clark,' she says, 'Why would I want to go out with him?' The mate replies 'He's one of the most interesting people I know.' She replies, sensibly, 'So why don't *you* go out with him?' But in *The Big Steal*, the possibility of homosexuality is rejected almost as soon as it has been raised, as the single-minded pursuit of Joanna from opening voice-over to concluding birthday present makes very clear. A similar possibility is raised when the Clarks give their beloved car, a Nissan Cedric, to their son for his birthday. For Danny and his two mates, Vangeli (Angelo D'Angelo) and Mark, who are there for the presentation, this is not an appropriate car for the masculinity which the boys all want to exhibit. As Joanna later notes, a Cedric 'sounds more like a Qantas steward than a car'. Again, though, the opening voice-over has already informed the audience of the kind of image which Danny is seeking, and there's no danger of his driving the Cedric, or living out a masculinity that is outside what Bob Connell calls 'the circle of legitimacy'.[5]

It might seem surprising to describe *Death in Brunswick*, a film whose chief protagonist is in his late thirties, as a film about growing up, but an early shot of Carl Fitzgerald's (Sam Neill) untidy room is only the first of many signs that he is still a boy. In this film the chief step in the transition to adult masculinity is breaking free of the mother. In fact, one of the early images of the film – Mrs Fitzgerald (Yvonne Lawley) lying prostrate on Carl's kitchen floor with her head in the gas oven suggests that the death in Brunswick in question is to be hers, but it turns out that she is merely cleaning her son's kitchen. For most of the film, she does his washing, opens his mail, frowns at his dirty magazines, and generally interferes in and criticises all aspects of his life. *Death in Brunswick* shows Carl going through a rather belated adolescence in order to establish a relationship with Sophie (Zoe Carides) that will replace his relationship with his mother, whilst making knowing jokes about Freudian accounts of the growth to manhood along the way. Carl's second sexual experience with Sophie is a hurried encounter in the coolroom of the Bombay Club in which they both work. To his obvious discomfort, Sophie asks Carl about his mother while they are having sex. In replying, he commits something akin to a classic Freudian slip, explaining that his mother is staying at his house because 'she gets horny–lonely. She gets lonely'. By the end of the film, Carl's anger with his mother has induced a stroke, and she has been relegated to a radio-controlled wheelchair, with him holding the controls. She might not be dead, but she's not going to push her son around any more.

In their attempts to maximise the audience for *Strictly Ballroom*, the promotion team spent some time arguing about which angles to stress, deciding not to follow the filmmakers' initial desire to push 'the high camp comedy' and the prominence of ballroom dancing. Instead they chose three lines which stressed the conventional narrative at the film's core: 'The hero doesn't always use a gun', 'The girl isn't always blonde' and 'The fight isn't always fair'.[6] In accordance with these slogans, the film's central narrative does involve the gradual 'masculinisation' of Scott Hastings (Paul Mercurio), a plot which both demonstrates and endorses the culture's smooth policing of masculinity. As in *Death in Brunswick*, the achievement of what *Strictly Ballroom* sees as a proper adult masculinity first involves the son rebelling against his mother's strict control. Barbara Creed argues that Scott's compulsion to dance his own steps 'comes to signify his desire to fulfil his proper oedipal destiny as a man and not as a boy slavishly following his mother's dictates'.[7] *Strictly Ballroom* suggests that boys need role models in their growth to adult masculinity, and when Doug Hastings (Barry Otto), Scott's biological but emasculated father, is obviously inadequate, the boy turns to model himself on Rico (Antonio Vargas), Fran's (Tara Morice) father, with instruction from her grandmother, Ya Ya (Armonia Benedito).[8] The film is initially somewhat critical of the patriarchal control which Rico exerts within his family, but it shifts quickly to approve of his demonstration of a particular masculinity, and he operates as a kind of surrogate father. In effect, Rico's stereotypical Latin passion (he even lets out an 'olé' at one point) invigorates Scott's flaccid performance of the *paso doblé*, so that the boy becomes a kind of bullfighter–proud, forceful, and dominating. Scott learns the proper *paso doblé* with its 'proper' masculinity; in other words, he learns Rico's masculinity. And in the closing segment of the film, his successful performance of dance and gender is given centre stage. As David Buchbinder has suggested:

> the *Paso doblé* which Scott learns lends a new phallicism – absent in ballroom dancing – to his physical presence. This is particularly so in

the closing sequence, when Scott and Fran defy Fife and the Federation and dance the *paso doblé* as it should be performed: Scott wears a highly decorated and spangled, but traditional, toreador's jacket lent to him by Rico. This item of clothing exaggerates the shape of the male wearer, widening the shoulders and narrowing the hips and providing a sort of gilded carapace that suggests a heavily muscled body; and it refers us to the tradition of the bullfight, in Spanish culture deemed a true test of a man's strength, agility and power.[9]

A parallel, if compressed, narrative is the re-masculinisation of Scott's father, Doug. Through most of the film we see him as hopelessly ineffectual – another example of subordinated masculinity – barely opening his mouth, unless to give himself a spray of Cedel breath freshener. Shirley (Pat Thomson), his wife, constantly belittles him, addressing him as 'you stupid man' and berating him for not doing anything (with some justification). But finally he insists that Scott listens to what he has to say, and then, more importantly, he defies his wife by telling the truth about what happened in the past. The film finishes with Doug and Shirley dancing together, him leading, as we are told should be the case in ballroom dancing, and therefore in life – so that hegemonic masculinity is restored twice over at the film's conclusion. Evidently that's what you needed to do to have a ballroom dancer as the male lead in an Australian film in 1992.

Although *The Heartbreak Kid* is probably slightly more interested in twenty-two year-old Christina (Claudia Karvan) breaking free of her strict and patriarchal Greek background, it also focuses in detail on Nick (Alex Dimitriades), her seventeen year-old student, and his transition from adolescence to manhood. In terms of masculinity, this film offers a more traditional narrative than *Death in Brunswick* and *Strictly Ballroom*, tracing Nick's development through playground fights, success on the sports field, the beginnings of a sexual relationship, and breaking free from his father.

Critical Dimensions

As the above outlines indicate, the four films have largely conventional narratives, the path to adult heterosexual masculinity at their heart, but in the course of telling their stories, a number of stereotypical notions are challenged. From an early shot which shows Danny stroking a model Jaguar strategically placed on his lap, *The Big Steal* signals its awareness of the connection between cars and adolescent male sexuality, concurrently showing that it is prepared to laugh at that connection. Joanna demonstrates her disinterest in cars from her first conversation with Danny, and when he has a drag with a carload of hoons on their first date, and the Jaguar's motor blows up, she storms off, pouring scorn on 'little boys and big cars'. One of the markers that Danny has, indeed, grown up by the end of the film is his discovery that he no longer likes Jaguars. Another moment which calls into question the macho behaviour of some of the men in this film is when Gordon Farkas (Steve Bisley) is caught with his pants down, so to speak. For most of the film Farkas veers between an ingratiating blokiness and macho aggression, but when he emerges from his car after having been caught going through a red light by the police, he is revealed wearing stockings and high heels. One critic has said that this scene is 'the only comic moment in the film that doesn't click',[10] but this insight into the private pleasures of the chief bad-guy operates as an effective way of undercutting the aggro-masculinity he exhibits elsewhere in the film. One of the attractions of *The Big Steal* for Australian audiences is the way it takes narrative elements that are the staple fare of Hollywood teen movies and locates them in distinctively Australian contexts, often deliberately parodying the original. The film's version of a car chase is not a means by which the hero proves his tough masculinity as it would be in the classic formula. Instead Danny is driving his parents' Nissan Pintaro, and has not realised that the family's ancient caravan is still attached. Van, driving his Monaro, is dismayed that his first car chase is against a Volvo, and hopes desperately that none of his cousins see him.

   The Heartbreak Kid provides a powerful critique of the control which Christina's father has exerted over her, and the way in which this kind of behaviour is largely to be replicated by her lawyer-fiancé, Dimitri (Steve Bastoni). One of the turning points for her in breaking free of her parents is when she is taken by Dimitri to the house that he (with a $50,000 contribution from her father) has bought for them. She is appalled not to have had any say in the decision, and appalled that she might never escape the eye of her parents – the new house is situated across the road from their place. Dimitri is only slightly more liberated than the older generation, and his expectation is that Christina will give up her job to become the mother of his children, and to support him in his career. While *The Heartbreak Kid* is strongly critical of the control exerted by some traditional Greek men, its harshest criticism is levelled at Brian Southgate (William McInnes), a particularly unattractive example of hegemonic masculinity. Brian, a teacher at the school and the Australian rules football coach, is established as an emblem of all the worst excesses of the traditional Anglo male. As well as being a sneering bully, he is both racist and sexist, blocking many attempts to establish soccer at the school, and ridiculing Christina's suggestion that she could be the team's coach. *Death in Brunswick* is similarly critical of various forms of masculine power, focusing its attention on Laurie (Boris Brkic), the bullying bouncer, and the other thugs who work for Yanni (Nicholas Papademetriou), and also on the patriarchal control exercised by Sophie's father. One of the damning images of her father is the photograph which Carl notices, depicting two big men on a hunting expedition, displaying their guns and their kill. The film uses particularly crude stereotypes to depict Greek men as violent, patriarchal, and dumb, and Turkish men as maniacally violent and criminal.

Barry Fife (Bill Hunter), head of the Dance Federation in *Strictly Ballroom*, wields power ruthlessly to control ballroom dancing competitions with an iron fist, and an early close-up depicting his delight in that power establishes him as the villain of the film. Fife resembles Bruce Ruxton, long-time president of the Victorian Returned Servicemen's League (RSL), and an emblem of a bygone authoritarian and patriarchal era, fittingly *Strictly Ballroom*'s dance competitions are held in RSL halls. The film's gradual unveiling of Fife's decades of machinations, and his increasing desperation to cling to power, offer a more sustained critique of hegemonic masculinity than that in the other films discussed here.

At times *The Big Steal's* criticism of adolescent macho behaviour overlaps with ethnic stereotyping, such as in its treatment of Vangeli Petrarkis. Right from the start the film gets laughs at Van's expense – at his Monaro and his simple view that the easiest way to attract a woman is with a powerful set of wheels. *The Big Steal* is ambivalent about this view, on the one hand showing Van's success – he spends a good deal of time in the back of the Monaro with different partners – but also showing that a woman like Joanna would never be attracted to a version of masculinity such as his. One scene which draws attention to the difference between private reality and public posturing is when Danny and Joanna overhear Pam (Sheryl Munks) in the back of the Monaro criticising Van's sexual performance as 'weak as piss'.

Where *The Big Steal, Death in Brunswick* and *Strictly Ballroom* depict differences in masculinity relating to differences in ethnicity using a handful of crude stereotypes, *The Heartbreak Kid* gives a much more subtle and sympathetic picture, demonstrating that there are differences in masculinity *within* particular ethnic groups.[11] Nick's father is also strict in many respects but where Christina's parents and fiancé's efforts to control her are largely determined by the impact which her behaviour might have on their standing

in Melbourne's Greek community, Nick's father, George, usually has his
son's own long-term interests at heart. George is also able to change his
attitudes on occasions, and one of the most moving moments in the film is
when he arrives to act as coach for his son's soccer team, after having earlier
condemned Nick's obsession with the sport. But in spite of his ability to
shift ground, George strongly disapproves of his son's relationship with his
teacher, partly out of what the film presents as traditional Greek attitudes
towards the sanctity of the marriage which is soon to take place. The
father's shifting approval and disapproval makes him a believably complex
character, struggling to do the best for his son, unsure of his own wisdom
on how best to achieve this.

Another sympathetic father is Desmond Clark (Marshall Napier),
Danny's father in *The Big Steal*. Mr Clark is an eccentric character,
spending much of the film in a dressing-gown, playing Scrabble, and prone
to having what he describes as 'visions'. But his deep love for his son and
his wife, his wisdom, his ability to state his opinions of Danny's actions
and yet offer him support even when disagreeing with him, are portrayed
as positive and endearing attributes. In some ways the father-figure in the
film has been split in two, for Joanna's father is also called Desmond. Mr
Johnson (Tim Robertson) is the patriarchal father, permanently angry, and
struggling with incestuous desires for Joanna – 'you don't know what it's
like having a beautiful daughter', he tells Danny. Instead of struggling to
break free of his own parents, Danny competes with Mr Johnson for
Joanna.

Mateship Reconsidered

A good indication that the old stereotypes of Australian masculinity are in
the process of change is the way that the once revered institution of
mateship is presented in these films from the early 1990s. In *The Big Steal*,
Danny Clark and his mates consistently and unproblematically support
each other through the narrative, although the epilogue which shows the
three boys' futures, suggests that, as adults, they move in very different
directions. *Death in Brunswick* takes a closer look at the bond of mateship,
showing some of its positive and negative elements. On the one hand,
when Carl has accidentally killed Mustafa (Nico Lathouris) and is
floundering in circumstances too difficult for him to deal with, he turns to
Dave (John Clarke), and the mate fulfils the time-honoured role of offering
substantial and generous assistance. In addition, Carl is able to discuss with
Dave, albeit in a rudimentary way, aspects of his relationship with his

mother and with Sophie. On the other hand, the two mates behave like a pair of boys, particularly when Dave's wife, June (Deborah Kennedy), is around, and, for Carl, the friendship with Dave operates as a way of avoiding responsibility for his own actions. It is only when the mateship bond breaks down, with Dave refusing further assistance, that Carl finally attempts to confront his own problems. Mateship is thus seen as a stage through which it is necessary to pass before attaining adult masculinity. In *The Heartbreak Kid*, Nick clearly has friends at the beginning of the film, but no effort is made to depict the nature of the relationships, and they are quickly displaced by his relationship with Christina. In *Strictly Ballroom*, Scott seems unreliable as a friend to his male co-dancers, and has no close links with men. Mateship is clearly not the heroic and fulfilling bond it once was in Australian culture; if anything, these films represent it as an adolescent relationship which needs to be outgrown for a boy to reach adulthood.

Perhaps not surprisingly, given that all four of these films have a romance as one of their chief structuring elements, the supposed inability of Australian men to express their emotions is called into question. In *The Big Steal*, Danny's initial difficulty in speaking to Joanna is gradually overcome, and he is rewarded with a kiss when he reveals to her his affection for his parents, and his regret that they have been hurt by his using the Cedric as a trade-in to obtain the Jaguar. As for being able to express love, one of the funniest scenes in the film occurs when Danny tells Joanna that he loves her through a megaphone at five o'clock in the morning, in the presence of her father, and, presumably, within earshot of the Johnson's neighbours. Similarly, in *Death in Brunswick*, Carl is allowed to express his feelings for Sophie in ways which are at variance with stereotypes of non-Anglo masculinity, also in ways that differ from the archetypal laconic Anglo male, and he does so several times to his mate, Dave. His breaking of the conventions for the circle into which he has been thrust is made clear in a scene where he tries to convince Sophie's friend, Carmel, to intervene on his behalf. Carl declares, somewhat weakly, 'I love her'. Carmel replies, 'You're weird, Carl'. But it's a weirdness that the film ultimately regards as positive.

One of the ways in which Carl is able to live out a gentle and sensitive masculinity in a film that depicts a good deal of aggression and violence is through a series of sleights of hand, as it were. It is true that Mustafa is killed by the carving fork which Carl is holding, but Carl doesn't stab him, Mustafa impales himself. Similarly, Carl is able to get revenge against his enemies, and regain the face he has lost through being bullied, without directly being the agent of that revenge. In one scene, Carl's inability to perform macho masculinity is demonstrated when, confronted by Laurie and with nowhere to run, he fails several times to break a bottle to use as a weapon. Laurie and the film's audience dissolve into laughter, but when the bouncer demonstrates how it's done, it is he who immediately doubles over in agony, as the bottle cuts his hand. Carl's ineffectual efforts are laughed at, but in the process of setting up a better joke at the expense of Laurie's macho posturing. More usually, Carl's revenges are displaced, as others do for him what he should have done himself, if he was conforming to the patterns of hegemonic masculinity, set out by many Hollywood films. Dave elbows Laurie in the balls and retrieves Carl's money for him, and Mustafa's friends firebomb the club; in both instances Carl is present, and, in the terms of traditional economies of masculinity, has the motives for taking the action. When Carl takes his own revenge, it is generally in creative and non-macho ways, such as when he prepares a pizza for Laurie and his henchmen, spicing it with dead cockroaches and mouse droppings. Finally, the film does make a concession to traditional expectations of the male lead, when Carl elbows Laurie in the testicles as he and Sophie flee the club for the last time. To some extent this operates as a marker that Carl is beginning to act on his own behalf, but it is not given much prominence, and is immediately followed by Mustafa's friends taking over the fight against Laurie, and ultimately beheading him.

Carl might be over-dependent on his mother for most of *Death in Brunswick*, but he is depicted as a likeable, if ineffectual character. There are positive aspects to the kind of masculinity that he lives out, Sophie tells him that he is 'different than the guys around here'. Her first assumption about him, and that of most of those who work at the Bombay club, is that he's 'a poof', but she soon learns that his difference is not one of sexuality. He stands out partly through his Anglo background, and partly for reasons concerning class; one of the aspects of his mother that he must shake off is her snobbishness. But it is also true that what sets Carl apart from Yanni, the club's owner, and his henchmen, is the kind of masculinity that he represents. The way Carl is depicted offers the film's audience modes of behaviour that differ from traditional notions of Australian masculinity, and from stereotypical ideas about non-Anglo masculinity. Although *The Heartbreak Kid* has the most traditional plot of the four in regards to the growth to manhood, it also goes out of its way to depict a nurturing side to masculinity, showing Nick caring for his sister affectionately, doing the family's shopping and cooking, and. of course, presenting him as churned up over his relationship with Christina. His involvement in these non-traditional activities for men is facilitated by the fact that his mother is evidently dead.

In its depiction of masculinity, *Strictly Ballroom* proposes, in many ways, the most radical shift from the tradition of heroic male leads like Bryan Brown, Paul Hogan and Jack Thompson. Scott Hastings might embody the anti-authoritarian values that have been seen as an essential part of Australian identity, but the wild colonial boy has become a ballroom dancer, played by someone known for his ballet roles, in a film with a conscious emphasis on camp. While acknowledging that *Strictly Ballroom* privileges heterosexual romance, John Champagne has analysed, in detail, the ways in which the film might appeal to a gay male spectator, and the ways in which homosexual possibilities are highlighted, pointing, among other things, to the connections between ballroom competitions and drag performance, the erotic focus on Paul Mercurio's body, the 'homoerotic bonding between Scott and Fran's father', and Scott's dancing the tango with Les who is, at one point in the film, called 'a pathetic little fag'.[12] Kerryn Goldsworthy notices the eroticism of 'the moment when Rico ... lays his forehead lightly and briefly in the beautiful curve of Scott's neck and shoulder at the end of an inspired flamenco lesson under the coloured lanterns on the back veranda across from the railway line, while the trains, thunder by in the dark'.[13] Another critic has wondered 'if the closet in which *Strictly Ballroom*'s Doug Hastings keeps the secret reminders of the life he might have led doesn't have a certain symbolic resonance'.[14] Whatever one might think of these suggestions, without doubt Scott Hastings is breaking new ground for the male lead in a mainstream Australian film, partly by his interest in artistic self-expression, and partly by the presentation of the male body as spectacle.

David Buchbinder suggests that 'Scott's triumph masks the fact that he, like all men, must *continue* to compete and will always find rivals',[15] however, there is another way of looking at the way that *Strictly Ballroom* deals with the notion of competition. Throughout there's a strong tension between the desire to compete and the desire to express oneself. For most of the film Scott, Fran and Doug (although, in his case, the audience is not aware of this until the end) are more interested in the latter, and stand against all the other characters who cannot see beyond winning. The final happy scene is a utopian moment when the very notion of competition is overthrown – audience, judges and instructors join the competitors in a joyful celebration of unity, and of participation for its own sake. *Strictly Ballroom* is, in this final image, drawing on archetypally Australian ideas of egalitarianism to depict a contemporary culture of people from different classes and ethnic backgrounds dancing happily together. Buchbinder is, of course, correct to suggest that this is an ideological picture, in the sense that it hides the reality of contemporary Australian society. But, in terms of the idea of competition, correctly identified by Buchbinder as such a central aspect of the way that contemporary masculinity is constructed, this ending takes up one of the film's most important questions, and resolves it firmly in favour of non-competition. Certainly it is utopian, but *Strictly Ballroom* concludes with an uplifting rejection of competition.

Men and Women

Crucial to the kind of masculinity these films ultimately endorse is the way they depict the relations between men and women. In *The Big Steal* Danny's parents seem to live out a mutually supportive relationship, both having inner strength, and both able to act independently when they wish. The relationship between Danny and Joanna is not sketched in any detail, but it is clear that she is by no means the junior partner. She begins the film more confident and self-assured than Danny, and demonstrates her decisiveness and competence by engineering his rescue from Gordon Farkas's car yard. By the end of the film, Danny has matured enough to allow the hope of a relationship between two equals. Although *Death in Brunswick* depicts a terrible relationship between Dave and his wife June; Barbara Creed suggests that a scene where a dead woman's body is crushed might be interpreted as Dave 'giving vent to his real feelings towards his dominating wife', it, too, holds out some hope of an equal relationship between the two leads.[16] Their relationship is a substantial departure from the patriarchal family which Sophie is leaving, and she has a considerable strength, demonstrated right from the beginning in her active role in the courting process.

Although one might expect the teacher to hold all the power in her relationship with a student, *The Heartbreak Kid* clearly establishes that they both must learn from each other. Nick's introducing Christina to the arts of dope-smoking and roller-blading might not be of extreme significance in the narrative, but is indicative of something wider which he is doing – helping her to challenge her previous conformism with regards to the expectations of her parents and the Greek community. More specifically, he consistently pushes her, both intentionally and unintentionally, towards questioning whether she should marry Dimitri. She remains, however, five years older than Nick, and in a position of authority over him, so that the film finishes with her resolving to go away for a couple of years, in part to allow him to mature into an independent young man. The patriarchal model has not been replaced by one where the woman dominates; again it has been replaced by a relationship with the possibility of equality.

Perhaps because *Strictly Ballroom* has to work so hard to counteract the potential feminisation of its male lead, it gives much less attention to presenting an equal relationship between Scott and Fran than the other films in this group. The first interactions between the couple show Scott holding all the power, and are more than a bit uncomfortable for those with any awareness of feminism, but the audience is reassured when Fran is able to show him some steps she's been working on at home, and he suddenly becomes her pupil. The moment is short-lived, however, and Scott's treatment of Fran continues to vacillate between the poles of tenderness and heartlessness. The romance narrative requires the hero, like Mr Darcy in *Pride and Prejudice* and Mr Rochester in *Jane Eyre*, to soften, to turn from tyrant into acceptable romance hero. Scott does finally realise that he loves her, and that he should not abandon her as his partner, and, like a traditional romance heroine, Fran discovers that if you persevere long enough with a man who behaves like a bastard, he'll eventually reveal the nice guy underneath. But that final image of Scott performing as a toreador, operates among other things as proof that he is not over-softened, and is not under the heroine's thumb. Hopes for an equal relationship here, are not nearly as strong as they are in *The Big Steal, Death in Brunswick* and *The Heartbreak Kid*.

Strictly Ballroom may offer a more strident critique of hegemonic masculinity in its depiction of Barry Fife than any of the other films discussed here, but, in its efforts to have a ballroom dancer as the male lead, it seems simultaneously to need to make a range of concessions to an only slightly different form of hegemonic masculinity, with Rico its initial exemplar. By the end of the film, Scott has proved that he possesses a heterosexual masculinity which is powerful but not excessive, and has been awarded the prize of the heroine in recognition of this; the strong women have learnt their place; and the importance of firm but nurturing fatherhood has been re-endorsed. However, as Kerryn Goldsworthy has pointed out, 'time after time in *Strictly Ballroom* that surface structure–causality leading to the closure of restored order–is ruffled and broken by hints of possibility and images of rupture'.[17] The possibilities identified by Champagne and others, listed above, are certainly present for some viewers, as is the questioning of the competition so often identified as central to contemporary masculinity. In the final analysis, the wild colonial boy *does* appear as a ballroom dancer, permanently altering the spaces available for

masculinity in Australian film. Without *Strictly Ballroom*, a film like
Priscilla, Queen of the Desert would not have been possible.

Conclusions

The basic structure of these four films is roughly what you might expect in
narratives about growing to heterosexual adult masculinity: a boy must free
himself from his parents' control, prove that he can stand on his own two
feet, and establish a relationship with a woman. But within those generic
restrictions, it is clear that the pressure of changing ideas about masculinity,
femininity and gender relations is having an impact on the stories which are
told, and which audiences want to hear. All four may be conventional and
heterosexist, but they also all make profound criticisms of hegemonic
masculinity, show that the old unitary notions of masculinity are no longer
sustainable in a multicultural society, and offer some ways of behaving that
are outside the traditional stereotypes.

To become an adult male, according to the films, it is necessary to have
backbone, but this is not the same as the toughness identified by West in
Fathers, Sons and Lovers. Instead there's a stress on gentleness, on
nurturing, and on being able to express emotions. It's true that none of the
four propose a 'sensitive new age guy' as an attractive model of masculinity
(the marginal figure, Graham, in *The Heartbreak Kid* is probably the only
character to qualify for this label, and his is a very minor narrative function)
instead they propose sensitivity coupled with the strength to stand on one's
own two feet. In spite of West's conclusions, none of the films mention war
and, although there is some fighting, the hero usually manages to avoid
being involved. *The Heartbreak Kid* is the only film which has the hero
involved in several fights, and it also shows achievement in sport as
important in the hero's road to adulthood.

Although West's study found that sex was helpful for gaining peer
approval, the films do not present it in this way. The hero does have sex with
a woman in *The Big Steal* and *The Heartbreak Kid*, but not to impress his
mates; in fact, the first of these films makes fun of Van's public display of
his sexual prowess. Instead of depicting men as needing to be stronger than
girls, or feeling the need to provide for loved ones, the films generally go
out of their way to establish the possibility of equality in the relationship
between men and women. It may be that the boys in these films need to
'prove their masculinity', but this is not in the sense of proving their
'manliness', which is what the phrase means in West's study. The
'masculinity' they need to prove is the ability to live independently of their

parents in a potentially non-exploitative relationship with a woman. In fact the characteristics set out by West sound very much like the hegemonic masculinity which all four films carefully critique.

But it frequently seems to be a struggle for the films to move away from older patterns of masculinity. Often it is as if there's a need to compensate, so that to have a ballroom dancer as the hero, he must undergo a remasculinisation, or to present ethnic difference in any more than crude stereotypes means that the narrative must be traditional in other respects, or to depict a non-violent hero, others must be violent on his behalf. And while the films might put together a version of the ideal father as firm but nurturing, perhaps critical of his son's attempts to move towards independence, but not hindering him in the long run, they are much less positive in their depiction of mothers. According to all but *The Big Steal*, for a boy to grow to adult masculinity, the mother needs to be rendered silent and immobile (*Death in Brunswick*), or to learn her place (*Strictly Ballroom*), or to be already dead (*The Heartbreak Kid*).

These four films show that a significant shift in the representation of masculinity was taking place in the early 1990s. No doubt some of the elements that marked that change were present in isolated films in earlier decades, but the substantial box office success of a group of films showing the impact of new ideas about masculinity indicates that Australian audiences were ready for a different set of images and narratives. The boundaries for Australian masculinity were to be pushed further as the decade continued, in films like *The Adventures of Priscilla, Queen of the Desert* (1994), *The Sum of Us*, (1994) *Blackfellas* (1993), *All Men Are Liars* (1995) and *Doing Time for Patsy Cline* (1997), but the successes of the early 1990s were crucial in giving the industry the confidence to move even further away from traditional icons of Australian manhood.

NOTES

1. Graeme Turner, *Making it National: Nationalism and Australian Popular Culture* (Sydney: Allen & Unwin, 1994), p.127.
2. Peter West, *Fathers, Sons and Lovers: Men Talk About Their Lives From The 1930s To Today* (Sydney: Finch, 1996), pp.29–32.
3. Ibid., pp.58–60.
4. See Tom Morton, *Altered Mates: The Man Question* (St. Leonards; New South Wales: Allen & Unwin, 1997).
5. R. W. Connell, *Masculinities* (St. Leonards; New South Wales: Allen & Unwin, 1995), p.79.
6. Mary Anne Reid, *Long Shots to Favourites: Australian Cinema Successes in the 90s* (Sydney: Australian Film Commission, 1993), p.52.
7. Barbara Creed, 'Mothers and Lovers: Oedipal Transgressions in Recent Australian Cinema', *Metro*, No.91 (Spring 1992), p.18.

8. David Buchbinder, *Performance Anxieties: Re-Producing Masculinity* (St. Leonards; New South Wales: Allen & Unwin, 1998), p.62.

9. Ibid., pp.63–64.

10. Jim Schembri, '*The Big Steal*', *Cinema Papers*, No.81 (December 1990), p.53.

11. Turner, p.130.

12. John Champagne, 'Dancing Queen? Feminist and Gay Male Spectatorship in Three Recent Films from Australia', *Film Criticism*, Vol.21, No.3 (Spring 1997), pp.66–88.

13. Kerryn Goldsworthy, '"…not always strictly ballroom": The Phenomenon of *Strictly Ballroom*', *Arena Magazine*, Vol.2 (December 1992–January 1993), p. 45.

14. Karl Quinn, 'Drag, Dags and the Suburban Surreal', *Metro*, No. 100 (Summer 1994–95), p.26.

15. Buchbinder, p.68.

16. Creed, p.17.

17. Goldsworthy, p.45.

6

His Natural Whiteness:
Modes of Ethnic Presence and Absence
in Some Recent Australian Films

DAVID CALLAHAN

The Comfortable Ethnic

At the beginning of the film *Glass* (1989), a flower-seller looks up at a skyscraper, faced with sheets of mirror glass. The modern city is opaque, unyielding to scrutiny on the part of its street-level inhabitants, reflecting only other buildings. At the end of the film we find that the flower-seller has been the murderer whose activities have driven the narrative. He had been transformed into a devious killer because his former patch as flower-seller had been appropriated by the new building's developers, 'developers' of the kind which have come to occupy centre stage amongst the most consistent villains in Australian film over the last two decades.

Significantly, for our purposes here, this flower seller is patently 'ethnic' in what used to be the formulation 'southern European'; full of emotion and picturesque charm, but marginal to the operations of real power in this society. Among many possible meanings that could be constructed out of this, one may be that such immigrants have been in Australia long enough to be dispossessed of their territory, in a way that is distantly analogous to the dispossession on which the country's history is based. From such a perspective, this narrative is in some way legible as a displacement of that greater but altogether too sensitive and too problematic theme of dispossession. While the flower seller has not been dispossessed explicitly because he is Italian, it is precisely because he is an immigrant that he exists on the margins of power and can therefore play no part in decisions about the occupation of territory.

At so many levels of Australian filmic representation, 'ethnicity' within the nation operates in this troubled way: both as activator of meanings and concealer of them. 'Obviously' ethnic characters often exist uneasily on the edge of their ethnicity, partly constructed in terms of that ethnicity and partly as the individual functions of classic (Hollywood) cinema. For the murderer in *Glass*, his status as a southern European immigrant is at least a semi-concealed factor in the aetiology of his actions: restrict a person's access to power and they will take it into their own hands. However, when it comes to Australians of British/Irish origin, not to mention the totally invisible non-Maori New Zealanders, the question of ethnicity becomes even more concealed, as concealed as what lies behind the mirror glass.

Authority Politics

European, and even Asian, ethnicities have long been a godsend to Australian filmmakers, for they give less contentious scope to that basic element in all advice to scriptwriters: conflict. Despite the fact that Australian history is built on conflicts of various kinds, not all of them are available or at least comfortable for white Australian filmmakers. The need to examine the original and psychically most significant conflict on which the nation is based, that between Aborigines and colonisers, has proven difficult in most contemporary Australian film. White filmmakers who attempted to deal with the issues involved in the recent past, no matter how well-meaning, tended to be scalded by the response, so that the films made by white filmmakers that most enthusiastically deal with Aboriginal-White conflict or relations, albeit in ways that various constituencies find seriously flawed, date from the 1970s or 1980s. Few contemporary films by white directors take the risks of *Walkabout* (1970), *Backroads* (1977), *The Last Wave* (1977), *The Chant of Jimmie Blacksmith* (1978) or *The Fringe Dwellers* (1986).

In the mainstream cinema, it seems as if white filmmakers, which is to say almost all filmmakers in Australia, have been largely cowed by the intensities of authority politics and swerved away from this conflictual element in the national makeup. It might be argued that Aborigines represent only a small proportion of the population of Australia and that therefore it is only to be expected that narratives dealing with them would be marginal to the country's film production. However, I side with Bob Hodge and Vijay Mishra with respect to the symbolic significance of issues dealing with the relation between Aboriginal peoples and others; as they say, 'their [Aborigines'] importance in the construction of Australian identity is disproportionate precisely because these issues have not been resolved'.[1] And the central issue is that of *belonging*, with which, in one way or another, so many Australian films appear to deal.

The discomfort aroused by the psychic manoeuvres required to accommodate dealing with belonging without dealing with Aboriginal/ white relations ensures, then, that other non-Aboriginal ethnicities provide welcome material through which belonging can be dealt with as a theme and, in more general terms, through which conflict and narrative opposition can be generated. The liberal enthusiasm for inflecting Australia with non-British ethnic aspects, earnestly yearned for at all turns in Australian cultural life – from the alacrity with which the cultural establishment leapt at first to include the story of a putative Ukrainian within the range of national stories in the Helen Demidenko affair, through the desire, even at the official level of the Victorian state government, to find a Portuguese origin for the first European footprint – is also clearly apparent in Australian filmmaking.[2]

One of the principal contemporary mediations of this yearning, *Strictly Ballroom* (1992) seems to be craven in its representations of up-tight Anglos as compared to the fiery and passionate Spanish. Admittedly caricatural, the film nevertheless picks on such repeatedly-battered-as-to-be-supine conventions of liberal Australian culture – such as that suburban white Australians are emotionally dysfunctional – that it ends up offering little more than a degraded version of Anglo wish-fulfilment. That is, if only we were not descended from Poms how happy we'd be. The tired representation of 'Spaniards': the tourist cliché of the Andalusian gypsy – ironically violently marginalised in Spanish society – even gets its dance steps wrong: the reiterated *paso doblé* that the ardent Spaniards are teaching out the back of their dwelling (undeveloped because their values are above such 'suburban' materialism) is not a Flamenco routine at all, but a sort of village fiesta military two-step. Who cares? 'Ethnics' are made to be used in the representation of British-Australia as a psychically damaged place, but also as a place where the injuries of this inheritance mask the fact that the British-Australians' position is erected upon their taking themselves as the base of what constitutes identity in Australia. Richard Dyer states the problem clearly at the outset of *White* (1997): 'as long as white people are not racially seen and named, they/we function as a human norm. Other people are raced, we are just people'.[3]

To some extent, *Strictly Ballroom* redeems itself by setting up ethnic opposition in order to critique what passes for the Australian norm, but it partly foxtrots away from any worthwhile implications of this critique by using Spanish as its contrastive ethnicity. As a migrant group in Australia the Spanish are not one of the most numerous or noticeable and cannot do duty as a really viable, or visible, alternative model, except by way of cultural meanings that have been circulating not simply in Australia but in Western cultures since the Romantics. Moreover, the clichés by which these meanings are mediated have been ironically transmitted through very British/Northern European (and middle-class) traditions of romanticising the Spanish/Andalusians/Gypsies, so that *Strictly Ballroom* wistfully denies its middle-class rigidities, ultimately as innovative in cultural politics as any nineteenth century sentimentalisation of the southern European.

Ethnic Comedy

One obvious contrast with the values of white Anglo-Australia is not with Spaniards but with the country's indigenous peoples. Yet *Strictly Ballroom* insinuates what may still perhaps be true in the politics of ethnic representation in Australia: it is too early for white filmmakers to assay comedy in the relations between white Australians and Aborigines. Admittedly, Aboriginal peoples might have been a bit tricky to accommodate in a film about ballroom dancing, but the basic values of bodily expression and recuperating the legacy of an oppressed father seem at first sight certainly capable of comparison with the relations between Aborigines and non-Aborigines. Bruce Beresford's attempt to envision a warm-hearted and yet comic register in which to represent Aborigines in *The Fringe Dwellers* was not received comfortably, and has not led to the installation of this register in Australian film, although the film was popular with Aboriginal audiences in Australia when it first appeared.

Helen Garner suggested in 1996 that 'it's hard for Australians to make light, playful movies. Our film comedies tend towards a broad, raucous style which risks dropping earthward and turning gross'.[4] The comic register can, however, be used when continental Europeans are involved, as in any number of films since *They're a Weird Mob* (1966). The black comedy *Death in Brunswick* (1991) operates by means of the same caricatural strategies as *Strictly Ballroom* but at least represents a plague-on-all-houses and does not sentimentalise any particular ethnic position. Envisioning Melbourne as a pullulating cauldron of ethnic cross-purposes, misunderstandings, hostilities and failure, all ethnic groups are situated as bloody-minded and dysfunctional. In its hearty swipe at whatever ethnicity gets in its way, however, the film does what most films do not: it grants everyone an ethnicity. In *Strictly Ballroom*, we have the stiff and anxious whites existing as 'society', with the Spanish clearly marginal both culturally and spatially (living in a marked-off zone with little connection to the rest of society, on the edge of the iconic badlands represented by railway tracks). Fran (Tara Morice) has to mask her ethnicity to belong, at one point responding to Scott's (Paul Mercurio) asking what her surname is by saying 'Just Fran', presumably because her surname would disclose her 'ethnic' status. Only the first generation are open and impassioned; by Fran's generation, Anglo shyness and withdrawal have already set in. In *Death in Brunswick*, on the other hand, the mixture of ethnicities leaves everyone inscribed as positional. This is a society whose dominant relation is conflict. The caricatures fly in all directions, and their crudity is certainly not in the spirit of multicultural harmony, with Greeks on the make, Turkish thugs and drug dealers, a Pommie lout and that stock-in-trade of liberal Australia – the would-be refined Anglo matriarch. Indeed, Anglos are nicely gradated from the recent lower class arrival (the crude and violent bouncer at the restaurant/bar), Dave's (John Clarke) lower middle-class background in all its confused readjustments of power within the family, to the genteel Anglophile pretensions of Carl Fitzgerald's (Sam Neill) mother (Yvonne Lawley).[5]

In this discrimination among various forms of Anglo ethnicity, *Death in Brunswick* can perhaps be seen as affirming at least their numerical centrality within Australian culture, but the film is certainly not an affirmation of either their moral hegemony or their assumption of themselves as unmarked 'society'. Indeed, it is precisely the exasperation with which Mrs Fitzgerald attempts to construct a version of respectable and well-bred difference from her surroundings that reveals her awareness that such a construction is under threat and cannot assume its centrality. Peter Lawrence, is either being ironic or misses the point when he suggests that 'Brunswick, Melbourne, is an inner-urban sprawl populated with Greeks and Turks and a few Australians'.[6] In fact the film slyly presents a world in which to be Australian could be to be anything: where, in any event, what is important is not so much identity as various forms of survival, from the survival of the cultural forms of Mrs Fitzgerald through the marital survival of Dave and June (Deborah Kennedy), the economic survival of Yanni Voulgaris (Nicholas Papademetriou), and the survival of life and limb on the part of most characters. In this environment, ethnicity constitutes more of a liability than something to be supported or fought for, interfering in characters' struggles for happiness and even in their efforts to stay alive.

Invisible Ethnicity

In addition to the tendency to use minority ethnicities to generate narrative and ideological conflict, in which nonetheless the majority ethnic groups are rendered negatively, there is also the reverse tendency, as noted by contemporary writers on whiteness: to simply ignore ethnicity as a factor in Australian culture, not only for white people, but for everybody. In this way, Australians simply inhabit 'society', which becomes equivalent to Australia's 'culture'. That is, there is no need to draw attention to anyone's ethnicity because we are all the same, or perhaps, all in the same boat. Given that the majority of people represented in such scenarios are white, this can also be seen as the naturalisation of whiteness, and occurs in those films in which nobody apparently belongs to any specified ethnicity. John Dingwall's *The Custodian* (1993) or Emma-Kate Croghan's *Love and Other Catastrophes* (1996) serve as my examples here.

In *The Custodian* there is a certain attentiveness to the ethnic mix of Australian society, but no attention to this ethnicity as culture. That is, it exists as a visual sign of the differences within Australian society but doesn't activate anything beyond that. For example, the film begins in a Japanese restaurant. The portrayal of the Japanese is generally negative in Australian films, in part precisely because there is no significant presence of Japanese people living in Australia and so they can function as the somewhat unproblematised threat of the rich and powerful, the vulgar and simplistic meanings of which are only half-parodied in Yahoo Serious's *Reckless Kelly* (1993). In *The Custodian*, the restaurant is simply backdrop, although one could also say that it exists as a sign of an easy assumption of the country's multicultural habits, if nothing else.[7] Throughout the film, ethnicities are not only made specific but function only at a continental/transnational level. We see an unspecifiedly 'central European' police psychologist (shades of Hollywood avatars of Freud), a 'European' administrator at the TV station, and an 'Asian' senior figure also at the TV station, his smoothness inflecting the threat of the slick and manipulative oriental. There are also gestures to the country's multi-ethnic composition in the presence of a black gambler in the raid toward the beginning, and later a black detective in on the take (as are most of the white ones). Neither of these is, however, Aboriginal, so ethnicity remains unmarked, as if it were a colourful element but hollow of cultural impact. The principal characters in the film are simply majority whites, and the other ethnicities are not treated as possessing any difference other than their accents. The implicit suggestion is thus that belonging to the majority ethnicity is without need of self-definition, and that social problems, in this film, police corruption, and individual ones, are dealt with by individuals for whom ethnic status is irrelevant. Quinlan (Anthony La Paglia), the detective who becomes obsessed with the corruption among his fellow detectives, is also going through a profound personal crisis connected to the breakdown of his marriage, so that the film's hermeneutic code connects the social malaise with his personal difficulties. La Paglia's brooding performance gains some of its power from the claustrophobic dead-end this sets up, wherein the personal becomes the social becomes the personal. As in the familiar traditions of Hollywood narrative, social problems boil down to the confrontation of individuals, whose strengths and weaknesses are no more than personal. In this trial the lone avenger naturally has no parents, no children, no aunts, cousins or brothers and sisters, and certainly no ethnicity, an isolation that is perhaps part of the problem.

In *Love and Other Catastrophes*, we have a comedy version of the same sort of things. Ethnic status is not a factor, only individual problems and solutions. None of the characters refers to anything other than their wishes, dreams, desires or problems, personalities and relationships, and in none of these perfectly acceptable areas of concern does ethnicity intrude. Although Laura Miller, in *Sight and Sound*, referred to the film as 'Woody Allen lite',[8] the self-consciously New York Jewish focus of Allen's chronicles finds no parallel or echo in Croghan's film. More locally significant is the fact that although we might imagine student life to be a time when issues of social inequality and government oppression are burning concerns, there is no indication in the film that anything exists outside, as the title has it, love and sex. The absence of reference to ethnicity is just one of the ways the film collapses the social into the personal, but once again the personal becomes as much a mask as a site for display. The ease with which Mia (Frances O'Connor) and Danni (Radha Mitchell) represent their lesbianism clearly suggests a liberation from the homogenising constraints of the past in this area, but the homogenisation of whiteness as personhood persists. Similarly in Kevin Dowling and Geoff Burton's *The Sum of Us* (1994), in which Harry (Jack Thompson), a suburban blue-collar dad, relates easily, warmly even, to his gay footie-playing son Jeff (Russell Crowe), we get humorous and good-hearted transgression of formerly fearful and rigid boundaries; however the film is not interested in deconstructing the codes it is transgressing as partly ethnic. The values of normality and straightness are not connected to the assumptions of ethnic superiority with which white ethnicities, especially Anglo male ones, connect themselves.

Whiteness as an Ethnicity

Lola Young, in *Fear of the Dark: 'Race', Gender and Sexuality in the Cinema*, suggests that work such as Richard Dyer's on whiteness in British and American cinema might be useful but that it shouldn't 'become yet another opportunity for white experiences and attitudes to be foregrounded'.[9] It is difficult to know how to read this statement. In the first place, such work as Dyer's scrupulously reads white experiences with reference to other groups, instead of simply naturalising those experiences, and this seems properly responsible. Secondly, white people do have experiences and can scarcely be expected to ignore them, and in places where they are the vast majority it does not seem unduly oppressive that they should often be foregrounded. Dyer, however, is equally nervous about the same possibility and makes a similar point, when he suggests that his 'blood runs cold at the thought that talking about whiteness could lead to the development of something called "White Studies"', that studying whiteness might become part of 'a new assertiveness ... amounting to a statement of "white ethnicity", the acceptable face of white nationalism'.[10] Nonetheless, we can only become self-conscious about whiteness itself as an ethnicity by realising that its meanings come from its relation to what is characterised as not-white. The further task – of breaking down the assumed naturalisation of this centrality – is undertaken precisely in stories about white people in which their whiteness is shown to be cultural and just as ethnic as any other position. This need not be an assertion of whiteness at the expense of other ethnicities.

In reflecting on these issues, one of the most penetrating analyses is that of Toni Morrison, who can hardly be accused of wishing to institute aggressive whiteness studies, in her book *Playing in the Dark: Whiteness and the Literary Imagination*. To bring whiteness into the foreground is precisely to subject it to an enquiry of its naturalised presence as unmarked and the measure of all others. As Morrison claims, 'in matters of race, silence and evasion have historically ruled literary discourse. Evasion has fostered another, substitute language in which the issues are encoded, foreclosing open debate'.[11] In her incisive reading of these codes, Morrison reveals how this certainly does not privilege whiteness but rather brings into focus the ways in which African Americans have been used to sustain the encoded centrality of that whiteness. At the same time, this also masks other more problematic nexus:

> images of blackness can be evil *and* protective, rebellious *and* forgiving, fearful *and* desirable – all the self-contradictory features of the self. Whiteness, alone, is mute, meaningless, unfathomable, pointless, frozen, veiled, curtained, dreaded, senseless, implacable. Or so our writers seem to say.[12]

At first sight *Romper Stomper* (1992) appears to be a film that does take white ethnicity seriously and, to the extent that it represents its white protagonists as preoccupied with such concerns it brings white supremacism to the surface. Moreover, it appears to do so in such a way as to confront Australians with violence in a way that, according to Jane Mills, Head of Screen Studies at the Australian Film, Television and Radio School, is not generally attempted in Australian film. 'Few Australian filmmakers portray humankind's inhumanity; this deprives audiences of a means of discovering reason to help control and lessen individual and government-sanctioned violence.'[13] However, it is doubtful whether *Romper Stomper* is quite the film to achieve the portrayal of humankind's inhumanity that Mills might want. More of a conflicted representation of issues of maleness, a sort of Australian version of the New Zealand movie *Once Were Warriors* (1994) – without the Maori culture to fall back on. The violence between whites and Vietnamese in *Romper Stomper* becomes an inner-city pirates set piece, now one side in the ascendant, then the other flowing back and swarming up the rigging. The inhumanity is not dwelt on because the results of violence on its victims are not dwelt on, there are some sensitive scenes among the Vietnamese before the fighting in which can be seen the mixture of fear and bravado the occasion generates, but in the end the personalities they had begun to build up become flattened, so to speak. We see lots of fighting but we know little what has happened to the injured, the effects that it has had in their lives, what it means to have had your spleen ruptured or your teeth impacted in your gums.

The revelation that one of the two principal members of the skinhead group, Davey (Daniel Pollock), is of German ancestry rather muddies things by swerving from their rootedness in the majority culture. This is the only member of the group whose family background we see, and yet, as a German, Davey can be seen as marginal to the principal sources of power in Australian society and majority British-Australia can distance itself from the position he occupies. The clichéd identification of Germans with delusions of ethnic superiority lets British-Australians off the hook, moreover the revelation that Davey's family only goes back two generations at the most enables the older and more unresolved history of ethnic violence also to be subsumed into Davey's more recently European origins. Nonetheless *Romper Stomper* is a film that does dislodge something that is all too common in even well-meaning narratives dealing with relations between ethnic groups, in Toni Morrison's words: 'the pattern of thinking about racialism in terms of its consequences on the victim – of always defining it asymmetrically from the perspective of its impact on the object of racist policy and attitudes'.[14]

From Conflict to the Appropriation of 'Belonging'

When it comes to dealing with these issues in the context of relations between whites and Aborigines, it seems difficult for white filmmakers to imagine other possibilities, when they do, than those of conflict. Aleksi Vellis's *The Life of Harry Dare* (1997), to take one example among several, has its heart in the right place; an Aussie battler/ratbag cops comedy in which the battler is Harry Dare (John Moore), an Aborigine in Adelaide trying to deal with the various strands of his life: bonding with Jim (Aaron Wilton), his young son, making up with his wife, dodging the racist policemen who want to put him in jail, and getting back a Combi van he's been working on for years. The narrative drive and the engaging good humour ensure an upbeat vision of Aborigines getting the better of the cops and re-establishing family supports. Nonetheless, the establishment of an agonistic relationship between whites and blacks is such a common model of ethnic contact in the media, even in the liberal media, that one wonders whether the only well-known positive models of white/Aboriginal mates are going to remain the sentimental ones of Mick Dundee (Paul Hogan) and Neville Bell (David Gulpilil) in *Crocodile Dundee* (1986) or Fingerbone (David Gulpilil) and Mike (Greg Rowe) in *Storm Boy* (1977), in both of which we see models of natural savages, even if ironically inflected. At least there are efforts made to construct male friendships, while female friendships between Aborigines and whites appear difficult to approach.

One of the most surprising successes in recent years has been that of the low-budget comedy *The Castle* (1997), which has charmed audiences in Australia with its picture of what might be seen as a white natural savage, the battling Darryl Kerrigan (Michael Caton), and his family in their naive fight against the inevitable developers. The family's principal weapon appears to be the binding optimism of Darryl's love for the family, for anything they are interested in, and ultimately in life. Unable to perceive his family's tastes in comparison to anything, Darryl valorises unreservedly what the knowing audience laughs at: his gimcrack holiday house, for instance, which he cannot believe he got so cheaply, the camera panning back until we see the giant electricity pylons looming over it; or his wife's unimaginative and stodgy cooking, precisely things associated with dull and pre-multicultural Australia. We laugh at his naiveté, and this laughter establishes an uneasy complicity between the film's point of view and that of the audience. Despite Darryl's absurd optimism and enthusiasm, brilliantly rendered by Michael Caton, nobody in the film laughs at him; only the privileged audience does. In conversation at the recent European Association of Studies on Australia conference in Klagenfurt it was suggested that the constituency *The Castle* might be appealing to is that to which right wing politician Pauline Hanson also appeals (so much wider than that of Oxley). Darryl's warm inclusiveness, in which good Aussie blokes hover semi-permanently on the edge of tears, expatiating in lachrymose fashion on the wonders of his wife's unimaginative cooking, is not simply a bulwark against the dysfunctional domestic life that exists as one of the film's determinate absences, but it shades into a valorisation of ignorance and clannishness that is at odds with its would-be optimistic vision of the Aussie battler winning out against the system.

   In Darryl's battle with the wealthy, the powerful and the tasteful, he succeeds precisely because of his ignorance of and thus failure to act in accordance with the accepted procedures and protocols of society, like some antipodean version of Forrest Gump. While this has a certain Candide-like charm, it also suggests that one is morally healthier by not knowing anything about how one's society functions or having any idea whatsoever about how other people might be. The film attempts to have it both ways, for Darryl's predicament is rescued by the intervention of a kindly QC (Charles Tingwell), who has been touched by Darryl's fatherly warmth and naive optimism. That is, Darryl succeeds through the system rather than against it, suggesting that it is only on the level of the personal that the system can be made to work; one can have no faith in civil mechanisms in the maintenance of civility.

   What is interesting in this version of the agonistic relationship between the individual and the social – so central after all to every narrative tradition since the beginnings of the folk tale (not to mention Kafka's nightmarish parable of the same name, *The Castle*) – is the signs of the appropriation by white Australia of the discourse of belonging that has been generated so forcefully in recent years by the other determinate absence in this film, Australia's originally dispossessed people. It is echoed when Darryl laments: 'This house is our memories, our stories', the terms here relating the family not simply to possessions but to a History as the space wherein they ground themselves. And it is starkly summoned up when Darryl says 'I'm starting to feel how the Aborigines feel'. While this may be seen as appropriation, it can also be seen as a positive attempt to ally Aboriginal issues with those facing the average bloke, the establishment of an axis of sympathy along which the Aussie battler can relate to what is happening/has happened to the most severely dispossessed of the nation's peoples.

This sly introduction of ethnicity at the heart of the film's central concern, when the audience's identification has been well and truly achieved, may indicate, in a favourable reading, one direction in which such issues can become inclusive rather than divisive. However, that the use of such discourse is severely context-determined can be seen by the use of a similar statement in *Romper Stomper*, where the racist Hando (Russell Crowe) snarls 'I don't want to go the same way as the fucking Abos'. Such discourse claims the same moral right to belong as the Aborigines and places white Australians in the victim position, eliding complicity with their part in instituting such a victim position in the first place. Many contemporary commentators have picked up on this tendency to appropriate the markers of marginality by groups desiring to use the sympathies such markers might arouse for their own purposes. I have commented elsewhere on this tendency of white Australians to allocate to themselves signifiers formerly associated with Aboriginal peoples, concentrating on the proud use in contemporary Australia of the rhetoric of great age as just one more in the national paradigm of items of great size: 'Aboriginal history here has also become a counter of true-blue Australianness, sliding neatly in alongside the rhetoric of distance and extension'.[15] Peter Beilharz, reviewing Jane M Jacobs, notes that:

> the modern need for primitivism collapses the other into the dominant self. As we, white Australians are positioned by our northern superiors, so do we position ourselves over and against others, patronising our predecessors as we seek to make ourselves authentically indigenous.[16]

That Hando should read his fear of Vietnamese immigrants in terms of Aboriginal dispossession both highlights the heavy ironies involved in appropriating the Aboriginal victim position and is indicative of the displacement of Aboriginal peoples from their moral centrality in narratives of belonging. On the other hand, Hando's cornered stridency to the discourse of dispossession associated in Australian public life with the Aboriginal peoples, could be seen to imply that both are simply versions of the same whinging aggression. I feel that the former reading edges out the latter, but that could clearly be a function of my desire that such readings should prevail. In any event, *Romper Stomper* manages to build a narrative around white people who are aware of their ethnicity, who do not erase the issue in the easy assumption of themselves as simply 'society' or 'humanity', the film does not simply place Aboriginal or migrant peoples in the victim position, a 'problem', to be anguished over. This in turn brings us back to Lola Young and Richard Dyer's concern that 'Whiteness Studies' could lead to yet more concentration on the lives and problems facing white people.

Jennifer Lawn writes about this in a New Zealand context in her interesting article 'Pakeha Bonding' in *Meanjin*. There she talks of how 'members of a hegemonic group ostensibly abject themselves to an idealised other, while diverting the terms of the debate from material conditions of oppression to their own psychic malaise'.[17] This suggests that the terms of the debate were concentrated on material conditions of oppression in the first place, which is an exaggeration I feel, in both countries. Indeed, the terms of the debate were moved away from simplistic discourses of material progress and advancement (always conceived in white majority terms) toward wider identity issues – which are also material – precisely by the upsurge in Aboriginal visibility since the 1970s. While we do not want too much syrupy identity-speak, from any sector of the community, these issues do not resolve themselves into a question of land title or heart attack statistics. No material acts can adequately recompense for colonial actions, but they do have symbolic value in terms of recognition. It may be that British-Australians also have a need to be recognised, but are unable to fully admit it without the abjection Lawn speaks of, for it would mean significant readjustments in the ways they have constructed themselves. Moreover, to activate this need for recognition also activates in a much more visible form the painful possibilities of misrecognition or denial. Even though white identity needs cannot be reduced to one source, that of white ethnicities, neither can they be reduced solely to psychosexual and interpersonal sources, as many films seem to suggest.

Enclave Politics

With this problematic relationship to a discourse of belonging that excludes Aboriginal peoples, even as it appropriates references to them, a typical Australian response is to construct narratives whose energies are directed toward the promotion of what I term *enclave politics*, and ultimately this term might be applied to many Australian films in that their principal moral centre consists in shoring up the enclave against the social, the individual against the public, the group against the wider polity. In this way, belonging can be examined in terms of the culturally-sanctioned group of mates holding out against the rich and powerful without requiring any reference to the more troubling theme of ethnic and cultural dispossession upon which the nation's history is based, not to mention the complexities of living in a more variegated multicultural society. At the same time, the tensions involved and the displacements they engender can, like all significant displacements, generate absorbing and even powerful narratives as films deal with these questions.

In a more scabrous treatment of the dysfunctional family dynamics of the would-be enclave, we have a dark version of Darryl's Candide-like innocence in Rolf de Heer's powerful *Bad Boy Bubby* (1994). As in *The Castle*, Bubby's (Nick Hope) innocence serves as a vehicle for commentary on a shallow and self-serving society, moreover the alternative is not posited upon a retreat from society. Bubby's confinement for more than thirty years is represented as incarceration, slavery and abuse, and his escape is experienced by the audience as an escape into freedom. However the ambiguities of the society he escapes into, as in all such tales, soon become apparent. Michael Rymer's *Angel Baby* (1996) is another film dealing with people on the very edge of social acceptability: two psychiatric patients and their passionate relationship in the face of officialdom. While the intensities of marginal states are part of film's territory, it is also possible that Australian cinema's investment in individuals on the borders of social acceptability may be another way of eliding ethnic politics in favour of the personal. Once characters are pushed so far to the boundaries of the normal, they become particular cases and cannot do duty as representatives of identifiable social groups or tendencies. One can hardly suggest that *Bad Boy Bubby* is a revelation of the social and ethnic issues surrounding men kept locked up by their incestuous mothers; only the most severe metaphorical constructions could suggest there was much of a directly-involved constituency here.

In a critical success from the same year, *The Well* (1997), we have Elizabeth Jolley's version of the attractions of the enclave. Typical of her work these attractions are subverted concurrently as they are celebrated; unlike what happens in, for example, the sub-Forsterian events of John Duigan's *Sirens* (1994). Indeed, the most fascinating thing about *Sirens* is not so much the male heterosexual wish-fulfilments of this vision of Norman Lindsay's household in the Blue Mountains, its various female members in full frontal, but the fantasy that such a community might be left alone by local yobs, respectfully tipped the hat by the working class, and left to concentrate on prancing naked among the trees and talking about bourgeois hypocrisy. At no stage is this vision destabilised or is there any suggestion that this privilege is built upon the erasure of an indigenous culture which, in other colonial cultures, might have served as a reference point for any activity that claimed to be celebrating the natural or the sensual. The principal contrast here is with Jane Campion's *The Piano* (1993), in which the claustrophobic enclave and its inhabitants' more troubled and urgent encounter with their sensuality is unsettled constantly by the presence of the Maori people and their alternative approaches to the film's central issues of property, negotiation and power.

In the establishment of the enclave as the central bulwark of would-be Australian values, issues can be made to relate to the inwardness of the group in ways that position society as the eternal Other, often as overt enemy as in *The Castle* or *The Well*. By establishing the life of the enclave as central, such narratives need not engage with a wider society and can turn all issues into psychological ones. This attraction to the dynamics and values of the enclave can naturally be triangulated with the financing structure of Australian film, for it is cheaper to make a film not simply with few characters but in a confined setting, preferably distant from as many as possible of those variables that need to be controlled by way of liasing with local councils, building owners, traffic police and so forth. This does not explain the attraction in Australian writing for such stories, such as the *Tourmaline* type of narrative, that of the charismatic individual who irrupts into the group and destabilises it, in its own way a development of the nineteenth century bush narrative of the individual who comes from an unknown place bringing the threat of that unknown origin into the hitherto stable group or family. As a topos in Australian literature it is not surprising that it should be taken up and mediated by Australian cinema.[18]

Positive Directions

The Crossing (1990) is a growing-up film in which not much growing up gets done. The young men who experience a series of misunderstandings in their relationship with the same young woman end up in a generic test of strength or resolve, and in the ensuing confusion one of them is killed. As a film about young men and women in small towns it is blandly generic. However, it does attempt to represent a relationship between whites and Aborigines that is relatively infrequent in Australian cinema: a relationship of easy familiarity and integration. One can appreciate the energies that have gone into establishing a vision of ethnic harmony, except that nobody really does have any ethnicity; what they have is colour doing duty as ethnicity, and this is of course part of the problem. When I say they have no ethnicity, what I mean is that what we have is a picture of assimilation, in which indigenous peoples are approved of in terms of their disavowal of their own cultures and their approximation to that of the colonising people. The Aboriginal people in *The Crossing* are such sterling types, such good mates, that the only thing that differentiates them from the others is their colour. Thus they represent a situation in which there is no ethnicity, simply a human norm; a norm invariably established by whites in which even earnestly assimilating individuals (for it must not be forgotten that people do have the right to assume whatever ethnic positioning they judge appropriate) will nonetheless always be 'othered' by virtue of norms that take whiteness as an unmarked category. I am not suggesting that difference can be or should be elided but rather the reverse. As Richard Dyer says: 'whiteness needs to be made strange'.[19]

Australian historian Stuart McIntyre affirmed in the *Australian Book Review* in 1995 that:

> Historians have been successful in deconstructing the story of triumphal material progress that used to prevail ... They have been less successful in reconstructing a history that can encompass these new elements and enable them to be seen together. They have been conspicuously unsuccessful in restoring a history that can span cultural difference ... to excite wonder in the continuities and discontinuities of time and place.[20]

Similarly for Graeme Turner, 'If it is worth attempting to revive the national imagination, this must proceed from a thorough critique of current mythologies of Australian nationalism, aimed at producing multiple, hybridised formations'.[21] What these observers feel are the types of meanings that would be more responsive to the multifarious nature of contemporary Australian cultures, as opposed to one Australian culture, are also meanings they feel would be healthier for the culture to produce.

I have indicated areas in several contemporary Australian films where whiteness is unselfconsciously assumed as an ethnically unmarked position, or range of positions, however it is also true that despite the sensitivities attendant upon these areas, Australian cinema (and television) do often treat the issues of ethnic politics with sincere interest, even if the complexities involved mean that there will always be constituencies that feel unhappy with the results.

Contemporary mediation of the issues with respect to the representation of Aborigines emerges in three ways: first, in the number of films made with a large input from Aborigines themselves, which is obviously a pleasing development unless it goes on to suggest a *de facto* authority politics in which only Aborigines can speak about themselves; second, in films made by white filmmakers, desiring to intervene in positive fashion in the circulation of representations of Aboriginal peoples and yet probably not attaining that celebration of relaxed multiplicity Turner or McIntyre believe would be healthy; third, or in such sites as the saccharine and anachronistic inclusion of Aboriginal topics in television drama, such as *The Man from Snowy River* (1993-94) or the worthy touching on, say, issues of Aboriginal artefacts in *Blueheelers*. In both these latter cases, the issues remain resolutely controlled within the framework of white power, which is never threatened by its good-willed but undisturbed assumption of its right to act as guarantor of social values. Nonetheless, goodwill is not so ubiquitous a quality that it should be spurned in the drive for a questionable purity of ethnic representation. There is a difference between such earnestness and, say, the cynical casting of blond bombshell Cameron Daddo as Boney in the eponymous 1990 Grundy Entertainment pilot and series, after auditions that did not consider a single Aboriginal actor.

Tracey Moffat's *Bedevil* (1993), defuses the issue of authority politics by assuming its right to deal with the ghosts of the entire community, an exploration of the presence of the past in three separate scenarios. This splitting of the film into three linked narratives cleverly eases the pressures on Aboriginal filmmaker Tracey Moffat to become only a spokesperson, to speak only for her ethnicity rather than about whatever it is around her that intrigues her. Thus she is able not only to represent Aborigines within the film, and to do so in an impressively nuanced fashion, but also to avoid the suggestion that theirs were the only stories she was qualified to tell. In this way the issues are seen not simply as ones of representation, but of the production of the representations themselves in the context of an intertwined community of multivalent ethnic positions and possibilities. Moffat's move into feature-length filmmaking endorses this multivalence on the levels of both representation and production. Still, *Bedevil* was not a commercially-oriented film, and may be thought to have been directed at an audience less in need of simplistic or agonistic representations of ethnicity, even if recognising whiteness as an ethnic factor remains difficult.

Rachel Perkins's *Radiance* (1998) has been described as 'the first commercially oriented Australian movie directed by an Aborigine, let alone an Aboriginal woman'.[22] Perkins sees her version of Louis Nowra's comedy dealing with the tribulations of three young Aboriginal woman coming together for their mother's funeral during twenty-four hours in steamy north Queensland as not simply a screening of Aboriginal issues but rather as a step in the development of an 'indigenous film industry',[23] reminding us of the severe discrepancies in control over the generation of representations, discrepancies that might partially forestall objections to the imperatives of authority politics, at least at an early phase in the development of Aboriginal-controlled film. Perkins was clearly attracted to the narrative for its focus on Murri issues, but appears to have become more excited by the significance of Aboriginal input itself at this stage of the filmmaking process. After all, the celebration of a putative rainbow nation in Australia could only be considered provisional until at the level of production the celebrating is not limited to restricted and relatively privileged sectors of the community.

However in the production of representations, in the making strange of whiteness as ethnic, there needs to be a certain confidence in the right to represent the Other and to make 'mistakes'. In the desire to disavow the insensitivities of the past, to avoid compounding them with those of the present, a certain postcolonial diffidence can set in. As Satya Mohanty writes:

> cultural relativism of any kind is unlikely to be of help in engaging another culture in a noncolonising dialogue. If 'we' decide that 'they' are so different from us that we and they have no common 'criteria' (Lyotard's term) by which to evaluate (and, necessarily, even to interpret) each other, we may avoid making ethnocentric errors, but we also, by the same logic, ignore the possibility that they will ever have anything to teach us. Moreover, we may gain only an overly general and abstract kind of tolerance that is divorced from an understanding of the other culture.[24]

Given that there will inevitably be viewers who negotiate meanings at variance with those imagined by any film's makers, the rough and tumble of the relationship between variously-sponsored meanings is part of the task of redefining ethnic presences in Australian cinema. This article itself is no more than, one hopes, an ideologically self-conscious intervention that makes no claims to anything other than its provisionality and partiality, and yet, I realise, it is a lot easier to do this when one is not laying the average Australian film's budget of $4 million on the line in doing so. If it has seemed not to have demonstrated much tolerance, at times, of any type, I hope it will be taken in the spirit of constructive evaluation that Mohanty supports.

NOTES

1. Bob Hodge and Vijay Mishra, *Dark Side of the Dream: Australian Literature and the Postcolonial Mind* (Sydney: Allen & Unwin, 1991), p.xiv.
2. Indeed, there is even a film that uses the possibility of the existence of a lost Portuguese ship at the centre of its plot, *Sweet Talker* (1991).
3. Richard Dyer, *White* (London: Routledge, 1997), p.1.
4. Helen Garner, 'Home Movies', [reviews of the videos *Fool for Love* and *Così*], *The Independent Monthly* (May 1996), p.67.
5. Interestingly, the conjunction of three of New Zealand's most notable actors, Sam Neill, Yvonne Lawley and John Clarke, in *Death in Brunswick*, has led to this movie being included in a series of New Zealand films on video in that country.
6. Peter Lawrance, *'Death in Brunswick'*, in Scott Murray (ed.), *Australian Film 1978–1992: A Survey of Theatrical Features* (Melbourne: Oxford University Press, 1993), p.312.
7. There is another Japanese restaurant in Pino Amenta's *Heaven Tonight* (1990). There, the ageing rock star Johnny Dysart (John Waters) is unable to get his career going again and, after a series of vicissitudes, accepts that the musical times have changed and takes the advice of his wife Annie (Rebecca Gilling), and invests in a Japanese restaurant. Here, the restaurant does signal that Australia is not the place it was when Johnny was younger.
8. Laura Miller, *'Love and Other Catastrophes'*, [review] in *Sight and Sound*, Vol.7, No.5 (nos) (May 1997) p.49.
9. Lola Young, *Fear of the Dark: 'Race', Gender and Sexuality in the Cinema* (London: Routledge, 1996), p.33.
10. Dyer, p. 10.
11. Toni Morrison, *Playing in the Dark: Whiteness and the Literary Imagination* (London: Picador, 1993), p.9.
12. Ibid., p.59.
13. Jane Mills, 'Cinema's Portrayal of Violence is Cathartic', [letter], *The Australian* (18 August 1997), p.10.
14. Morrison, p.11.
15. David Callahan, 'The Narcissism of Distance – Australia and the Rhetoric of Extension', *Antipodes*, Vol.8, No.2 (December 1994), p.103.
16. Peter Beilharz, 'Radical Geography', [review of Jane M Jacobs, *Edge of Empire: Postcolonialism and the City*], *Australian Book Review*, No.189 (April 1997), p.12.
17. Jennifer Lawn, 'Pakeha Bonding', *Meanjin*, Vol.53, No.2 (Winter 1994), p.295.
18. *The Well* is not the only work of enclave literature to have been filmed recently. John Ruane's *That Eye, The Sky* (1994) took Tim Winton's story of the charismatic individual who appears from an unfamiliar distant place with a brand of hope and explanation that destabilises the

small rural family, partly positively, partly not, but in any event causing them to question themselves and what they want out of life.

19. Dyer, p.10.
20. Stuart McIntyre, et.al., 'Symposium: Why History?', *Australian Book Review*, No.177 (December 1995-January 1996), p.18.
21. Graeme Turner, 'Discipline Wars: Australian Studies, Cultural Studies and the Analysis of National Culture', *Australian Studies*, Vol. 12, No. 1 (Summer 1997), p.19.
22. Helen O'Neill, 'Women on The Verge of A Breakthrough', *The Australian* (22 August 1997), p.16.
23. Ibid.
24. Satya Mohanty, 'Colonial Legacies, Multicultural Futures: Relativism, Objectivity, and the Challenge of Otherness', *PMLA*, Vol.110, No.1 (January 1995), p.112.

7

All Quiet on the Western Front?
Suburban Reverberations in Recent
Australian Cinema

BEN GOLDSMITH

When I get home, I put the telly on
for the noise.
I hate the quiet.
I fucken hate it.

       – Mick the Poet, *Idiot Box* (1996)

For Tom O'Regan, the characteristic feature of Australian cinema is its
hybridity. It is an 'unprincipled assemblage', an intricately interwoven and
imperfectly aligned skein of 'people, texts, elements, social practices,
discourses and technologies'. Unburdened in the 1990s of the policy
expectation of previous decades that filmmakers should produce and
promote a singular version of Australian national identity, Australian
cinema in the 1990s has become a cinema of 'noise'. For O'Regan, it is the
task of the critic in assessing the industry and its products to 'foreground
[its] intrinsic noisiness and mixed character', to 'exemplify' the noise, 'to
sort it, to emphasise its incommensurate values and ends'.[1] Over the last
three decades, Australian cinema has grown from virtual silence to being a
noisy, conversational cinema which readily and wryly acknowledges
generic or technical influences from Hollywood and the cinemas of Europe,
and returns them, with a twist. This image of a noisy cinema conjures some
sense of its heteroglossic or multi-accented character in the 1990s, as well
as figuring that cinema as fundamentally demotic: popular, populist, filled
with the sounds of contemporary multicultural Australian society.

  This vision of Australian cinema as polyphonic contrasts with the
preference of the major funding bodies from the mid-1970s for 'quality' films
which could be 'the cultural flagships of the nation'.[2] As Karl Quinn has
written of the emergence of a new and popular 'Australian style' in the 1990s:

'No more bullshit costume dramas; no lingering shots of rural beauty; no wordy, European art-house aspiring dialogue. These films are young, funky, irreverent. Above all, they refuse to take themselves too seriously'.[3]

From the mid-1970s to the mid-1980s, the critical and commercial success of what Dermody and Jacka have described as the 'AFC genre' films, worked to reinforce a reliance upon literary source material for their high cultural resonances.[4] This made a great deal of sense to funding bodies in the early years of the revival, when generating a public psychological investment in the feature industry was not only a core concern, but a condition of the industry's very survival; the stories were already familiar to many Australians, and it was felt, the popularity of some would readily translate to the screen. But at the same time, the preference for historical rather than contemporary and adapted rather than original stories worked to further embed conservative values in the industry, whereby respectability was valued above innovation, and emphasis was placed on comfortable reaffirmation of, rather than critical engagement with, preferred constructions of national identity.[5]

In the 1990s the stock of literary reference points continues to feed a film industry hungry for cultural credibility, although adaptations from other sources, particularly the stage (*Strictly Ballroom, The Heartbreak Kid* (1993), *No Worries* (1993), *The Sum of Us* (1994), *Hotel Sorrento* (1995), *Cosi* (1996), *Blackrock* (1997)) are increasingly visible. However there is a welcome trend toward original screenplays which demonstrate the development of a distinctively cinematic sensibility (as opposed to simply adapting literary voices and preoccupations). Equally importantly is the allusion in many of the period films to past constructions of national character or identity which revolve around notions of the bush as the site of the 'real' Australia and which work to discourage critical engagement with the realities of contemporary, urban Australian society which is no longer so prominent. Urban-set films and films which increasingly interrogate the stock of received mythology are increasing in number in the Australian cinema of the 1990s.

The 'noise' of Australian cinema of the 1990s marks then, in part, its difference from, and disruption of, the preferred models of the earlier period. Noise is here a positive feature of Australian cinema, emblematic of its healthy response to the diversity of contemporary Australian society. For Mick (Jeremy Sims) the poet in David Caesar's *Idiot Box* noise is equally desirable, a familiar, comfortable state to which he aspires. But noise also has a different resonance for Mick. For him it is disruptive, an intervention in, and an obstacle to, the transfer of information along established and privileged channels from which he is excluded by virtue of his social status (unskilled, unemployed) and his geographic situation in the outer suburbs.

In traditional communication and information theory, noise is the demon Other, an unwelcome disruption in the passage of information. Noise is 'anything that is added to the signal between its transmission and reception that is not intended by the source ... anything that makes the intended signal harder to decode accurately'.[6] It is, in Michel Serres' formulation, akin to a 'third man', who in a dialogue is always assumed, and whom interlocutors continually struggle to exclude.[7] Noise is therefore simultaneously a condition and a by-product of the act of communication, it represents the ever-present possibility of disruption, interruption, misunderstanding. In sonic or musical terms, noise is cacophony, dissonance; as Peter Bailey observes, 'In any hierarchy of sounds it comes bottom, the vertical opposite of the most articulate and intelligible of sounds, those of speech and language and their aesthetic translation into music. In the official record such expressions 'make sense', whereas noise is nonsense'.[8] For economists, noise is an arbitrary element, both a barrier to the pursuit of wealth and a basis for speculation. For *Idiot Box*'s Mick and his mate Kev (Ben Mendelson), as for Hando (Russel Crowe) and his gang of skinheads in *Romper Stomper*, or (to a lesser extent) Dazey (Ben Mendelson) and Joe (Aden Young) in *Metal Skin* (1994) and all those like them starved of (useful) information and excluded from the circuit – the information poor – their only option, their only point of intervention in the loop, is to make noise,[9] to disrupt, to discomfort, to become Serres' 'third man', the very 'prosopopoeia of noise'.[10]

This article will focus on three films which disrupt the tendencies of Australian film in the 1990s outlined above in a number of ways. Each takes as its focus the experience of suburban working class life and in particular the (lack of) place of working class men, but it is as much their dissimilarities in story-line, style, access to audiences and reception that amplifies their noise, and ultimately reaffirms some of the diversity of Australian cinema in the 1990s.

'There are things ... powerful ... and he just doesn't understand': Anomie and Abjection in *Metal Skin*

That divine moment of expectation, the threshold between the worlds of the real and the cinematic, when the lights dim, the screen darkens and all around is pitch black and anticipation, is lacerated by a screech, a scream, a shriek of such agonising intensity that all possibility of a comfortable, distanced spectatorship is shattered. Initially the scream scarcely sounds human, but more like the terrifying, sharp rasp of metal on metal. Long and drawn out, it gathers emotion as it fades to a whimper. Suddenly there is no doubting its origin. It is a woman's scream, seemingly of terror, pain, anger, frustration, resignation, all balled-up together. Then the picture kicks in before there is time to process this heart-rending intrusion. Opening titles are inter-cut with images of huge metal containers piled high at a dock. The camera follows a young woman, Roslyn (Nadine Garner), flecks of blood speckling her sky-blue kimono as she wanders through the metal labyrinth between the containers. The camera leaps forward to face her as she walks, leading her deeper into the maze of metal. Fleeting shots of a road, the brutal sound of an engine pushed to its limits, flit across the screen. Reaching the heart of the maze she stops, sits, and wide-eyed and smiling enigmatically, slowly lifts her face to stare at the sky. The camera pauses for a moment on her face before we are unceremoniously dumped in the passenger seat of a car racing at its limits through deserted outer-suburban streets. The noise of these first moments, both aural and visual, offer some clues in what is a complex and difficult film, to director Geoffrey Wright's world view and work as a filmmaker, and to the directions taken by Australian film in the 1990s.

Michel Chion, theorist of film sound, describes sound like that original scream in which the originating cause is not seen as 'acousmatic'. Chion goes on to note: 'A sound or voice that remains acousmatic creates a mystery of the nature of its source, its properties and its powers, given that causal listening [defined by Chion as listening to a sound in order to gain information about its cause or source] cannot supply complete information about the sound's nature and the events taking place'.[11] The source of the scream in *Metal Skin* is never made apparent as it is never repeated with visual accompaniment. This unrevealed source, in Chion's terms, is the acousmêtre, a character 'whose relationship to the screen [and, by implication, to the spectator] involves a specific kind of ambiguity and oscillation' which may be defined as:

> neither inside nor outside the image ... It is not inside, because the image of the voice's source – the body, the mouth – is not included. Nor is it outside, since it is not clearly positioned offscreen in an imaginary 'wing', like a master of ceremonies or a witness, and it is implicated in the action, constantly about to be a part of it.[12]

The scream is a noise-as-framing device. Its occurrence evokes the constant threat of disruption, creating the expectation of its imminent return and acting as an ever-present reminder of the spectator's ambiguous relationship to the screen image, questioning identification while simultaneously transgressing and reinforcing distance. But while the subsequent images and story appear to indicate that the scream is Roslyn's, the expectation or desire for confirmation is never directly satisfied. As a result, the scream itself and the intention of its acousmêtre remain extra-filmic, its function to shock the spectator out of their complacency and draw them through the rim, the screen/meniscus, into the abject world which Wright's characters inhabit.

Wright employs a similar technique in his first film, *Romper Stomper*, to draw the spectator in to the fringe world of his skinhead characters. The film opens with the camera/spectator moving at speed at street level, sharing the viewpoint of a teenager sitting on a skateboard, laughing and talking animatedly with his companions in Vietnamese. A subtitle places the action at Footscray Station, Melbourne, as the skateboard/camera descends a ramp into the subway between the platforms. As the skateboard/camera moves underground, the image decelerates to emphasise the threat and other-worldliness of the environment into which the teenagers have descended, as in slow-motion, the camera passes the leering faces of a menacing skinhead gang. The board's motion is abruptly halted by the cherry-red booted foot of Hando, the leader of the group. Wright reverts to normal speed as Hando tells the terrified teenager 'This is not your country', and the skinheads proceed to beat up the hapless Vietnamese. This pre-credit sequence ends with the on-screen naming of the main skinhead characters Hando and Davey (Daniel Pollock), before another as yet unnamed skinhead yells 'Fuck off!' directly into the camera. Immediately in these scenes Wright has introduced the key themes of the film, and signposted the controversial and problematic issue of spectatorial identification which will recur throughout. Not surprisingly, anxieties about the subject positions on offer underlay much of the virulent criticism that Wright and the film have received. It is this key question of audience positioning which the acousmatic scream that opens *Metal Skin* reiterates, and which the film never satisfactorily resolves.

Metal Skin revolves around four characters, the series of love triangles and intrigues which evolve around them, and their negotiation of life in what one reviewer described as the 'industrial-park nightmare' of the western suburbs of Melbourne.[13] Joe is a loner, taunted mercilessly by his peers for his looks and dysfunctional family background. He lives in a fortress-like house in a run-down part of town with his father, a Rumanian immigrant who won medals for pistol shooting at the Melbourne Olympics in 1956, but who is now in the advanced stages of dementia. In his spare time, he tinkers with his beloved Chrysler, and attempts to perfect the supercharger that will make him rich, and provide his escape from the impoverished circumstances in which he is trapped. Joe has been unemployed for four years before landing a night job as a supermarket shelf-stacker, where his co-workers include the charismatic romeo Dazey and Savina (Tara Morice). Savina is, like Joe, a loner, distanced from her peers and her profoundly religious mother by her long fight against the blood cancer leukaemia. Dazey shares Joe's passion for cars. His father builds and races Nascars, souped-up production models, which Dazey used to drive until his recklessness and over-confidence caused a road accident in which his girlfriend, Roslyn, was seriously burnt. Realising his desire for Roslyn will always remain unfulfilled, Joe is drawn to Savina, but she in turn is obsessed with Dazey, over whom she believes she can cast a spell to control him and make him love her. At first it appears that the spell has worked, but after making love to her in her mother's church, Dazey leaves Savina to go to work in his father's garage. To overcome his resistance to her spells, Savina resolves to perform the most sacrilegious rituals and convince the devil to bring Dazey back to her. With Joe's help she desecrates the church; they upend the crucifix and perform a marriage ceremony before she sends Joe away telling him she needs to be alone to pray. She sacrifices several chickens before drinking their blood, however she is interrupted by the return of the priest. She climbs into the bell tower, hanging by her fingernails from a ledge to avoid detection, but loses her grip and falls to her death. The next day Joe goes to meet Savina at her house, only to be confronted by the family in mourning. Devastated, he returns home to find his house has been trashed by his nemesis, Paul, whose car Joe had inadvertently incapacitated some nights previously while escaping a police raid on an illegal street race meet. Joe tries, but fails, to commit suicide by overdosing on pills.

Savina appears to him in his hallucinatory state crucified on the ceiling above him. He levitates up to her, but just as he is about to kiss her and succumb to the everlasting darkness, he is struck down by Savina's mother who attempts to drive a metal spike into his head. Joe screams and is awoken from his stupor by his father who, tortured by his own demons, is bashing the ceiling with a broom. Joe tries, but fails, to calm him. Overwrought, Joe shoots his father with his own gun, all the time yelling Dazey's name, believing him to be responsible for the madness that surrounds him. Joe goes in search of Dazey. At Dazey's father's garage Joe shoots and kills a mechanic, and steals the prized Nascar. He drives to Roslyn's house to which Dazey, stunned by Savina's death, has retreated for sanctuary. Dazey hears the Nascar arriving, and goes outside to see what is happening. Joe wrestles him to the ground, shoving the barrel of the pistol in Dazey's mouth. Joe forces Roslyn to show him and Dazey the extent of her burns, which cover three-quarters of her torso. Joe returns his attention to Dazey, but Roslyn manages to hit Joe over the head with a wooden mask and she and Dazey escape in Dazey's car. Joe pursues them, and after a long chase through empty warehouses at the docks, both cars crash and Joe is killed. Roslyn, dressed only in a sky-blue kimono, staggers from Dazey's car into the maze of containers piled at the dock. The film ends as it began with Roslyn sitting, surrounded by containers. The camera pans up to reveal the city skyline in the near background.

Riding on the success of *Romper Stomper*, the full $2 million production budget for *Metal Skin* came from the Film Finance Corporation's Film Fund for 1992, supplemented by earlier script development funding from Film Victoria. Roadshow Distributors, Australia's largest distribution company had picked the project up at an early stage and provided further backing. After a difficult nine-week shoot in mid-1993 during which the director himself admitted the film was 'really too ambitious',[14] In addition, the production budget ran out with over 100 shots still needed. These shots were eventually taken in just three days (an immense effort for all concerned). Post-production took five months, with the majority of time spent on the editing which is so important to the look and feel of the film. The film's release was delayed because of the release of *Muriel's Wedding* (1994) and *The Adventures of Priscilla, Queen of the Desert* (1994), and put back even further by the polarising of publicity around the Oscars ceremony in March, which denied advertising space to any but those films in competition for awards and currently in release. Despite the backing of Roadshow and the benefits of its ties with two of Australia's major exhibition chains Village and Greater Union, producer Daniel Scharf's belief that the strength of the cast, the story and the interest in Wright after *Romper Stomper* would enable the film to 'generate its own momentum' was not borne out by the film's performance once post-production was completed.[15] The resonances of the movie's original title (*Speed*) may have helped attract the young audience so crucial to its success, but when Wright was forced to change the title after a threat of legal action by the producers of the Keanu Reeves/Sandra Bullock film of the same name, such 'momentum' as the project had generated quickly dissipated. Harsh or indifferent critical treatment did not help, David Stratton, movie reviewer for the Australian newspaper and SBS Television's *The Movie Show*, damningly described *Romper Stomper* as '*A Clockwork Orange* without the intellect. In many ways genuinely appalling', refusing to discuss the film at all.[16] The film grossed a disappointing $825,000 in three weeks in May 1995 before disappearing from the top 20 films, the victim of bad reviews and bad word of mouth.[17] Its final theatrical gross was close to just $1million, although the film has since performed well on video after initial sales of approximately 5,000 units.[18]

The bleakness of the environment inhabited by the characters in *Metal Skin* is emphasised by the almost complete lack of sunlight in the film; daytime scenes are shot against unforgiving grey skies, or at twilight, or in the rain. Industrial or dockside or suburban scenes are drained of colour, with occasional flashes of maroon or lime green in the characters' clothing the only breaks in the monotony. Much of the film is shot at night to emphasise the characters' separation from the mainstream and lack of interaction with 'normal' city life; as their night work at the supermarket indicates, they are not even full members of the service economy, but are marginal even here. Incessant and intrusive editing (sometimes described as 'MTV style'), numerous jump- and cross-cuts, and confounding time-shifts work to disorient the spectator and prevent a distanced critical appraisal of the characters and their world. Bill Murphy and Jane Usher's editing (which reportedly took five months) emphatically conveys Wright's aggressive filmmaking style and the primary emotion driving his work (which is one of the resonances of the opening scream): frustrated anger (much of which, it must be said, is reflected back on Wright by unsympathetic audiences), anger which can never be usefully channelled, and which can only ever be self-destructive.

The director's proclaimed sympathy with the marginalised, the outcast, the fringe-dwellers of society extends only to the desire to document, not to offer hope, solutions, options, where he knows (or thinks he knows) there are none. Of all the characters in *Metal Skin*, only Dazey has agency, only Dazey initially has the power to make things happen, although ultimately all, and particularly Roslyn and Savina, are victims of circumstances which are beyond their control. Joe first encounters Dazey on his first night at the supermarket when he stumbles into the tea-room, catching Dazey and another co-worker *in flagrante delicto*. The next night, at the end of the shift, Dazey seeks Joe out, concerned to ensure that Joe does not tell Roslyn what he has seen. He tells Joe 'I hope you can keep your mouth shut about what you saw the other night. Things happen, you know. I mean, I love Ros, but … things happen, you know? You know what I mean?' Joe looks blankly back at Dazey who takes his half-nod to mean understanding. But Joe, who has never been able to make 'things happen' with women the way Dazey so effortlessly does, knows it is Dazey who does not understand the repercussions of his actions, or even that he is able to act where others are not.

This is reinforced in a later scene when, after making love to Savina, Dazey seeks out Roslyn who is sitting by the water's edge at the docks. Roslyn talks about leaving the city, and getting a job on a cruise ship as a hairdresser. As they embrace Roslyn notices teeth marks on Dazey's neck. Pushing him away, she says 'I know you screw other girls. Why do you hang around? Why don't you just leave me alone?' She turns to walk away, but he calls her back. She turns to face him and says again 'Why don't you just get out of my life?' She walks away. In voice over we hear her whisper, 'Please'. As the camera cuts to a long shot of the shoreline at dusk she whispers again 'Please ... get out of my life'. Throughout this exchange, she implicitly acknowledges that just as he is responsible for bringing her to this state, only his action can end their relationship. She can never leave him, only he can leave her.

In the final tumultuous scenes following the deaths of Savina and Joe's father, Joe tries to make Dazey understand that his actions have consequences, and that he as much as the others is bound by forces beyond their control. With his gun in Dazey's mouth Joe tells Roslyn 'There are things ... things that nobody understands. There are things ... powerful ... and he just doesn't understand'. Finally, plaintively, with righteousness born of a lifetime without love, a lifetime spent looking after his father, who drifts in and out of his own personal hell, Joe cries 'Dazey doesn't deserve to be loved'. This, it seems to me, is one of the fundamental components of the acousmatic scream, the wail of the repressed, patient, unloved, finally demanding to be heard. But the logic of the film demands that these characters are doomed to a pitiful and violent fate because of these nebulous 'things' which they do not understand and cannot control. Joe, however hard he tries, is a perpetual loser: he loses a drag race at the railyards early in the film, he loses a fight after the race, he loses Savina to Dazey, he loses his job helping Savina steal catfood from the supermarket. He is unable to overdose successfully, and he is finally unable to kill Dazey. As he lies dying, half crushed under the Nascar, the last thing Joe hears is Dazey taunting him, saying 'I beat you' over and over again. But in the end, everybody loses: Joe and Savina are dead, Dazey has lost Roslyn and wrecked his father's car, and Roslyn has finally lost her mind.

This dystopic ending, which has become something of a hallmark in Wright's work, further distances him from the mainstream of Australian cinema and from the slew of quirky comedies which invariably end on an ambiguous if upbeat note, offering the audience the pleasure of speculating about the characters' future, consider the reuniting of the sisters in the act of disposing of the lothario who came between them in *Love Serenade* (1996). The dystopic ending underscores the director's denial of empathy with his characters. Wright prefers to unsettle his audience through story and style, to 'engage the senses in a very aggressive way, rather than stand off and have the audience judge the characters at a distance'.[19] But this tactic often alienates the audience as it denies critical distance while forcing the spectator to endure Wright's characters' torment and the inexorable movement towards their tragic fate, and to relive the terror of the acousmatic scream. As

Mendelsohn recalls of his first viewing of the completed film, 'I remember feeling ... that it was an incredibly intense thing. I remember going `Whoah' at the end, and being glad to be out of there.[20] With *Metal Skin*, Wright has moved away from an investigation of the limits of mateship – in *Romper Stomper*, Davey ultimately chooses Gabe, (Jaqueline McKenzie) over Hando and kills him to stay with her – to a portrayal of a world from which its tender certainties and devotions have been banished. Joe desires nothing more than human connection, particularly with Dazey in whom he searches for a mate, a father-figure, a mentor, but one such he must ultimately destroy or risk being destroyed himself. In contrast with David Caesar's take on mateship in *Idiot Box* which the characters' devotion to each other sustains them, Wright's two halves of masculinity can never be perfectly aligned, and will always result in (self-) destruction.

Gallipoli in the Suburbs: *Idiot Box*

The key differences between Wright's take on the margins of urban Australian society and that of David Caesar lie in their sympathies, in their intent, and in their understandings of the legacies and burdens of mateship. This is emphasised at various levels of their work, with such differences impacting directly on very formal questions of film style: editing, for example, works rather differently. Wright uses jump- and flash-cutting to perpetually disorient the spectator, to force continuous questioning of the audience's own subject-positioning, and to routinely deprive the spectator of an empathetic response to the characters on the screen: Caesar and his editor Mark Perry employ jerky, speedy cuts that index a developing televisual style of Australian cinema,[21] which seeks a complicity with the audience through a ream of in-jokes and sly references to other texts this generation shares in common.[22] At heart Caesar is obviously extremely fond of his characters, and the constantly moving camera, coupled with a soundtrack which incorporates snippets of the noise of the city and life in the suburbs, creates a definite sense of place and works to draw the audience in, to acquaint them with *Idiot Box's* characters and their environment, and to create an empathetic relationship between spectator and characters that is wholly absent in *Metal Skin*.

Like *Metal Skin* in 1994, *Idiot Box* was one of three films funded in the Film Funding Corporation's Film Fund for 1995, to a maximum amount of $2.5 million. The Film Fund represents a departure for the FFC from its usual commitment to funding only those projects which have attracted a significant amount of private funding and which promise financial returns to the Corporation. The Fund is aimed at directors with no more than two feature film credits 'who have not yet established a sufficient track record to attract marketplace support' although consideration requires that projects have an international sales agreement in place.[23] The scheme, popularly known as 'the chook raffle', attracted 130 original submissions, which produced a short-list of a dozen. Conscious of the importance of place to his characters and in his cinema, in publicity for the film, Caesar reiterated his desire for the film to screen in multiplex cinemas in environments Kev and Mick would be familiar with. Distributed by UIP, Australia's second largest distribution company, and Globe Films, *Idiot Box* opened on 42 screens in February 1997, with a healthy screen average of $6,630. The film was unable to sustain this performance in Caesar's preferred venues, and was reduced to just 16 screens after three weeks, having grossed just under $700,000. Ironically, the film drew a strong response in the more typically middle-class domain of the art-house cinema circuit, although it has since performed well on video which, in truth, would probably have been its protagonists' preferred medium.

Kev and Mick are long-term unemployed, living in the western suburbs of Sydney with little prospect of gainful work. They spend their time watching videos at each other's houses, and make rare trips to the pub on the day they collect their dole. While watching a video, they hatch a plan to rob a bank, albeit not with any grand end in mind. The robbery is simply something to do, something to break the monotony of their lives. Interwoven with Kev and Mick's story is that of Greg (Andrew. S. Gilbert) and Luce (Susan Prior), a couple in their thirties. Greg, it becomes apparent, is 'Laughing Boy', a bank robber who targets suburban banks on pension day. Luce is a heroin addict, whose intake Greg struggles to control. By process of elimination, Eric and Leanne (Graeme Blundell and Deborah Kennedy), two world-weary detectives assigned to investigate Laughing Boy's series of robberies, narrow his options down to one bank in the western suburbs. By chance this is the bank Kev and Mick have their eyes on too. The action spirals to its inevitable tragic conclusion, as Kev unconsciously does all he can to make his and Mick's plan fail. They obtain some guns from Colin (Steven Rae), the sleazy local man-with-connections, but Kev beats up Colin's right-hand man, Jonah (John Polson), during the transaction, and as a result Colin supplies information on their plans to the police. Kev shoots a dog that has been annoying him; his failure to kill it becomes for him a premonition of doom. They steal a getaway car, but encounter its owner on their way to the bank and are forced to return it and suffer the indignity of walking to the bank.

In this moment Caesar's film is set apart from its contemporaries, the raft of blackly comic road movies that appeared in 1997. Where these films, the Australian-Japanese co-production *Heaven's Burning* (1997), Stavros Efthymiou's *True Love and Chaos* (1997), Bill Bennett's *Kiss or Kill* (1997), and Chris Kennedy's *Doing Time for Patsy Cline* (1997), utilise the conventions of road or chase movies to literalise characters' journeys towards self-discovery, *Idiot Box* like *Metal Skin* is a 'going nowhere' movie. Yet while Kev and Mick are trapped in their environment (without a car they literally have no means of escape), they do have a sense of it as *their* place, as home. Unlike the characters in *Metal Skin*, whose environment is unremittingly bleak, the characters in *Idiot Box* are 'at home' in their environment, although this is not to say that they do not long to escape or find some way of breaking the monotony of unemployed routine.

Idiot Box opens with a series of aerial shots of a city at night, as if from a police surveillance helicopter tracing a path through a familiar web of roads and buildings. Short grabs of dampened sound collide: telephone conversations, car horns echoing, television or radio broadcasts: the noise of the city, before an electric guitar crafts a rhythm and a melody from the cacophony and the camera glides down to ground level. Tracking through long grass the camera picks out car headlights travelling straight towards us, as effortlessly we stand and follow a young man, Mick, nonchalantly crossing the busy road. As he reaches the other side Mick turns to wait for his mate, Kev, who slowly and defiantly walks towards him. Cars surge past, horns blare, a driver yells 'Get off the road', but Kev does not hurry or lengthen his gait. A car fills the screen, Kev barely steals a glance out of the corner of his eye. The camera swoops around, before Mick pulls Kev out of the line of fire of the car's blinding headlights, both of them falling into a ditch as the car screams past. Rolling above Mick, Kev puts his face to Mick's and yells, laughing maniacally as Mick rolls away panting 'You mad bastard!'. It is this rippling undercurrent of sexual tension between the two with Kev testing the bounds of brotherhood and Mick responding devotedly to the call, repeatedly saving Kev from himself, which sustains them and lies at the heart of the film. The bond between mates defines and reaffirms their identity from the outset as it is explored at a variety of levels.

The bond is all the stronger for the absence of father-figures in their lives. Indeed, only one paternal relationship is alluded to in *Idiot Box*, that of Lani (Robyn Loau) and Arri (Cramer Cain), and he appears only through the agency of Arri who keeps a protective eye out for his sister because 'Dad says I've got to look after ya'.[24] Kev lives with his mum, Mick with his brother. There is no mention of either's father. The absence of a father-figure places *Idiot Box* firmly in a line of recent Australian films running all the way back to *Walkabout* (1970), and marks it out from its quirky contemporaries for whom the relationship between main characters and their father-figures hinge the plot, whether they appear as mentor or teacher (Wal the wise old garbage truck driver in *Garbo* (1992) Fran's father Rico in *Strictly Ballroom*) or best mate (Harry in *The Sum of Us* which is really a movie about the mellowing of ocker Australianness and the place of its personification, Jack Thompson, in Australian cinema) or whether their failings drive characters to escape or madness (Muriel's father Bill in *Muriel's Wedding*; Morris in *True Love and Chaos*, whose absence impels Mimi across the Nullabor to Perth; or Lilian's father in *Lilian's Story* (1996)).

Kev exudes simmering aggression and sexual tension; like a walking fault-line he is the prosopopeia of noise, unstable, constantly on the verge of eruption. Mick by contrast is a freethinker and a poet, his talent unrecognised by his peers because, as the barmaid in their local pub tells him, 'Poems are about flowers and sunsets and shit like that. You can't have a poem about being on the dole'. Mick's philosophy is that 'if you say something's a poem, then it is': he refuses to be bound by the unwritten rules which his contemporaries unquestioningly assume exclude them from the realms of poetry and the imagination.[25] This in part, Caesar implies, is the legacy of television, the *Idiot Box* of the title, simultaneously the great entertainer, the great educator, the great seducer. Together Mick and Kev have a chance of overcoming the banality and circularity of the daytime soaps and cop-dramas that blare from the corner of their lounge rooms and kitchens. It is as if in their attachment, in the things they bring to their mateship, Mick and Kev will only succeed if they stick together. The bond between Mick and Kev is the most crucial in their lives, since in the absence of fathers this is their paramount male-male relationship. It is so powerful that unlike Davey in *Romper Stomper*, Mick chooses his mate over the girl, and, unlike *Gallipoli* (1981), does not watch his mate die alone.

No Place Like Home: *The Castle* (1997)

The Castle, perhaps more than any other single film,[26] reinforces Adrian Martin's definition of Australian cinema in the 1990s as increasingly 'televisual'. As Stephen Crofts has argued, the film is a hybrid of film and television aesthetics and production processes.[27] It was made for just $700,000 by the production company Working Dog, best known to Australian audiences as the makers of the spoof of current affairs television, *Frontline*.[28] Written in two weeks and shot in eleven and a half days, the film has minimal production values, with few elaborate set-ups. The film's distributors, Roadshow, earmarked just $50,000 for publicity, but on the strength of weekend advance screenings in New South Wales and Queensland, the film entered the Australian box-office top 20 grossing films before its scheduled release date. In its first week the film screened at 34 locations around the country. Despite largely negative critical reviews, in its second week the film took over a million dollars on 86 screens, and went on to gross $10 million after just nineteen weeks, the second Australian feature film in a year to so do. As Tina Kaufman concluded, given the film's small promotional budget, poor reviews and lack of name actors, the film's success can only be put down to 'good word of mouth'.[29] *The Castle* was released on video in August 1997 while still screening theatrically, and it was the top rental over the following Christmas period. *Variety* reported in February 1998 that American mini-major Miramax had paid US$6 million for American and selected foreign rights after the film screened at the Sundance Film Festival.[30]

While Kaufman may be correct in noting that the film contains no 'name' film actors familiar to Australian audiences, the television celebrity of the crew and several of the lead actors provided an immediate point of connection in the local market (Michael Caton and Sophie Lee are recognisable from their television work on the long running wartime soap opera *The Sullivans* [Channel 7], and *Bugs Bunny* and *Sex (with Sophie Lee)* [both Channel 9]). In addition, in its style and means of production the film plays much more to the demonstrated audience appeal of local television productions and distances itself from the majority of Australian film product. The events of the film are seen initially through the eyes of the Kerrigan family's youngest son Dale (Stephen Curry) in the direct-to-camera style of a video-diary, and later presented as the kind of personal, on-the-spot current affairs show report of the kind satirised so mercilessly in the satirical television show, *Frontline*.

The Castle has a simple message rooted in the egalitarian spirit of the 'fair go', which enervates the phrase on which the Kerrigans's court case (and the film) turns: 'on just terms'. The Kerrigan family, Sal (Anne Tenney), Darryl (Michael Caton), sons Steve (Anthony Simcoe) and young Dale, live in a house in Highview Crescent, Coolooroo, next door to Melbourne airport. Another son, Wayne (Wayne Hope), is serving time in Pentridge prison, and daughter Tracey (Sophie Lee) has recently married after completing a hairdressing course at Sunshine College of TAFE (Tertiary and Further Education). When their beloved family home is compulsorily acquired and scheduled for demolition to make way for airport expansion, Darryl, takes the council to court. This image, of the family fighting faceless corporate/government bureaucratic procedures, lies at the heart of the film, and is perhaps the key to its reception at a time when the familiar Australian scepticism and mistrust of politicians and corporate executives was heightened by revelations of expense rorts perpetrated by elected members, and by the successful prosecution of crooked corporate highfliers of the 1980s like Alan Bond. Darryl and his hopelessly ill-prepared solicitor Denis Denuto (Tiriel Mora) cite the precedent of the Native Title Act 1993 (popularly known as 'Mabo'), which they believe enshrines in Australian law the connection between a family and its home, its roots. While the court is adjourned awaiting judgement, Darryl meets Lawrence Hammill (Charles Tingwell), a retired QC specialising in constitutional law, who later agrees to take their case to the High Court, and to act without pay. Basing his arguments on an interpretation of Section 51, 31 of the Australian Constitution which states that the state's dealings with citizens must be 'on just terms', Hammill convinces the bench to dismiss the compulsory purchase order, in the process recognising the strength of connection to place that, the film suggests, lies at the heart of indigenous and non-indigenous cultures alike.

Where *Metal Skin* proffers a vision of an abject suburbia, and *Idiot Box* glories in its rough edges, *The Castle* constructs a sentimentally appealing, cosily domestic suburban idyll which clearly struck a chord with Australian audiences. The intimacy of the televisual style permits what one reviewer identified as the 'element of familiarity with the Kerrigans, as if they were our own family, or our neighbours or friends'.[31] Thus the film celebrates the qualities of the 'battler' working-class family: loyalty, perseverance, a fundamental sense of justice, and hooks in to a set of established myths about Australian social and cultural life which allow the Kerrigans to appear very much as 'ordinary Australians' who are Prime Minister Howard's touchstone. As such, they are entrepreneurial and upwardly mobile: Steve, 'the ideas man' as Darryl calls him, is constantly on the lookout for a bargain in exchange-sheet *The Trading Post*. At the end of the film we learn that the family's success in court has coincided with a growth in Darryl's tow-truck business; and Darryl is proudest of all about daughter Tracey's hairdressing certificate which he believes will allow her to 'better' herself. They are self-sufficient and self-reliant, and reluctant to make themselves a burden on the state. In many ways the family stands for a core set of conservative values more suited to the 1950s than the 1990s, based on the family as the critical social unit .

Emphasising this point and setting *The Castle* apart from *Metal Skin* and *Idiot Box* is the figure of Darryl Kerrigan, patriarch and moral centre of the film and of his community. It is around Darryl that the neighbourhood gathers when it is threatened from outside, and it is his faith in the innate justice and fairness of the system that leads to their ultimate triumph. By retaining faith in the system, Darryl is able to act and to succeed; his immediate affinity with Lawrence the barrister reinforces the film's message that by working within the system in partnership with representatives of the professional, paternal middle classes, the respectable working class family can contribute to the creation and maintenance of a socially harmonious, equitable, just society.

Conclusions

In its upbeat ending and in the portrayal of the father as the lynch pin of the community, *The Castle* constructs a very different suburban reality to that envisaged by *Metal Skin* or *Idiot Box*. However the three films discussed here are linked by a number of underlying themes which organise their action and address. Despite radical differences in their apparent sympathies and emotional distance from their characters, these films are concerned fundamentally with the same issues of place and placelessness, home and homelessness, the meaning and consequences of love in all its many forms, the possibility and absence of hope in the suburbs, the effects of, and reaction against, their characters' exclusion from and negotiation of the information society. They are films which intimately address the question of agency; of who is, and who is not, able to act, to influence, to have a voice, to make (and ignore) noise.

Both *Idiot Box* and *Metal Skin* are 'noisy films' in a number of ways which set them apart from the simple intimacies of *The Castle*. In purely aural terms, both lay great emphasis on sound as much more than simple accompaniment to the image track; where noise or melody is often used in conventional ways to strengthen the emotional tenor and pitch of a scene, both films use sound as a disorientation mechanism, to force the spectator to question and avoid easy assumptions about plot, characters and their own investment in the film. Both films reject the tendency of the 'quirky' cinema to recycle the sights and sounds of the 1970s as a means of garnering a sympathetic, nostalgic response from their audiences.[32] Both also provide a counterpoint to what David Caesar has called the 'toned-down working class films of the 1990s' which smooth out their characters' rough edges to emphasise their endearing eccentricities and unthreatening idiosyncrasies.[33] While Caesar was referring in particular to *Strictly Ballroom* and *Muriel's Wedding*, his remarks are equally applicable to *The Castle*. Given the commercial success of the latter film, and the relative failure of his own, it seems to be the case that Australian audiences prefer diluted rather than fractured or disruptive representations of suburban life. Given the coincidental success of the independently-financed *The Castle* at a time when the major agencies of federal support for the film industry, the Film Finance Corporation and the Australian Film Commission, were coming under increasing pressure to be 'accountable' and to revise their sense of cultural mission to concentrate on the bottom line,[34] it may be that the flurry of suburban noise will dissipate and die away like *Metal Skin*'s acousmatic scream. While the success of *The Castle* has worked to reacquaint sections of the Australian audience with Australian film, the noise of its success may potentially drown-out dissonant suburban voices and undercut the hybridity that characterises contemporary Australian cinema.

NOTES

 1. Tom O'Regan, *Australian National Cinema* (London: Routledge, 1996), p.40.
 2. Graeme Turner, 'Art Directing History', in Albert Moran and Tom O'Regan (eds.), *The Australian Screen* (Ringwood, Victoria: Penguin, 1989), p.103.
 3. Karl Quinn, 'Drag, Dags and the Suburban Surreal', *Metro*, No.100 (Summer 1994– 95), p.23.
 4. Susan Dermody and Elizabeth Jacka, *The Screening of Australia: Anatomy of a National Cinema* [Vol.I] (Sydney: Currency Press, 1988), pp.28– 37.
 5. Brian McFarlane, 'Conservatism in the New Australian Cinema', *Australian Cultural History*, No.7 (1988), pp.37– 48.
 6. John Fiske, *Introduction to Communication Studies* (London: Methuen, 1982), p.8
 7. Michel Serres, *Hermes: Literature, Science, Philosophy* (Baltimore: The Johns Hopkins University Press, 1982), p.67.
 8. Peter Bailey, 'Breaking the Sound Barrier: A Historian Listens to Noise', *Body and Society*, Vol.2, No.2 (June 1996), p.50.
 9. '… noise is what makes our observations imperfect. It keeps us from knowing the expected return on a stock or portfolio. It keeps us from knowing whether monetary policy affects inflation or unemployment. It keeps us from knowing what, if anything, we can do to make things better'. (Black 1986: 529) Noise as rumour, conjecture, misheard or half-heard or overheard hypothesis, is information's Other. But noise, like information, can drive a market, though its condition is, unlike information's, irrationality; noise is 'bought' by the uninitiated, the uninformed, who act on it, irrationally, 'as if it were information that would give them an edge' (Bradford De Long *et al.* 1990: 704).
10. Serres, p.67.
11. Michel Chion, *Audio-Vision: Sound on Screen*, [trans. Claudia Gorbman] (New York: Columbia University Press, 1994), p.72.
12. Ibid., p.229.
13. McCarthy, 1994
14. Wright, *Encore*, (19 Aug.–1 Sept. 1993), p.10.
15. Ibid., p.10.
16. Anon, *Variety*, (25 May 1992), p.54.
17. Anon, *Encore* (12– 25 June 1995), p.29.
18. I am grateful to producer Daniel Scharf for this information.
19. Anon, *Time Off* [Brisbane] (April 1995), p.14.

20. Tim Hunter, 'Ben Mendelsohn: Hometown Boy ... Not!', *Cinema Papers*, No.119 (August 1997), p.22.
21. Adrian Martin, 'Ghosts ... of a National Cinema', *Cinema Papers*, No.97/98 (April 1994), pp.14–15.
22. At 'one point Caesar offers a distinctively Australian take on the "Royale with cheese" hamburger conversation in Tarantino's *Pulp Fiction* (1994), when Colin, local middle-man, fixer and dealer in junk of all persuasions refuses to eat the burger his right-hand man Jonah has brought him because it contains pineapple. He later discusses the qualities of pineapple and beetroot on burgers with the two detectives. Throughout the film there are numerous references to early Australian television shows, particularly police dramas like *Homicide*, and kids shows like *Skippy*. The film also taps in to the vernacular of the suburbs in its multiple use of the word "dog", variously taken to mean a four-legged canine, an unattractive woman, a police informer, or an unmanageable piece of livestock and used in defiant rebuke as in Kev's t-shirt exhortation to "Get a dog up ya". Kev also has several run ins with a barely restrained rottweiler, culminating in Kev shooting the dog but failing to kill it. The incident reveals a hitherto unseen vulnerability in Kev; he takes the dog's pained whimper as a sign of impending doom, telling Mick "It's like an omen, something bad's gunna happen to me. I'm gonna get punished, I fucken know I am"'.
23. *Australian Film Finance Corporation Annual Report* (1995–96), p.25.
24. David Caesar, *Idiot Box: The Screenplay* (Melbourne: Text Press, 1996), p.26.
25. Ibid., p.29.
26. Adrian Martin uses the term in response to 'the fondly elaborate television pastiches that litter Australian film' as part of an attempt to set up new critical frames and ways of looking at Australian films which override the tendency to compare its products to those of Hollywood or to European art cinema, in Martin, p.15.
27. Stephen Crofts, '*The Castle*: 1997's "Battlers" and The Ir/Relevance of The Aesthetic', unpublished paper delivered at 'Cultural Crossroads: Ownership, Access, Identity' conference, Sydney, Nov. 1998. A revised version of this paper is published elsewhere in this volume.
28. Working Dog is based in Melbourne. Its principals are writer/producers Santo Cilauro, Tom Gleisner, Jane Kennedy, Ron Sitch, and executive producer Michael Hirsh. The team is familiar to Australian television audiences through their work on *D-Generation* (ABC) and *The Late Show* (ABC). As well as the television series *Frontline*, the team has also produced the series *Funky Squad* which spoofs 1970s cop shows, and *A River Somewhere* in which Sitch and Gleisner profile fishing spots around the world.
29. Tina Kaufman, 'Finding an Audience: The Challenge for Australian Cinema', *Metro*, No.112 (1997), p.10.
30. Anon, *Encore* (11– 24 Feb. 1998), p.16.
31. Tim Hunter, '*The Castle*', [review], *Cinema Papers*, No.116 (May 1997), p.45.
32. This is not to say that the musical soundtrack and the benefits of using tracks liable to gain radio airplay were unimportant in promoting the films, particularly *Idiot Box*. The use of new music by bands like Snout, Hoss, The Mark of Cain and You am I (whose frontman, Tim Rogers, was instrumental in the soundtrack's production) featured strongly in publicity for the film and reinforced the film's attempt to appeal to the same audiences.
33. Anon, *The Australian* (11 Feb. 1997), p.10.
34. In May 1997 it was announced that the Film Finance Corporation's total investment in 111 features since 1989, amounting to $267 million, had returned just $51.41 million to federal coffers.

8

Romance and Sensation in The 'Glitter' Cycle

EMILY RUSTIN

Introduction: The Individual Versus the Environment

In 1986 Graeme Turner argued in an influential assessment of Australian fiction in film and literature that:

> The dominant myth of the Australian context sees the imperatives of the self surrender to the exigencies which are imposed by the environment ... Regardless of whether that environment is a 'natural' one or a 'naturalised' one, there seems to be little that the individual can do to affect or change his condition ... In narrative the result is most often the construction of the condition of enclosure, restriction and entrapment.[1]

Almost as Turner wrote, however, parts of Australian cinema at least seemed to be undermining the mythology's dominance. In the later 1980s, films such as *Malcolm* (1986) and *Young Einstein* (1988) portrayed the transformative power of the individual, whilst the early 1990s brought a cluster of films – popularly termed the 'glitter' cycle on account of their luminescent and colourful visual style – which effectively re-wrote the place of the individual within the Australian 'context'. Although the works in question differ in various respects, *Strictly Ballroom* (1992), *Muriel's Wedding* (1994) and *The Adventures of Priscilla, Queen of the Desert* (1994) all feature protagonists who act decisively to change the circumstances of their lives, and who move forwards in directions which deviate in some way from the 'restriction and entrapment' of the norm. In the worlds constructed by the glitter pictures, there is, apparently, much that the individual can do to affect his or her condition. Through acts of courage and faith, the protagonists of these films assert themselves in contradiction to the social/familial backgrounds which have enclosed and restricted their desires. The films thus share more than a particular visual style, and in the comedy they provide much is suggested about the nature of contemporary Australian society.

Independence and Identity in *Muriel's Wedding*

The heroine of *Muriel's Wedding*, Muriel Hesslop (Toni Collette), is a large, endearing and dreamy girl who lives with her family in the Gold Coast town of Porpoise Spit. Unhappy, mistreated by her father and her circle of bitchy female friends, Muriel decides to take action on her own behalf, and makes a bid to escape her circumstances. Absconding with a large sum of her parents' money (courtesy of a blank cheque intended for her employer), Muriel books a stay on Hibiscus Island, an exclusive resort on the Great Barrier Reef, where her former friends are holidaying. Here she encounters an old acquaintance, Rhonda (Rachel Griffiths), and embarks on a series of adventures which represent a new and more exciting phase in her life. Siding with her new friend against the girls from Porpoise Spit who had rejected her, Muriel and Rhonda win the resort's talent contest with a superb rendition of ABBA's 'Waterloo', and create chaos amongst the girls by exposing a range of infidelities within the group. On returning home, Muriel only stays in her parents' house long enough to anticipate the full extent of her father's rage, before getting back into her taxi and fleeing to Sydney and the joys of a shared apartment with Rhonda. The initial sequence of narrative events are thus initiated as a direct result of Muriel's actions, although these do display a blind selfishness in respect of her mother's feelings and her substantial theft. Muriel, however, escapes the boundaries of Porpoise Spit, a small-minded and vulgar town whose mould is entirely unsuited to her personality and appearance. Her nasty group of friends tell her she is too fat; wears the wrong clothes; likes the wrong music; sports the wrong hairstyles; embarrasses them with her behaviour – as when she sobs loudly in a bar after they have delivered this harsh commentary. However these girls are consistently ridiculed by the film, and appear petty, shallow and cruel. Played for comic effect, they are nevertheless more than a grotesque caricature. P. J. Hogan has stated in interview that the Porpoise Spit girls are based on real people he has himself encountered:

> The girlfriends are raucous and uncouth, and that's how I remember a lot of girls from the Gold Coast. They are absolutely in love with themselves and certain that there is no better world than this … It's just cultural cringe to pretend that these people aren't out there, because they are.[2]

The film's depiction of Muriel's dysfunctional family suggests that this unsupportive background ('You're all useless' her father is often heard to remark to his brood of overweight, listless children) has fostered both insecurity and fantasy in her. Although Muriel despises her background she has nevertheless internalised some of its materialistic and patriarchal values, for her greatest fantasy, and the event which she believes will prove her ultimate worth and success, is to get married. This thematic is the source of much humour: Muriel repeatedly visits bridal wear shops where she tells the assistants increasingly outrageous stories about the difficult family circumstances surrounding her upcoming (imaginary) marriage. Moved to pity, they invariably take photos of her dressed up which she subsequently puts in an album. This obsessive behaviour reflects the writer-director's own experience of small town life:

> I grew up in a small town and it always seemed to me to be harder for women ... especially to escape. Being a male, I always felt it was expected of me to leave home. But when my sisters were younger, they often thought that marriage was the only way of leaving home and establishing a future. They were encouraged that way by my parents.[3]

Muriel's father Bill Hesslop (Bill Hunter) is a local politician and businessman who holds much sway with those in positions of power. When his wife Betty (Jeannie Drynan) is caught absent-mindedly shoplifting, he manages to persuade the authorities to let her off, and when the same charge is levelled at Muriel he befriends the policemen who bring her home (knowing one of their fathers) and sends them happily away with crates of beer. This mutual doing of favours is part of the explicitly male culture of mateship, and is the key to Bill's political success. However, this trait, so widely celebrated in other Australian films – such as *Sunday Too Far Away* (1975) and *Breaker Morant* (1980) – is here the subject of serious critique. Bill Hesslop is exposed as an egotistical man, obsessed with his own success and popularity, failing utterly in his role as husband and father: unfaithful to Betty, abusive and tyrannical in his behaviour, he undermines the confidence of his family rather than providing them with love and support. Interestingly the representation has a distinctly regional dimension. In a chapter entitled 'Screensland: The Construction of Queensland in Feature Films', Bruce Molloy has discussed the cinematic representation of this large Australian state (twice the size of Texas), charting a movement from a mythical to a more ironic view. He argues that *The Overlanders* (1946) and *Sons of Matthew* (1949) both 'represent Queensland as the destination of a journey of epic proportions ... (and) celebrate the spirit of enterprise and the virtues of hard work.'[4] However, later films made during the revival such as *Colour Me Dead* (1970) and *Final Cut* (1980) associate the Gold Coast with corruption and duplicity, while in *Goodbye Paradise* (1982) 'politicians are presented as weak or venal or both ... Stacey (Ray Barret) alludes to the political climate when he explains to an American interrogator, "This is Queensland – I can tell as many lies as I like"'.[5] The portrayal of Bill Hesslop in *Muriel's Wedding* is clearly continuous with this critique of Queensland's political culture; however the film's overt use of parody and humour makes the point even clearer. His schemes to engineer meetings with his lover Deirdre are rendered laughable by the repetition of an episode in which she appears as if by accident while he is dining with his family. 'Bill? Deirdre? What a coincidence!' they exclaim in mock surprise on both occasions, emphasising their clumsy duplicity. Bill is embroiled in a corruption scandal in the later part of the film, confirming hints of a dishonest and unscrupulous nature, but perhaps his most distasteful act occurs at his wife Betty's funeral. Here he smugly revels in the notoriety bestowed on him – and noted by journalists – by a telegram from former Prime minister Bob Hawke, expressing sympathy. Even his wife's tragic suicide serves to pamper his ego.

Molloy further argues that the style of *Goodbye Paradise* appropriately represents 'the cultural pastiche and semiotic excess of the Gold Coast streetscape, its postmodernist treatment capturing the melting pot of blatant affluence, hedonism and tastelessness that overlay the natural beauty of the coast.'[6] I would suggest that the overblown characterisation and brash visual style used to depict the setting and inhabitants of Porpoise Spit serves a similar function. P. J. Hogan has described the Gold Coast in interview as 'a chaotic mess of neon and plastic, with blue skies above and beach below',[7] and in the Porpoise Spit of *Muriel's Wedding* this is what we see. As Todd McCarthy of *Variety* has observed:

> Visual style highlights the crassest elements of middle-class Aussie lifestyle, with an emphasis on vulgar colour schemes, bad clothes and touristic consumerism.[8]

It is very noticeable when watching the film that as Muriel becomes settled in Sydney (seen as the city where happiness and freedom may be found) she begins to wear more tasteful and attractive clothes. This symbolises her break with the 'tackiness' of the Gold Coast. In *Muriel's Wedding*, the cinema audience received a less celebratory portrayal of Queensland than those traditionally evoked in the popular imagination by feature films. Molloy identifies these as 'the construction as mythic destination, exotic playground, utopian backdrop, even final resting place.' He continues that 'these dominant images of Queensland ... are unlikely to change until a regional feature film industry develops. Until then, Queensland runs the risk of always, like Texas, being defined by outsiders.[9] We must therefore be grateful that P. J. Hogan was able to make a 'local production' set on the Gold Coast where he grew up.

Muriel's Wedding is unusual within the Australian cinema for depicting a female character who begins as a victim yet ends the film full of hope and independence. Muriel abandons her false marriage, despite some growth of affection between herself and her 'arranged' husband, and returns to Porpoise Spit to face the aftermath of her mother's death. She then decides to go back to Sydney with Rhonda, leaving her father to take responsibility for her brothers and sister, a task long overdue; she has clearly matured and achieved the ability to assert herself. This thematic of marriage and female independence does have a history in earlier Australian films, notably *My Brilliant Career* (1979). This film charted a period in the life of Sybylla (Judy Davis), an intelligent and rather tomboyish young woman lacking in conventional beauty. Sybylla's maternal relations all try to persuade her of the necessity of marriage as the only suitable option for a woman. 'Marriage gives us respectability, dear,' says her aunt Helen (Wendy Hughes). Sybylla, however, desires a career in the arts, and ultimately rejects the offer of marriage from her close friend Harry Beecham, in love with her for several years. This decision is riddled with difficulties: she does care for, although not love, Harry and displays a sense of insecurity and vanity which is flattered by his attention; the antithesis of this is possibly condemning herself to a life of solitude and social ostracism. Nevertheless Sybylla's main objective is to write books and find things out about and for herself. Parallels with Muriel Hesslop can clearly be drawn. Both films construct powerful and successful female protagonists. Although nowhere near as intelligent or headstrong as Sybylla, Muriel does display both selfishness and strength of will when she steals money from her parents to go to Hibiscus Island. Both women know what they want; both are in some way constrained by society's desire for them to marry (Muriel has internalised these values while Sybylla is consistently pressured by others to conform to expectation); neither adheres to conventional standards of beauty and desirability. However, by the end of *My Brilliant Career* and *Muriel's Wedding* Sybylla and Muriel have both rejected a marriage which was theirs for the taking, asserted their own needs and desires to close friends and family, matured in their acceptance of responsibility and begun a new and independent phase of life. What places *Muriel's Wedding* firmly in the present of the 1990s is that utopia is to be found not through isolated (if brilliant) writing in the outback

– happiness through art – but in living the excitement of Sydney with another single woman. She has found the support that Sybylla lacked.

The Restriction of Culture Versus the Freedom of Nature

The Adventures of Priscilla, Queen of the Desert tells the story of the journey undertaken on a bus across the Australian desert by three drag queens. Departing from Sydney, their destination is Alice Springs, where they are due to perform. During the course of the film the three protagonists, Tick/ Mitzi (Hugo Weaving), Adam/ Felicia (Guy Pearse) and Bernadette (Terence Stamp), encounter both the extraordinary vastness and beauty of the Australian outback and the differing attitudes and lifestyles of its people. In this film, which is at the same time a comedy, a musical and a road movie, we see what happens when a straight society is confronted with its gay counterpart, and when rural values are put into conflict with modern and liberated representatives of the city. The following observation by Graeme Turner provides a useful starting point for a discussion of the film:

> Survival is all, resistance is futile, and ideals are to be tempered by contingency. The alibi is provided by the representation of the land as harsh, hostile, impervious to human endeavour – but eternal.[10]

In *Priscilla*, however, it is people who provide obstructions to the self-expression and liberty of the three protagonists (as I shall discuss in detail), while their relationship to landscape, achieved through stunning use of cinematography, emphasises freedom and adaptability. In one scene, having spent a night in the desert as a result of their bus breaking down, the three protagonists share a luscious breakfast. Seated at a table in the middle of the outback, they appear perfectly at ease. To kill time while they wait for assistance, Adam decides to paint the bus lavender. Tick practises dance steps in full costume and is shot centre frame in the midst of the vast and beautiful desert, a certain security about his place within it. Bernadette sets off alone, breezily declaring she will be 'back with the cavalry'. There is nothing to be feared from this alien landscape; rather it is Tick and Adam who scare off the middle-aged couple who initially seem willing to help Bernadette. By contrast the group of Aborigines, who appear similarly at home in the desert, have no difficulty accepting the sexuality and bizarrely costumed (flowered wigs, all-in-one flared trouser suits, lavish make-up) appearance of the protagonists. They clap along appreciatively to the drag performance – of Gloria Gaynor's 'I Will Survive' – and the young

Aboriginal man who had originally befriended them joins Tick, Adam and Bernadette in costume, dancing enthusiastically. On the soundtrack a didgeridoo plays along with the recorded music, suggesting a fusion of cultures. This scene could also be read politically: two marginal groups (homosexuals and Aboriginals) engaged in mutual acceptance. The flamboyant appearance of the drag queens is used both to emphasise their difference and as a source of visual beauty. Some of the images used suggest that they have effectively conquered the Australian landscape, and found peace within it, in a way which would be impossible in the backward towns of the bush. One shot, for example, features the pink bus in long shot, centre frame, with a pink cloud of smoke billowing behind and above it. Atop the bus in a massive silver high-heeled shoe sits Adam, wearing a red cape which flows dramatically behind him. The expansive pink-brown desert landscape matches perfectly the colour scheme of Adam and the bus. The camera pans slowly around from a great height to observe this spectacular vision in its full glory. The stop-overs which punctuate the bus's journey towards the red centre provide a series of varieties of the kind of juxtaposition between artifice and nature; communities encountered.

Graeme Turner has also suggested that:

> the attraction of the idealised bush community as the paradigm of the authentic Australian existence derives part of its attraction, one guesses, from the fact that it is in the middle of the opposition; it is an invention which is neither wholly nature nor culture, but a compromise between the two.[11]

Priscilla, however, depicts the meeting of Tick, Adam and Bernadette, who represent the heterogeneous and progressive nature of life in Sydney, with the backward, oppressively heterosexist culture of the bush community, and firmly positions the audience's sympathies with the three gay protagonists. For the film's treatment of the bush towns visited by the drag queens on their route to Alice Springs does not expose a group of people living in harmony with nature, but rather a macho society deeply suspicious of outsiders, and evincing chronic homophobia (with the significant exception of Bob, played by Bill Hunter). *Priscilla's* gay characters, like Muriel in *Muriel's Wedding*, and Scott (Paul Mercurio) in *Strictly Ballroom*, are not powerless, although they are vulnerable to the scathing and cruel judgements of society, many aspects of which are exposed as narrow-minded and repressive. Tick, Adam and Bernadette live their lives outside society's heterosexual norms. Bernadette is a transsexual – she has had surgery to physically confirm her status as female; during the course of the film she begins a relationship with heterosexual Bob and decides to stay with him in Alice Springs. These are affirmative actions, going against the grain of social convention in order to achieve personal freedom and fulfilment. The casting of Terence Stamp in this role has a significant effect on how we view the character. One could argue that the trans-sexuality of Bernadette is rendered doubly subversive by being played by a well-known heterosexual male icon of the 1960s. The casting certainly adds to the comedy, but it is possible that this undermines the character's seriousness. When Tick, Adam and Bernadette arrive in Coober Pedy they descend from their bus in drag attire. While Bernadette dresses soberly in a white caftan, Tick and Adam sport high heeled boots, brightly coloured and feathered costumes and wigs and lots of flamboyant make-up. Their appearance is extraordinary, as in all sequences where they are in drag. They are stared at by the town's inhabitants, at whom they wave cheerfully, and the mood remains playful until they enter the local pub. The music cuts, the people gather round and a local woman defies Bernadette's attempt to order drinks with sneering insults: 'Well, look what the cat dragged in. What have we got here, eh? A couple of showgirls. Where did you ladies come in from? Uranus? We've got nothing here for people like you.' However, Bernadette turns the tables on her by making a sexist joke at her expense in the crude tradition of ocker humour. To the rather short, middle-aged and unattractive woman (who appears to be the only female in the pub) she says:

> Now listen here you mullet. Why don't you just light your tampon and blow your box apart, because that's the only bang you're ever going to get sweetheart.

After a moment's hesitation all the men in the pub burst out laughing, affirming the humiliation of the local woman. From that point on, Tick, Adam and Bernadette are made to feel welcome: we see them ceremoniously singing, and participating in a drinking competition with the women humiliated by Bernadette, who wins, impressing male bystanders. However, despite their apparent victory over the small-mindedness of the community (which was achieved, though humorously, at the expense of a woman), the drag queens are later made the object of outright prejudice and hostility. They discover the next day that 'Aids Fuckers Go Home' has been painted large on their bus. This critical depiction of the bush community – cruelly judgmental and two-faced – is contrary to the idealised version identified by Graeme Turner.

It is unfortunate that in a film so concerned to de-marginalise gay lifestyles – glorifying the aesthetics of camp and positioning gay characters as *Priscilla's* point of focus, identification and sympathy – that women are largely portrayed in such a derogatory fashion. The depiction of Bob's Filipina wife Cynthia (Julia Cortez) has been attacked for its racist and sexist use of stereotyping and humour, a criticism I would fully support. From her very introduction Cynthia is presented as a silly, unintelligent yet scheming woman who continually causes her husband Bob embarrassment. Her first appearance occurs when Tick, Adam and Bernadette are talking to Bob outside their bus (he is a mechanic). We hear Cynthia's squawking voice before we see her, calling 'Refreshments!', and, as the men turn towards her, Bob's embarrassment is immediately visible. Carrying a tray of lemonade and cookies, Cynthia smiles coyly but quickly becomes angry when Bob tries to get rid of her ('That's very nice, darling. Please, go back inside.') She answers him sharply in her own language, revealing an aggressive streak, and, when the camera again shows her observers, Adam is smirking derisively at Cynthia. Later, at dinner, she wears a short, tight, fuschia pink dress which exposes her cleavage – her femininity is portrayed as tacky artifice and her seductive manner rendered ridiculous, as her three guests are all gay. Pushing food around her plate distastefully, Bernadette says, 'Bob, Cynthia, thank you. I love lamb with meringue.' Cynthia's attempts to produce Western food are thus mocked, and her stupidity emphasised when she suggests putting face cream on the food. Bob has to interpret her attempts at English and his comments, added to the sarcastic and critical view taken of her by Adam, Tick and Bernadette, significantly affect the impression that we as viewers form. When Cynthia says, 'Me perform for you. Me dance too,' Bob explains that 'My wife used to be in the entertainment business,' and we later bear witness to her strip dance routine in the local pub. Melba Margison of the Centre for Filipino Concerns argued angrily that Priscilla portrayed Cynthia as 'a gold digger, a prostitute, an entertainer whose expertise is popping out ping-pong balls from her sex organ, a manic depressive, loud and vulgar. The worst stereotype of the Filipina'.[12] Her negative depiction is assured in a flashback sequence in which we see Bob waking up in a state of confusion to be confronted with a triumphant Cynthia brandishing their marriage certificate. The implication is all too clear: in a drunken moment Cynthia has enticed Bob to marry her so that she can emigrate to Australia. Bob also claims that Cynthia is not allowed in the pub anymore, as she has a problem with alcohol, and makes a fool of herself every time she gets drunk. This supposedly justifies him leaving her at home and locking the bottle cupboard. Cynthia stares at this furiously, ranting out loud in her own language, and having broken the cupboard open she appears in the pub, drunk and raunchy, wearing a revealing and tasteless leopard skin outfit.

This all suggests that Cynthia is lacking in self-control, attention-seeking, manipulative and, when drunk, reverts to her past behaviour as a stripper/prostitute. She arrives in the pub at the very moment when the drag queens' introductory number has been met with stony and unappreciative silence by the male audience, who (with the exception of Bob) do not know how to cope with this subversion of traditional sexual/ gender identity. We inevitably view Cynthia as a tawdry and pathetic rival who serves to confirm heterosexual norms: the men clap and whistle as Cynthia takes her place on the stage, but her act is crude in the extreme. Having seen how much work goes into the performances of Tick, Adam and Bernadette (and how spectacular they are) we cannot but resent Cynthia's intrusion. It is regrettable that in revealing the narrow-minded and oppressively traditional attitudes of the male bush community, *Priscilla's* filmmakers should have simultaneously utilised sexist and racist stereotypes. This is, in my opinion, a significant failing in a film which aims to be socially inclusive. Margison goes so far as to say that:

> While all the main and secondary characters in the film were treated with respect, humanised and dignified, the Filipina was treated with condemnation, dehumanised and stripped of any form of dignity. Her dignity was killed. That is the word. Violently killed.[13]

The next bush town is the site of the most unpleasant incident yet. When the protagonists arrive, Bob (who has joined their party since Cynthia left him following the pub incident) issues the following warning:

> Now look, you blokes watch your back. This is a pretty tough little town. They get up in the morning, they go down a hole, they blow things up and they come up again. That about sums things up.

Adam defies the instructions of Tick and Bernadette and goes out on the town in flamboyant drag attire. He approaches a group of men – who do not at first realise that he is a man – and behaves flirtatiously towards them. Catching sight of muscled arms one man is particularly incensed, and the atmosphere becomes violent. Adam runs away but is caught by a fence, and a brutal assault is only prevented by Bob's intervention. This macho bush community is a dangerous place for a gay man intent on declaring his sexuality in such visible form. The town's inhabitants are aggressive, fearful and intolerant, a result of their sheltered living conditions. This depiction represents a critique of the male group ethos represented by mateship and working communities. As Graeme Turner has noted, the classic shearer film *Sunday Too Far Away* celebrates the social and occupational group as a model of social relations, and stresses the importance of community values over those of the self. This film also fits into the generic category identified by Dermody and Jacka as the 'male ensemble film', which they argue was strongly influenced by the posture of the ocker: blunt, loud, hedonistic and conservative in the populist manner. Of the male ensemble film, they observe that:

> Its working-class or lower middle-class male figure is not an appeal for class solidarity, but a gesture towards the classless common man as last bastion of 'real' Australian virtues and vices. And, of course, the vices are cheered on as sardonically as the virtues; an Australian man is 'cut from a whole cloth', and the mix can't be argued or refuted.[14]

However, between the making of *Sunday Too Far Away* and *Priscilla*, much has changed. In the incident involving Adam's assault we are firmly positioned to identify with the (gay) individual over and against the judgements and demands of the (heterosexual) ocker group. Their communal work of 'blowing things up' has clearly raised levels of aggression, blinkered them to the heterogeneous nature of contemporary Australian society, and imbued them with a fierce homophobia. The vices of these men are not 'cheered on': they appear threatening in the extreme from Adam's perspective and thus from ours.

At the end of *Priscilla*, Tick and Adam return to Sydney, which is ultimately the place they feel most happy and comfortable in. 'Thank you, thank you. It's good to be home,' says Tick to the audience after their homecoming performance. Having conquered the landscape of the outback, if not its people, a return to contemporary urban life is seen as desirable. For as Bernadette comments after the frightening episode of Adam's assault: 'It's funny. We all sit around mindlessly slagging off that vile stinkhole of a city. But in its own strange way it takes care of us. I don't know if that ugly wall of suburbia has been put there to stop them getting in, or us getting out.' Here 'them' presumably refers to the backward inhabitants of rural communities, while 'us' signifies the members of the (male) gay community. Like *Muriel's Wedding*, *Priscilla* celebrates the city as the preferred habitation and site of liberation of its protagonists. However, the opposition set up in the latter film is between one male-centred culture and another. Women play little part in the film's representation of Sydney's gay community, and are similarly excluded, if not actively denigrated, in the depiction of outback communities (with the exception of Tick's lesbian wife Susan).

Graeme Turner has identified a central representative strategy of Australian film and fiction as the perceived split between nature and society:

It has become customary to talk about the representation of the Australian context as divisible into two separate and opposing terms; these appear variously as the country versus the city, rural versus urban, nature versus society. While each of these pairs differs from the others in certain respects, they are all attempts to label the perceived split between life within an Australian urban, social environment and life which takes place within, and is thus determined by the demands of, the landscape.[15]

The glitter pictures each explore the conflict between different sections of society and their associated values, and utilise the protagonists' struggle to deal with this opposition as the central narrative drive. However, in each case the split occurs within society (rather than between society and nature), serving to emphasise the often restrictive form of contemporary Australian culture, and exploring the possibilities of progressive change. *Priscilla* is successful in providing an entirely new angle on the traditional division between city and country, played out through the representation of male sexuality.

Strictly Suburbia?

In *Strictly Ballroom* the central opposition is located within the 'ugly wall of suburbia' identified by Bernadette. In this film the protagonist's struggle takes the form of Scott Hastings' battle to broaden the scope of dance steps in the arena of ballroom dancing. The film is set firmly in the suburbs of Sydney and the action moves between various (mostly interior) locations: the Hastings family home, the dance studio where Scott's mother teaches and where he trains, the ballroom arena, and Fran's (Tara Morice) home, which is located beside a railway marshalling yard, stressing the marginal status of her Spanish family. Writing in 1994 to coincide with the film's television screening, Peter Castaldi praised *Strictly Ballroom* for the way it combined a depiction of Australian suburbia with a tale of fairy tale romance:

> They (the film-makers) took the back streets of any town and dressed them up in the most colourful, outrageous and witty way. What is essentially the story of ugly duckling Fran (played by Tara Morice) getting her wish to dance with handsome prince Mercurio and (without kissing the frog) becoming a princess herself, is in fact a celebration like no other of everything Australian. *Strictly Ballroom* underneath its lavish frocks, its wonderful performances and crackerjack pace liberates the suburban from the grip of the realists and lets fantasy run free.[16]

The visual and acting style of *Strictly Ballroom* has much in common with *Muriel's Wedding*: a lurid colour scheme and hysterical bitchiness characterise Scott's social world, and the plot is highly melodramatic. Near the film's opening, Scott's parents are interviewed in their tacky pink-themed living room, filled with photographs and trophies, all won by the champion Scott. In documentary style 'to-camera' statements Shirley Hastings (Pat Thompson) and Les Kendall (Peter Whitford) (Scott's coach, pictured at the dance studio) recount what happened at a recent ballroom contest when Scott decided to dance his own steps, thus forfeiting all chance of success. The degree of seriousness which Shirley affords her subject is the source of much humour: 'I keep asking myself why ... did I do something wrong? ... did I fail him as a mother?' She breaks down into sobs and this is inter-cut with shots of Scott and his partner Liz (Gia Carides) dancing unconventional steps. Some critics have disparaged *Strictly Ballroom*'s mishmash of styles (in this instance, the contrast between documentary style interviews and the colourful visuals and fast-paced editing of the ballroom dancing scenes), and its brash, overblown quality. Pat Gillespie of *Cinema Papers* notes:

> it is hard to accept this film as a slice of life, when everything in it is exaggerated and parodic. The love story is a limp bridging device to hold together a number of cliched vignettes.[17]

Gillespie was especially critical of the use of social contrast between the backgrounds of Scott and Fran:

> Ethnic family life and its down-to-earth values versus the tacky Technicolor of the Australian ballroom. Drama is an integral part of Spanish life, whereas the Australians introduce drama into their otherwise bland lives. It is the classic us-and-them scenario.[18]

However, the melodramatic pace and colourful characterisation of *Strictly Ballroom* serves a number of significant purposes. The first of these is to provide a highly entertaining and humorous experience for the viewer. Secondly, the depiction of Anglo-Australian culture in *Strictly Ballroom* highlights both its crass nature and the degree to which it restricts personal freedom and fulfilment. Like Muriel, Scott has to get away from his family background in order to discover his true potential. Yet while she flees to the city, he finds solace in the suburbs, blossoming, along with Fran, under the guidance of her older and wiser Spanish relatives.

The fact that all of the film's major characters have such strong emotional (and in some cases, financial) investment in the ballroom dancing world means that the conclusion of *Strictly Ballroom* is heavily loaded with potential meaning. One could certainly argue that the film's denouement shows the way forward to a more inclusive and progressive society. Denying the fact that the music has been cut to prevent their dancing 'illegal' steps, Scott and Fran begin the steps of the *paso doblé* to the sound of the clapping of Fran's father Rico (Antonio Vargas) and grandmother (Armonia Benedito), joined by Scott's father Doug (Barry Otto). These characters, positioned outside the power structures of the ballroom world, help to unify the audience in its approval and admiration for Scott and Fran's performance. As Tom O'Regan has observed:

> (They) become central in the reconstructed public world from which they have been hitherto excluded. The institution of ballroom dancing is infused with the flamenco, remaking and rejuvenating itself so the son can fulfil his father's destiny.[19]

It is revealed in the closing scenes that Doug Hastings was coerced into giving up his role as Shirley's dance partner, and thus his chance to try out new and innovative steps in the Pan-Pacific championships. In justifying her part in this scenario, Shirley pleads, 'Our dancing career was on the line. We would never have been able to teach. I couldn't throw all that away on a dream. We had to survive!' Scott's eccentric and emasculated father – often pictured dancing alone at night in the studio – exemplifies a man whose creativity and ambition have been thwarted by social strictures. Scott, however, with his father's support, is brave where Doug was not, and asserts his rights as an individual within Australian society. He and Fran, who help each other through their fear, symbolise a new generation desirous of change.

The ending of *Strictly Ballroom* is also significant in representing the romantic sexual union of an ethnically unmarked Australian man and an ethnically marked woman. The film is an example of what Tom O'Regan has termed 'new world cinema', which he describes as 'populist in intent with its utopian ideological underpinnings.[20] The fact that it is the Spanish *paso doblé* which unites people against the rigid regulations of ballroom, (bringing joyous release to all but the film's corrupt villain, Barry Fife (Bill Hunter), who fixes competitions and manipulates the participants) suggests that the integration of European tradition into Anglo-Australian culture, and the concurrent dissolution of homogeneity, has a highly desirable potential. For, as James Walter observes, *Strictly Ballroom*'s portrayal of the positive contribution of multiculturalism takes place within the urban setting of most Australians, and thus transcends a purely individualistic standpoint.[21] The protagonists' fight against repressive strictures, which transpire to be rigged against the ordinary person, and their refusal to obey the corrupt bureaucracy of the ballroom, signifies a victory for one and all:

> When, in the closing scenes, the audience invades the dance floor, we can see that the protagonists have carried their 'community' with them: it is, in the end, a collective triumph.[22]

Conclusions

The style of the glitter pictures marks a significant departure from Australian film-making traditions. While using elements of established (Hollywood) genres – *Priscilla* is clearly one version of a road movie; *Muriel's Wedding* has strong echoes of teen movies; *Strictly Ballroom*'s director has claimed the influence of American 1950s musicals – they all display a boldness of address which is peculiar to this cycle. This is also a reaction to, and move away from, the features (in both senses of the word) of the Australian canon. Dermody and Jacka have written on the dominant aesthetic groupings in Australian filmmaking since the revival of the 1970s. The most prominent of these in representing national identity both at home and internationally, is the AFC genre, epitomised by such classics as *Picnic at Hanging Rock* (1975) and *My Brilliant Career*, and 'noted from time to time in the late seventies as a persistent tendency of Australian cinema to fall back on pretty, 'period', 'nostalgia' or 'history' films when it should be addressing the not-so-pretty, 'real', contemporary Australian world'.[23]

The release of *Breaker Morant* (1980), argue Dermody and Jacka, awakened the AFC genre towards the commercial possibilities of declared nationalism, and a male Australianness represented in the form of heroes/martyrs. The AFC genre films have strong ties to middle-brow fiction, and make a corresponding effort to be 'tasteful'. As Dermody and Jacka have commented:

> It is striking how morally inoffensive and bland the characters tend to be, as though in the hope of wooing a broad general audience.[24]

The cinematography of these films celebrates the beauty of the Australian landscape, with links to a romantic Australian post-impressionism. The use of *mise-en-scene* and editing is intended to charm, rather than stimulate or shock, the viewer. Dermody and Jacka pose the question of what it means for Australian cinema 'to have had such unexceptionable, "nice", even bland films at the centre of its field of possibilities',[25] and one answer to this in relation to the 1990s is the arrival of the brash cinematography and extravagantly drawn characters of *Strictly Ballroom*, *Muriel's Wedding* and *Priscilla*. For these films relish what the AFC genre had studiously avoided: popular culture (be it ABBA, ballroom dancing or drag performance), vulgar and offensive characters, and flamboyant visuals, reflecting the tackiness of much of contemporary Australian life. They each revel in artifice rather than aiming towards a picturesque realism (or its gritty counterpart exemplified by the social realist genre). Here is clear evidence of a break with the post-colonial ties to British high-brow artistic traditions, a heavy influence on the films of the AFC genre. In their place the style and thematics of the glitter pictures offer an evaluation of 1990s Australia using a more progressive set of aesthetic criteria.

NOTES

1. Graeme Turner, *National Fictions: Literature, Film and the Construction of Australian Narrative* (Sydney: Allen & Unwin, 1986), pp.50–51.
2. P. J. Hogan, interviewed by Jan Epstein, *Cinema Papers*, No. 101 (October 1994), p.31.
3. Ibid., p.28.
4. Bruce Molloy, 'Screensland: The Construction of Queensland in Feature Films', in Jonathan Dawson and Bruce Molloy (eds.), *Queensland Images in Film and Television* (St. Lucia, Queensland: University of Queensland Press, 1990), p.70.
5. Ibid., p.74.
6. Ibid., p.72.
7. Epstein, 1994, p.31.
8. Todd McCarthy, Review *of Muriel's Wedding* in *Variety* (23–29 May 1994), p.55.
9. Molloy, 1990, pp.76–77.
10. Turner, 1986, p.83.
11. Ibid., p.36.
12. Melba Margison, quoted by Jane Cafarella, 'Filipino Women Blast *Priscilla* for Portrayal of Worst Stereotype', *The Age* (7 October 1994). In *Cinedossier*, Issue 656, (11 October 1994), p.20. [reprinted in Tom O'Regan, *Australian National Cinema* (London: Routledge, 1996), p.154.]
13. Ibid.
14. Susan Dermody and Elizabeth Jacka, *The Screening of Australia: Anatomy of a National Cinema* [Volume II] (Sydney: Currency Press, 1988), p. 59.
15. Turner (1986), p.25.
16. Peter Castaldi, 'Movie of the Week', *The Sunday Herald Sun*, [TV Extra] (23 October 1994), reproduced in *Cinedossier*, Issue 656 (25 October 1994), p.52. [also reprinted in O'Regan, p.148.]
17. Pat Gillespie, *Cinema Papers*, No.91 (January 1993), p.52.
18. Ibid.
19. O'Regan, 1996, p.318.
20. O'Regan, p.318.
21. James Walter, 'From The Weird Mob to Strictly Ballroom: Politics and Public Culture in Australia Since The Forties', *Australian Studies* No.10 (December 1996) pp.7–21.
22. Ibid.
23. Dermody and Jacka, p.32.
24. Ibid. p.33.
25. Ibid. p.34.

9

A Pig in Space?
Babe and the Problem of Landscape

TARA BRABAZON

I was for the Pig before the Pig was famous.[1]

Oprah Winfrey

Every fairy tale requires a grand opening, a 'Once upon a time' delivered with panache. Births, deaths and marriages are effective, but Oprah has to be there to explain the meaning of it all. So, let's go with the big opening.

My parents spent the early years of their marriage in Broome, a town in the north-west of Western Australia. This ocean-side paradise features palms, boab trees and the chalkiest of white sand. Like all paradises, Broome possesses its own legends which details the fall of man. Many young Australians go to Broome, with the pioneering intention of making their fortune. This path to riches however, is always littered with tragedy. My parents, too, were tripped by the palisades of this evil landscape. The harsh, weathered terrain taught them a lesson. On their return from the north-west, my mother always reminded her children that 'whatever Broome gives you, it takes away before you leave'.

That opening was highly charged in terms of affectivity, but low in credibility. It was not sufficiently scholarly. Let's try again.

Once upon a time there was a chapter written about a little film that went a long way. To understand this text, the ficto-critical narrator engaged an old Australian filmic paradigm: the 'problem' of landscape. *Babe* (1995) signifies a pivotal shift in the cultural geography and historiography of Australian cinema. It is the culmination of a movement away from fetishised outback panoramas and dramas set in the colonial period. While

Proof (1991), *Strictly Ballroom* (1992), *Romper Stomper* (1992), and *The Big Steal* (1990) move the filmic frame into the contemporary, urban environment, *Babe* registers an innovative and unexpected vectoral shift.

In 1983, Ross Gibson suggested that the post-1970s wave of Australian films 'have been *about* landscape'.[2] Gibson's article, which changed the way in which national visuality is considered, is more than fifteen years old. The success of *Babe* provides an opportunity to rethink national cinematic imaginings and recognise that the passive, timeless and unchanging Australian landscape is the most lavish drag queen of all. By mobilising Hollywood tropes of film making, *Babe* provides an abrupt end point to debates about Australian content. The task of promoting national identity shifts from the text and towards the reader. As a popular film, *Babe*'s signifying mobility transgresses the ideological and critical demarcations of cultural space. This chapter therefore, explores how national meanings are gleaned from *Babe*'s semiotic landscape. Critical responses to the film have been soaked in nationalist renderings. From Oprah Winfrey's comment at the Academy Awards Ceremony ('I was for the pig before the pig was famous') to the *New Statesman* critic who located the Hoggetts' farm in Kent,[3] *Babe* has resisted critical closure. This deterritorialisation, when matched with considerations of accent, animatronics, funding and publicity, serves to locate *Babe* as a pivotal text in transforming Australian visual accents into an ocular Esperanto.[4]

Australian film historiography is like a Proppian folk tale: a morphology with a limited number of functions. The only analytical change is the end point. Each latest release becomes the most significant or the crucial closure to the narrative. These texts eventually fade from critical favour. From *Gallipoli* (1981) to *Crocodile Dundee* (1986), from *Strictly Ballroom* to *Shine*, (1997) each new film remakes the industry into a dazzling success story. Certainly clear obstacles face any non-American national film industry. During its moments of 'revival', Australian cinema has been reflexively (and at times embarrassingly) nationalist. Working against British codes of behaviour, Australian films like *The Adventures of Barry MacKenzie* (1972) and *Gallipoli* present a unified national ideology, rather than a contradictory amalgam of differences and historical discrepancies grounded in a recognisably national geography. In a remarkable reversal, Jonathan Romney's review of *Babe* in the *New Statesman*, the magazine of the British Left, tried to absorb the film into *British* cinematic narratives.

> Babe is set in idyllic countryside, a hyper-kitsch imagining of Enid Blyton England, all rolling hedgerows and skies candy-coloured in orange and yellow.[5]

At such a statement, Mick Dundee would weep into his beer. The review does however, demonstrate the malleability of the Australian landscape. Silence the broad accent, and deflect the camera from Uluru or Bondi, and the most adventurous of reviewers can discover the Famous Five darting amid the hedgerows.

The 'bloke', whether Breaker Morant or Mick Dundee, became a metonymy for the nation in the 1980s. Only as the industry entered its 'quirky' phase did *Proof* signal the timely arrival of a new man. Featuring the story of a blind photographer who, in proto-*X Files* fashion, trusts no one, Martin (Hugo Weaving), is so distrusting of people that he takes photographs to confirm that the world exists. The only problem with this proof is that Martin needs to find a trusted narrator to explain his images and thereby confirm his perceptions. This film verified that Australian cinema could ask complex emotional questions and render black humour. Similarly, *Strictly Ballroom*, although critically analysed and commercially exploited to the point of exhaustion, needs to be reclaimed as one of the most significant films of the last ten years. It featured urban, cosmopolitan life and imported film codes, such as the pseudo-documentary and 1950s Hollywood musical. It also articulated, through dance, a more critical, rather than celebratory, Australian multiculturalism through a conflictual yet consensual blending of Anglo and Spanish cultures. Australian masculinity was further re-inscribed and critiqued through *Muriel's Wedding* (1994) and *The Adventures of Priscilla: Queen of the Desert* (1994). Muriel's pathetic longing; to marry *anyone* and remake herself into a different person, positions the film as politically significant. *Priscilla*, too, transformed masculine ideologies and re-inscribed national narratives.

The connection between stories of drag queens and a pig who wants to be a dog seems somewhat tenuous, yet the treatment of the landscape in *Priscilla* opened the way for *Babe*. As Brian McFarlane and Geoff Mayer have realised, 'what "Australian cinema" might mean remains as elusive as ever'.[6] The concerns with iconography, ideologies and market have configured Australian film and televisual product as an export industry. With Australian films framed as different from Hollywood releases, internal divisions between the 'local product' seem arbitrary. The question remains: how does the *Australian* adjective operate within the phrase Australian film industry*?*

Phillip Adams states that 'our best films are, I reckon, our most culturally specific, the ones that don't attempt to integrate themselves with an audience in Los Angeles or, for that matter, at Cannes'.[7] Popular culture transgresses the boundaries of a nation, networked through electronic transfers of information. Yet debates about Australian culture are conducted, not surprisingly, at a national level. This policy discourse ties local, regional, subcultural, ethnic, Aboriginal and experimental cultures to the fate of the nation. It is a defensive discourse that evaluates the Australian film industry through the 'accuracy' by which it produces an effective image of the nation and its people/audience. By Adams' evaluation, *Babe* is not successful within the framework of the national industry. The desire for a cultural nationalism, the projection of an Australian advertising campaign for world consumption, shows an inadequate conceptualisation of film audiences. This manner of social imaging can be socially damaging, culturally narrow and oppressive. Making films *national* is a complex process of semiotic reclamation. As McKenzie Wark suggested in his assessment of *The Piano*:

> But was this an 'Australian' film? The answer is less interesting than what the question reveals; a New Zealand location, American principal cast, Australian development money, a French co-production with a major American distribution deal. This is 'Australian' cinema in the 1990s; a blend of the local and the international, the subsidised and the market-driven – a set of contradictions that have to be resolved.[8]

Wark's recognition of the contemporary impossibility of seamless national story telling, or even financing, profiles a larger problem: a recognition that inclusive narratives are not possible. Phrased another way, an Aboriginal drag queen, as featured in *Priscilla*, does not confirm the film's 'good politics'.

Babe's place in 1990s film historiography is similar to *Crocodile Dundee*'s in the 1980s, presenting a comfortable Australia for American viewers. The difference between these two films shows the increasing function of American imagery in Australia. Ruth Brown postulated that *Crocodile Dundee*:

> uses 'Australia' to restore America's sense of manifest destiny and to justify the use of superior weaponry by linking power with innocence and virtue.[9]

The only way for contemporary Australia to occupy this space as *America's manifest destiny* is to anthropomorphise animals. The signifier of *Australia* amidst the new world order relies on a landscape that is magical rather than national and a masculinity that is performed through soft, squeaky feminine voices. Tony Safford, Vice President of Acquisitions at Miramax Films, has stated that 'our ease with Australian cinema ... is knowing that it will be at once familiar (in language and culture) and unique (in character and setting)'.[10] *Babe* is clearly placed in this quirky, that is, familiar but comfortably different, niche.

Although the historiography of Australian film has worked through national discursive frameworks, there are alternative paths through the narrative. As Neil Rattigan has suggested, 'Australia has a long history of cultural schizophrenia regarding its national image'.[11] *Mad Max* (1979)[12] and *Priscilla*, for example, imported the American genre of a road movie and re-placed it over the Australian landscape. This form of generic movement does transform the terrain into a site for semiotic tourism, with little commitment to the ideologies, contradictions and problems of the place. As Aunty Entity (Tina Turner) from *Mad Max Beyond Thunderdome* (1985) proclaimed 'So much for history'. The movement from a frontier discourse to an affirmation of touristic consumption is not an apolitical journey. Australian films, from *Strictly Ballroom* to *Muriel's Wedding* have utilised the suburbs to prise open Australian nation-building myths. Suburban happiness is captured, critiqued and dismissed. The scene in *Muriel's Wedding* when the young 'try hard' protagonist is mocked by her 'friends' in a suburban night club for being fat and listening to ABBA articulates the superficiality of suburban values.[13] This pessimism is matched by Babe's realisation, upon asking Fly about his future, that pigs are eaten. While both Muriel and Babe, and Sybylla in *My Brilliant Career* (1979) before them, are successful at the conclusion of the narrative, they attain their realisations through being hyper-individualistic. Collective solutions to their problems, reaching beyond specific concerns with class, gender or species, were not pondered. These outcomes make the political field of these films highly ambivalent.

The land is the primary determinant of Australian ideologies. Both *Sunday Too Far Away* (1975) and *The Chant of Jimmy Blacksmith* (1978) feature opening scenes of the landscape. As McMahon and Quinn suggest 'the land becomes as powerful a force in the narrative as any of the characters'.[14] The land is configured politically, ideologically, economically and socially. Belonging structures are enmeshed into a place. Philip Drew recognises that 'space is a revealing dimension of any culture, and, as such, is just as important in its own way as language'.[15] Popular culture is mobile, circulating texts and styles through a myriad of cultural sites and spheres. To situate a community into a nationalised imagining involves piercing the surfaces of the landscape, inscribing it within the dominant forms of belonging. The increasing invention and proliferation of languages and practices within a nationalised frame makes the claims for solidifying national boundaries and territories more aggressive, conservative and deliberate. As Turner has suggested:

It is probably fair to say that in most Australian films today, national identity is simply not an issue ... something has happened to the way in which the nation is represented in our cinema, and this may be related to the fact that something has happened to the way arguments about the category of the nation are currently framed.[16]

Whilst Australian ideologies are changing, it is not surprising that the discursive dust from the cinematic landscape is still circulating in the semiosphere.

Landscapes provide the backdrop for stories, and the trigger for ideological conflict. They visualise Braudel's structure: the bedrock of history.[17] Colonisation, genocide, industrialisation and manufacturing decline are merely conjunctures: Pauline Hanson's[18] diatribes are events that wash over the environment. As an icon and a resource, the Australian landscape is increasingly vulnerable to sweeping, contradictory historical narratives of ownership, development and progress. In *The Man From Snowy River* (1982), even Tom Burlinson's horse could not ride over the contemporary contradictions within Australian nationalism.[19] Between the tortured, brutal imagining of *Mad Max* and the suburban park of *The Sum of Us* (1994) lies a web of inter-textual networks. Distinctively, *Babe* summons a pastoral ideology, revelling in the simple social conventions of country life. Industrialisation is a danger and technology is confusing. The Hoggett's farm is a site of safety and order. Only those forces from the outside, like fax machines, city dogs and the abattoir, are disruptive and evil. *Babe*'s visual field is enclosed by a fence of rurality. Mrs Hoggett's garden and Mr Hoggett's farm show a domesticated terrain. Both are distinctively demarcated, granting the landscape clear symbolic qualities.

Although *Babe*'s landscape is affectionate and nostalgic, it is also politically ambivalent. As a domesticated terrain, it is trapped between what Gibson has described as 'questions of habitat and terms of hermeneutics, between referent and reference'.[20] Traditionally, the land of Australian film exhibits agency: its irregularities roll cars and its hidden crevices engulf picnicking schoolgirls. Predictably such narratives favour frontier settings, which commentators on the 'landscape-cinema'[21] have seen as the articulatory nexus of national filmic difference. Yet *Babe*'s terrain is pastoral, green and safe. These binaries are:

farm	city
safe	hostile
traditional	modern
structured	disordered

These binary oppositions immerse *Babe* into a distinct ideological framework that moves beyond the bush, beach and barbecue. *Babe*'s landscape is neither dusty and red, nor sandy and white. The cinematic palette has changed.

Babe was filmed in Robertson, in the New South Wales southern highlands. Yet this location has gained little publicity. Eager small business proprietors had hopes of erecting signs welcoming a tourist into 'Babe country'. Such advertisements were rejected by Kennedy Miller Productions. Similarly, the lifestyle programme *Burke's Backyard* tried to promote the region by featuring 'the Babe angle' in a story. As Michael Freeman, general manager of Don Burke's CTC Productions discovered, such publicity was blocked:

> to protect the secrecy surrounding Babe, to maintain, if you like the myth of Babe living in 'Nowheresville', springing from nowhere, the imagination.[22]

Such a desire unravels the directives of Australian film historiography. The landscape is always plural, yet Heidelberg eyes grazing this cinematic field will find few pleasures. Ross Gibson asked in 1983 'why mainstream film-makers, audiences and critics in Australia are currently under the spell of some spirit of the land'.[23] It seems that the spell has been broken. *Babe*'s landscape is a metonymy for a significant shift in Australian films. Hoggett's farm could be anywhere: it is a home without a home. This little film went a long way, but to make that journey it had to ditch a long-standing national cinematic obsession.

The reconciliation of an identifiably Australian landscape framed by American cinematic techniques formulates an odd meshing of styles and symbols. *Babe* was a complex denial of Australian landscape traditions. Yet, as Cosgrove has suggested, 'we should not scorn the study of imaginative geographies'.[24] Landscape is enmeshed in histories of seeing and ways of representing the world. *Babe*'s frame is a heterotopic visuality, where multiple ideologies are collapsed and othered.

If a landscape could speak, what would its accent be? What glottal and gestural inflections shape the Sydney streets of King's Cross or the red rock of Uluru? Contemporary imaginings of the landscape, post-Mabo, summon a plurality of stories. Yet David Carter's suggestion that 'no representation of Australia is possible today without reference to Aboriginal cultures'[25] is premature. While Australian filmic landscapes may have slipped out of the European semiotic paradigm, they have not moved into a post-colonial space.[26] As Eric Michaels surveyed, the Warlpiri Media Association in Central Australia invokes solipsistic graphics that are evocative rather than denotative in meaning so that 'the apparently empty shot is quite full of life and history to the Aboriginal eye'.[27] *Babe*'s rendering of the landscape is not an 'empty shot'. Conversely, the filmic frame is crammed with animals, buildings, fences and gates.

National identity is imagined through a myriad of cultural industries. Few imagining sites are as important as the film industry. Films do not reflect reality, but provide a trace of how national identities are presented and re-inscribed. During the process of what Kay Anderson and Fay Gale have described as 'struggles for imaginative supremacy',[28] landscapes reify social structures and perform the processes of domination and justification.

While *Babe* was the story of a little pig who went a long way, it is also the tale of an Australian film industry that no longer requires a national adjective to verify its importance. By engaging Hollywood tropes of film making, *Babe* provides a denouement to debates about Australian content. Certainly, the film's success within magazine-based journalism was placed solidly within a national frame.[29] As a popular film, *Babe*'s mobility transgresses the ideological and critical demarcations of cultural space. The film does not seem Australian: there are no Australian accents, native wildlife or recognisable landmarks.

The problem with this new renaissance in Australian films is that perhaps a distinct, repressive nationalism is being summoned, one that is reliant on capturing an Australianness that is quirky, odd and humorous. The ideology in these new Australian films is individualist, flighty and dissatisfied. Graeme Turner argues that:

> for countries such as Australia, with multiple ethnic and cultural traditions, there can be no return to a unitary explanation of national identity. Rather, Australians need to explore ways in which we can make best use of the multiplicity of our possible identities.[30]

Babe is not the best use of national iconography and the tactics of place. Yet is must not be ignored or displaced in Australian film history.

A year after *Babe*'s success, *Shine* replaced the little pig as the nation's cinematic success story. Yet the 69th Academy Awards was troubling for American film makers. The success of *The English Patient* and Geoffrey Rush's award as best actor resulted in Billy Crystal proclaiming 'Oscar ... an American export industry'.[31] The pig seems lost to filmic history. Yet like the best of popular culture, textual residues remain.

During an episode from *The X-Files*' fourth season, Mulder and Scully were investigating the mysterious death of a mutant baby, buried under a baseball diamond. The resultant case involved the agents discovering a run-down farm and a family of mutant brothers, with their mother locked in a box. To distract the brothers from killing the agents, Mulder and Scully released the farm animals. Scully repeated the mantra 'BaaRamEwe', the statement used by Babe to train sheep during the film's climactic dog trial. Her mobilisation of the phrase suggests much about both *The X-Files* and *Babe*. The intertextuality of Chris Carter's programme is matched with the commonsensical knowledge of a pig who wanted to be a sheep dog.

This chapter commenced on the beaches of Broome, with sand weathered by the memory of my parents' trauma and disenchantment. My analysis concludes with a television programme made in Vancouver. If there is a truth *out there* in the Australian landscape, then cinema will continue to tantalise us with fairy tales that we still want to believe.

NOTES

1. Oprah Winfrey, *68th Academy Awards Ceremony*, Channel 9 (26 March 1996).
2. Ross Gibson, 'Formative landscapes', in Scott Murray (ed.), *Australian Cinema*, (St. Leonards: New South Wales, Allen & Unwin, 1994), p45.
3. Jonathan Romney, 'Pigs Swill Be Pigs', *New Statesman and Society*, (15–29 December 1995), p.55.
4. The issue of accent is one that is increasingly common to Australian popular cultural studies. John Fiske, Graeme Turner and Bob Hodge dedicated a chapter to accent in *Myths of Oz*, (St Leonards: Allen and Unwin, 1987). In this analysis, they argued that 'the Australian accent is one of the clearest markers of Australianness', p.163. Similarly, Ian Craven, in his 'Introduction' to the edited collection *Australian Popular Culture*, (Cambridge: Cambridge University Press, 1994) noted that 'one of the most noticeable phenomena evident to students of popular culture in the past ten years has been the increasing ability of an Australian "accent" amongst the languages and discourse that compose the field of their studies', p.1.
5. Romney, p.55.
6. Brian McFarlane and Geoff Mayer, 'New Australian Cinema: Sources and Parallels in American and British Cinema', *Cinema Papers*, No.88 (May–June 1992), p.28.
7. Phillip Adams, 'Introduction', from James Sabine (ed.), *A Century of Australian Cinema*, (Port Melbourne: William Heinemann, 1995), p.x.
8. McKenzie Wark, 'Cinema II: The Next Hundred Years', in James Sabine (ed.), *A Century of Australian Cinema*, (Port Melbourne: William Heinemann, 1995), p.202.
9. Ruth Brown, '*Crocodile Dundee* and the Revival of American Virtue, in Ian Craven (ed.), *Australian_Popular Culture*, (Cambridge: Cambridge University Press, 1994), p.80.
10. Tony Safford, 'Two Or Three Things I Know About Australian Cinema', *Media Information Australia*, No.76 (May 1995), p.26.
11. Neil Rattigan, '*Crocodile Dundee*: Apotheosis of the Ocker', *Journal of Popular Film and Television*, Vol.15 (Winter 1988), p.151.
12. As Delia Falconer has realised, 'Kennedy-Miller appear to weather the exigencies of international film-funding capital through 'original' appropriation of 'international' tropes of film making', '"We don't need to know the way home" Selling Australian Space in the *Mad Max* Trilogy', *Southern Review*, Vol.27, No.1, (March 1994), p.36.
13. For discussion of the place of suburbia in Australian films, see Ian Craven, 'Cinema, Post-colonialism and Australian Suburbia', *Australian Studies*, No.9 (November 1995), pp.45–69.
14. B. McMahon and R. Quin, *Australian Images*, (Marrickille: Science Press, 1990), p.33.
15. Phillip Drew, *The Coast Dwellers*, (Ringwood: Penguin, 1996), p.11.
16. Graeme Turner, 'Whatever Happened To National Identity? Film And The Nation In The 1990s', *Metro*, No. 100 (Summer 1994–95), p.33.

17. Ferdinand Braudel, *The Mediterranean and the Mediterranean World of Philip II*, (London: Fontana, 1986).
18. Pauline Hanson is the Independent Member for Oxley and was elected during the 1996 Federal Election. A one-time candidate for the Liberal Party, she was dis-endorsed because of her overtly racist and inflammatory comments about indigenous and Asian-derived Australians. She was elected to parliament and, after her Maiden Speech, has gained enormous publicity. The 'Hanson issue' is probably the most divisive moment in Australia's post-war history. It is also serving to unravel much of the effective political work assembled through the policy of multiculturalism.
19. In a wonderfully evocative essay about the iconography of Australianness, Robert Drewe stated that 'Speaking personally, I know that the coast still makes many of my Melbourne academic friends uneasy. They dislike the beach as personal terrain. English departments especially seem to find it ideologically unsound. They find the milieu common and vulgar, populated by sandy children and hoi polloi. Their Anglo-Celtic skins burn easily or they get grit in their private parts or get dumped by waves. Or they worry about sharks. In other words, it epitomises Sydney', 'The beach or the bush?' *Island*, Issue 60/61 (Spring–Summer 1994), p.5.
20. Gibson in Murray, p.49.
21. Ibid.
22. Michael Freeman, quoted in Shelli-Anne Couch, 'The Little Pig Who Could', *Who Weekly* (7 April 1997), p.129.
23. Ross Gibson, 'Camera Natura: Landscape In Australian Feature Films', *Framework*, No.22/23 (Autumn 1983), pp.26–29.
24. D. Cosgrove, 'Geography Is Everywhere: Culture and Symbolism In Human Landscapes', in D. Gregory and Walford (eds.), *New Horizons in Human Geography*, (New Jersey: Barnes and Noble, 1989), p.133.
25. David Carter, 'Future Pasts', in D. Headon, J. Hooton, D. Horne (eds.), *The Abundant Culture: Meaning and Significance in Everyday Australia*, (St Leonards; New South Wales: Allen & Unwin, 1995), p.10.
26. Jon Stratton argued that 'English, and more generally European, landscape painting presupposes a particular politics of the experiences of land', in 'Landscapes: Central and Western Desert Paintings and the Discourse of Art', *Theory Culture and Society*, Vol. 11, No. 1 (February 1994), p. 119.
27. Eric Michaels, *Bad Aboriginal Art*, (St Leonards; New South Wales: Allen & Unwin, 1994), p. 93.
28. Kay Anderson and Faye Gale, 'Introduction', in Kay Anderson and Faye Gale (eds.), *Inventing Places: Studies in Cultural Geography*, (Melbourne: Longman Cheshire, 1992), p.7.
29. During the early months of 1996, the currency of *Babe* was high. The pages of the Australian listings magazine *TV Week* were littered with references to 'Samantha and Babe!' (3 February 3 1996), p.70, 'Move over, Babe!' (17 February 1996), p.2 and excessive coverage of the 68th Academy Awards under the headline 'Aussie Oscar Glory' (6 April 1996) p.74. The story by Jenny Cooney stated that 'Aussie film *Babe* was one of the Oscar front-runners', p.74.
30. Graeme Turner, *Making It National: Nationalism and Australian Popular Culture*, (St Leonards; New South Wales: Allen & Unwin, 1994), pp.76–77.
31. Billy Crystal, *69th Academy Awards Ceremony*, Channel 9 (27 March 1997).

10

The Castle:
1997's 'Battlers' and the Ir/Relevance of
the Aesthetic

STEPHEN CROFTS

Beyond Alan Finney, who bought the film for Village-Roadshow, few could have predicted the remarkable success of the low-budget comedy movie, *The Castle* (1997). Having grossed over $10m before the end of its release-year, the film now ranks amongst the top ten Australian films at the domestic box-office. Low expectations had been set in many quarters with news of a film made by people from television with no prior filmmaking experience, a film written in two weeks, shot in 12 days and completed at the tiny cost of just $700,000 – production circumstances barely known since the French *New Wave* – and with a publicity budget of only $750,000. The creative team, calling themselves Working Dog, consisting of Robert Sitch (director and co-scriptwriter), Jane Kennedy (co-scriptwriter, casting, sound and music), Tom Gleisner (co-scriptwriter) and Santo Cilauro (cinematographer, co-scriptwriter) certainly seemed to lack a track record in cinema. Having achieved huge success with their small-screen spoof on current affairs television, *Frontline*, the group did most of the filming using their own money and enjoying total artistic control, before Finney saw a rough cut, funded post-production and signed up Working Dog to a three-picture, first-refusal contract.

Such a success story raises two vital issues for any consideration of Australian cinema in the third decade of the feature film revival inaugurated by Government funding in 1970. Firstly, there is the question of why and how the film elicited such popular responses in late-1990s Australia. To this end, a textual analysis is developed below in conjunction with a reception study of the film.[1] Secondly, the film articulates some unprecedented and significant cross-fertilisation between film and television in terms of aesthetics and production processes. It therefore provides a vantage point from which to explore the possibilities of such 'hybrid' projects for Australian cinema as it enters the new millennium.

Hind Sight

With these concerns in mind, I wish to initiate analysis of *The Castle* through a comparison with another canonically Australian film. This is from twenty-five years previously, namely *The Adventures of Barry McKenzie* (1972). Both *The Castle* and *Barry McKenzie* are self-consciously Australian, particularly in their use of the vernacular. But there are crucial differences. For *The Castle* inhabits a space somewhere between the ocker satire of Humphries' film and the populist domesticity of broadcast television's nuclear families, with their various cosiness' and dysfunctions, celebrated in genres and programmes including sitcoms, funniest home-video shows, lifestyle programmes and 'soapumentaries' such as *Sylvania Waters*. These televisual influences mean that the comic mode of *The Castle* somewhat distances itself from *The Adventures of Barry McKenzie*'s aesthetic and epistemology of the cartoon and the comic strip. The earlier film, as I have argued elsewhere,[2] is stylistically very much a cartoon-like filmic version of the *Private Eye* comic strip, *The Adventures of Barry McKenzie*, on which the 1972 film was broadly based. Witness its stilted appearance, aided by Beresford's opting for the 'cartoonish' look generated by harsh, flat lighting and poster-paint colour schemes. Likewise in terms of characterisation, *Barry McKenzie* has scant interest in realistic representations, or notions of characterial wholeness. This is decidedly not the 'serious' business of richly humanist characterisation, nor even of any substantial concern to engage audience attention with the characters. Like the comic strip, *Barry McKenzie* operates serially rather than sequentially; its attention is on the cameo, the one-liner or the gag rather than on narrative progression. Coincidence predominates over causality, with Bazza (Barry Crocker) drifting through events more than initiating them.

In default of any complex characterisation or strong narrative drive, the film's vernacular and wit offer very strong points of identification. This was especially likely at the time of the film's release, when Australian accents and humour were indeed novel on screen, and the vernacular represented a cultural–nationalist assertion against British stilted expression and plummy accents. Barry's many colloquialisms – many devised by Humphries and Beresford *for* the film and *then* passing into the vernacular – were, of course, a prime motor of the film and its success.

Like black American slang, there is a cultural assertiveness in such speech's densely metaphorical forms, arguably pathologically dense in this Australian case. The vernacular thus works against any syntagmatic drive in the film – whose narrative is episodic at best – and celebrates wordplay and metaphor throughout, including the absurdly oneiric ("Bloody Poms'd take the harness off a nightmare"), a kind of infantile contiguity aphasia in Sarah Gort (Jenny Tomasin) ("When he takes me in his thumbs and goes to the hospital, I mustn't suck his arms") and innuendo extraordinaire (as in Dame Edna's (Barry Humphries) designs, secateurs in hand, on Mr Gort's 'rhododendrons'). *The Castle* has no such investment in vernacular wit detachable from character and narrative. Rather, it reverses the earlier film's aesthetic hierarchy, subordinating and assimilating wit and vernacular to characterisation and narrative. Whereas the aesthetic of *The Adventures of Barry McKenzie*'s renders verisimilitude a largely irrelevant consideration, arguably preferring infantile indulgence to any serious construction of everyday lived experience, *The Castle*'s aesthetic draws more on the (relatively) verisimilitudinous modes of television sitcom, funniest home-video shows, and even the family photo album. If *The Castle* has none of the vitriol or nihilism of *The Adventures of Barry McKenzie*'s satire – witness Edna's waspish wit: 'How unusual to serve spaghetti bolognese without the taste!' – it nevertheless still shares several aesthetic characteristics: a certain visual stasis with restricted points of view, both visual and characterial; a simplification and exaggeration, sometimes grotesque, in characterisation; and often limited narrative development.

All these aesthetic tendencies are substantially incommensurable with, or at least in tension with, those of mainstream Australian fictional film. To the extent that we aim to recognise such texts as 'Australian', the national cinema – conventionally characterised as feature films – clearly needs to be contextualised in terms of other audio-visual production within Australia. Cinema *shown* in Australia remains predominantly Hollywood, and thus defines itself as grand-scale, high-budget, glamorous and escapist. Cinema *produced* in Australia largely differentiates itself from Hollywood in terms of the specialist national and international distribution circuits still known as art cinema, and thus defines itself as small-scale, low-budget, usually local and sometimes 'different', 'refreshing' or 'quirky'. In this context, television seems a more fruitful comparator for analysis of *The Castle* altogether. In the later 1990s, convergences and differences between film and television have, more readily than previously, encouraged the two mediums to be treated alongside each other in considerations of audio-visual production within Australia. Convergences in production and circulation; and differences in terms of the *popularity* of local material on television. Of the latter, Philip Bell has noted both the growing popularity of Australian programmes on Australian television, and also the corresponding growth in vernacular genres such as magazine-style programmes, lifestyle programmes, sitcoms, variety and consumer advocacy.[3] The comparison with Australian films reveals an imbalance – supported in part by television's Australian content requirements – between the strong popularity of Australian material on television and its fitful popularity in movie theatres across Australia. Statistical evidence abounds. The inside back cover of the production trade journal, *Encore*, for example, fortnightly lists the ten highest-rating television programmes and the twenty most popular films on the exhibition circuit. Over the last few years, in the former list, Australian product dominates –usually seven or eight out of ten – while in the latter, it ranges between invisibility and at most five out of twenty, the range accounted for by the seasonally fluctuating release patterns of Australian films. Sitch described *The Castle* as Working Dog's response to Hollywood's box-office dominance in Australia: 'You know your budget has got to be a tenth of an American budget, but the price people pay to go to see it is the same.'[4] It is a response made with direct reference to television: *The Castle*'s striking boldness lies in its readiness to *converge* television and film by transposing televisual aesthetics into the field of feature cinema. At the same time, production methods and budget more characteristic of television better allow for competition with Hollywood films at the local box-office. The film thus mobilises forms of audience address which are typical of Australian commercial television, and remain populist in their address to the everyday, the private/domestic and the consumerist; as Philip Bell describes television's vernacular genres: 'credible, ordinary, apolitical and above all 'ours' – Australian [...p]redominantly anglo-centric (Anglo-Australo-centric?), chattily optimistic, sentimental or mildly humorous'.[5]

What, then, characterises *The Castle*'s visual style? It is arguable that the creative team capitalised not only on their budgetary constraints and Sitch's unfamiliarity with film direction (this was his first film), but also on Cilauro's limited shooting experience (only on television, including *Frontline*, and prior to that, 'Holy Communion video, Christenings and things like that. My family handed me a Super-8 camera and it was my job'). Many aspects of the visual style contribute to the stilted, simple aesthetic. Much of the shooting has a flat frontality in appearance (quite inappropriately recalling Godard's *Made in USA* (1966) and adopted for very different reasons!). The Super-16mm shooting stock, blown up to 35mm cinema release-prints retains a decidedly grainy look, along with its connotations of the everyday. The camera is almost entirely static, with no hand-held shots and only about a dozen camera movements in the entire film. When they occur, these are stumbling rather than sweeping, providing coverage rather than dramatisation: this is very much the kind of film the family at home could make. There is also the awkwardness of much of the framing and the 'clunkiness' of the editing, dictated partly by limited numbers of takes and by filming within an actual house at the airport's edge. These aesthetic strategies variously invoke the home video and the family snapshot, which is used repeatedly in the film – both as a framing and freezing device for live action footage, and in the photo Dad Darryl (Michael Caton) often points out on the wall – as well as for the film's sole publicity image. Budget limits on location shots – very few expansive exterior establishing shots, fleeting glimpses at most of large legal buildings – actually reinforce the domestic/familial focus which the film takes from its principal audio-visual inspiration, the television sitcom. For many audiences, the film's aesthetic untidiness and reference to these familiar domestic genres are likely to be more engaging than the grander, more aesthetically considered and more expensive filming strategies of more 'cinematic' films, and may well have contributed to *The Castle*'s success. A popular *recognition* of the familiar, in other words, may have figured significantly.

Similarly, audience address here involves recognition of familiar everyday figures, closer to the inhabitants of *Burke's Backyard*, than of *Lifestyles of the Rich and Famous*. Yet, this being a comedy with some 'satirical' edge, identification is not as straightforward as in non-comic genres. As Steve Neale and Frank Krutnik point out, 'the process of comedy more acutely involves a *play* between identification and distanciation'.[6] In *The Castle* the central characters, the Kerrigan family, are constructed as foci for both distanced recognition and identification: sometimes mocked, sometimes celebrated, sometimes to be laughed *at*, sometimes laughed *with* – and narratively, as we shall see, 'felt good' with. However, the film's ambivalent attitude towards the class lifestyle of its protagonists differs from *Roy and H G's Club Buggery* (or *Bug House*, as Queensland television guides coyly label it). There, most of the time there is an ironic – and thus satiric – distance ensuring a clear separation between the types and attitudes represented, and the narration's attitude towards them. In *The Castle*, the grotesque tendencies – albeit muted compared with those of *The Adventures*

of Barry McKenzie – readily facilitate what sometimes might more
accurately be called mockery than satire (the latter implies at least some
clear and/or ethical position). A well-known recent example of grotesque
mockery is perhaps represented by the construction of the 'ockerines' of
Muriel's Wedding (1994), led by Tania, played by Sophie Lee, differently
cast as the daughter Tracy in *The Castle*. The earlier film separates off these
figures as easy objects of dismissive laughter, setting them up as foil to
developmental change in the far more complexly characterised Muriel, with
whom viewers are urged to identify through her shifting relationships with
her family and with best-friend Rhonda. Centring on one unified group of
characters, *The Castle*, conversely, moves between serious and mocking
treatment of them.

    This ambivalence towards its characters is instanced in the range of
types deployed in *The Castle*: the loving patriarch who dotes on his family;
the devoted domestic-carer wife; the gormless son (and apple of Dad's eye);
and the daughter with a promising career in hairdressing. The grotesque and
the mocked can be risible here, but are also endowed – by acting, by script,
as well as by narrative and televisual familiarity detailed later – with
sufficient humanising and pathos-encouraging traits to urge credence as
characters, to render them, in the words of one review, 'ridiculous but
believable.'[7] Elsewhere, *journal* reviewers broadly accepted the film's
ambivalence of address. Several *broadsheet* reviewers, though, had troubles
worrying about whether the film was 'patronising' its characters (which
might be read as worry about how keen such reviewers – in a possibly
patronising way – were to *see* such characters).

    The opening 12 minutes establishing the characters are those where the
Kerrigans are more obviously laughed *at*. Witness the exposition of the
types cited in the paragraph above, and also Dad Darryl proudly striding
forth into the yard in his ugg boots, the house praised for being right next to
the airport *and* some power lines, and lauded for its fake chimney and fake
lace metal, one son being lionised by Dad as the 'ideas man' who is
obsessed with buying bric-a-brac, and so on. The relish here is apparent: the
director – disingenuously, one wonders – suggested they 'could have taken
forty minutes' on the introduction! However the film's narrative modulates
the address to the viewer once the plot gets underway, detailing the
threatened compulsory purchase of the family's beloved home, the castle of
the title, and their stubborn resistance to removal. The film now seeks to
align viewer identification with the cause of the 'battler' family fighting
against the developers and government who would destroy what the family
values above all else: their home. The naiveties, gullibilities and lack of

middle-class taste that were mocked earlier in the film, now take on the qualities of simple good-heartedness and family love, human decency and dignity, Darryl becoming, in the words of the *Cinema Papers* reviewer, 'noble and simple, but never stupid', even modestly heroic.[8] (The film's ambivalence ensures that its version of heroism connects it with a long-standing Australian trope of ambivalence towards heroism.) Moments of pathos around the potential loss of the Kerrigans' and neighbours' homes, about their solidarity and generosity, sad songs and wistful guitar music, interleave with growing evidence of the smugness and violence of the developers, and are also leavened by further instances of laughter *at* the family's taste and gullibility, including running gags about buying questionably useful objects, such as a pulpit, from the small-ads columns of *The Trading Post*. With narrative information relayed through son Dale's faux-naive voice-over, the potential for irony is strong; at the same time, the lack of differential distribution of such information not only precludes any suspense, but also urges an experiential identification with the Kerrigans discovering and fighting the bad news.

The loving, happy family which the film celebrates stands in marked contrast to the virulent anti-humanism of *The Adventures of Barry McKenzie* – which savages all and sundry with an indiscriminate nihilism – and also to the more humanised but still dysfunctional families endemic in the Australian film revival and several television genres. The happy family was a point of constant return in promotional coverage of the film, which was the only film screened in the Australian Film Institute's Festival of the previous year's Australian productions to have a not just a happy family, but also a father (perhaps the latter's exceptional status suggests some cultural anxiety about authority). In the film itself, the happy family convivially neutralises any unpleasantness that might be associated with mockery of the Kerrigans. It vitally informs the 'feelgood' outcome of the High Court decision in favour of the Kerrigans' contention that 'a home is built of love and memories'. The force of the feelgood and laughter factors may explain why so few reviewers served negative notices on the film: only two reviews and commentaries from a broadsheet sample of fifteen were negative[9] and from the tabloid sample of nineteen, there was only one negative, and one undecided.[10]

The predominant restriction of narrative point of view to Dad Kerrigan similarly reinforces the feelgood outcome. The one apparent departure from this emphasis is provided by the voice-over of son Dale (Stephen Curry), who presents the film as his story. Dale is, however, very much one of the family: especially in the opening exposition, it is his gormlessness which acts as a relay, and thus licenses much of the laughter *at* the characters. Such a quasi-distancing device facilitates the film's ambivalence towards its characters, and authorises interview promotions such as that of Michael Caton, who plays Darryl, maintaining that the film is 'not a snide putdown of ordinary people, it's a very affectionate look at them'.[11] This is indeed the predominant stress of the Press Kit and publicity material deployed in reports on the film. Only Cilauro at one point asserts something different: 'We love that whole sort of gentle humour, like making nice points ... as long as you can then undercut them.'

Ambivalent address in *The Castle* can arguably be rated as something of a luxury perhaps as having a post-modern 'bob each way', so to speak. If comedy regularly plays between identification and distanciation, the form which distanciation takes here is distinctly *flattering*, a key factor of the film. Much as the television satire show *Frontline* encourages us to feel superior to the vain naïf, anchorman Mike Moore, so *The Castle* often urges us to feel superior to the Kerrigans; the comic hyperbole ensures that very, very few audience members could have homes encumbered with *so* much 'dagginess' as theirs. More specifically, the film's ambivalent address collapses the ironic – and thus satiric – distance which would ensure a clear separation between the characters and attitudes represented, and the narration's attitude towards them (interestingly, Kennedy cites *This is Spinal Tap* (1982) as one of his favourite films). *Frontline*, has often been cynical enough to undermine any belief in ethical values, if not also to evacuate any concern with them. Laughter at the Kerrigans' grotesqueries allows viewers, in Neale and Krutnik's terms,[12] to identify with the narration's aggression towards their attitudes, but also simultaneously to disavow that identification. Especially since this distanciation is so flattering, positing the viewer as superior to the Kerrigans, viewer-recognition of the social self is the more readily disavowed. *The Castle's* luxuriant 'feelgood' address may have been appealing to those in 1997 whose everyday lived experience – of retrenchment, for instance, or the shrivelling of the welfare state – did not quite tally with the 'relaxed and comfortable' Australia infamously promised by the Prime Minister in his 1996 Federal election campaign.

A further, cosy feelgood appeal draws on the genre which most influences *The Castle*. Neale and Krutnik argue the centrality of jokes to television sitcom's viewer address:

> The telling of a joke [...] serves to establish a demarcation between an 'inside' ('we who share the joke') and an 'outside' [...]. Such jokes

create a communal bonding between the participants which establishes a relationship of *power*, of inclusion and exclusion. [...] The sitcom, then, represents an institutionalising of the pleasures and processes involved in joke-telling".[13]

The Castle repeatedly uses a collusive direct address, both from Darryl and from Dale, to engage viewer-identification. Much as the television sitcom arguably *colludes* with its viewer against that which falls outside its own 'inside',[14] so the film limits its outside to the 'weekender' cottage, to immediate neighbours also under threat, and to places where the fight is undertaken. In contrast with the extended family and the extra-familial communities typical of soap operas, *The Castle*'s tighter narrative sets up all outsiders and other settings as either extensions or foils to its own family drama. This domestic solipsism posits that which is outside its own nuclear-familial space as potentially threatening.

A similarly cosy appeal is made by the quaintly nostalgic setting of *The Castle*, harking back as it does to some familiar 'constructions' of the 1950s. This decade is now routinely celebrated by anglophone politicians and audio-visual industries as an era of innocence and 'family values' in much the same way as the Victorian Medievalism of Pugin, Carlyle, Ruskin and others evoked an era of supposed harmony and stability in the face of the social havoc wrought by the rise of industrial capitalism. *The Castle*, of course, appeared amid the social havoc wrought by neo-liberal, post-industrial capitalism. It may be significant that members of the scriptwriting team referred often to basing the characters in part on their own parents, whose defining values would have been those of the 1950s. The film's drastically limited number of exterior urban shots assists this nostalgic impression, as does the crucial casting of the parental roles of Darryl and Sal Kerrigan. Kennedy observes that "we ended up with probably two of Australia's most loved television characters". Both are from long-running soaps: Michael Caton, whose most familiar television role was as Uncle Harry in *The Sullivans*, set in the 1950s, and Anne Tenney, best known for her role as Molly Jones in *A Country Practice*, whose rural setting facilitates a similarly nostalgic display of 'older values'. Director Robert Sitch avers: 'In Australia Anne Tenney holds a place in all our hearts ... *A Country Practice* ... was around those days I still believed in Father Christmas.' Significantly, this nostalgic setting licenses ethnic, gender and familial representations which can be read as comforting because they elide the anxieties and complexities of the present (not to mention the past also!). Hence *The Castle*'s community of white Anglo-Celtic and other established, but not recent, immigrant ethnicities; its happy family and its thoroughly traditional division of domestic labour. Evocation of the 1950s may indeed suggest an insufficiently tangible structure of retrospect operating through the film, whose narrative is actually more reminiscent of 1930s *Dad and Dave* films than of almost any more recent Australian production; these were films which regularly defended family and home against outside threats. Significantly, though, *The Castle* does reinstate the Australian mother/wife figure which the *Dad and Dave* pictures habitually omitted from its family *dramatis personae* out of respect for/deference towards the *mother*land of Britain, and which *The Adventures of Barry McKenzie* at the beginning of the film revival hysterically repressed with the very odd, inbred non-family of phallic 'mother', Aunt Edna, and surrogate son, Bazza.[15]

A related aspect of *The Castle*'s address is what Cilauro calls the film's 'suburban fairy tale' of the Australian Battlers defending their quarter-acre of home ownership against 'big' business and government. The ostensibly left- populism of the fairytale is undermined by the virtual impossibility in political reality of the *deus ex machina* of Lawrence Hammill, QC (Charles Tingwell) – met by chance; how else? – a figure who would likely never volunteer his services, let alone free, to defend the case of even affectionately eccentric battlers from Coolaroo. It is notable that in a promotional interview, Caton cites as his favourite moment of the film that in which Darryl and the QC 'meet [...] outside the court and they talk about bringing up a family'.[16] In this sweeping populist gambit – drawing some of its force from Caton's famous Uncle Harry role in *The Sullivans* – the family neutralises class differences; just as Darryl's incomprehension of legalese in the High Court pretends to nullify the importance of legal and cultural capital; the humour, of course, papers over the social improbabilities. Indeed, the avuncular, caring Queen's Council might be read not as the representative of a socially equitable, caring state, but as a narrative contrivance which in its in own small way contributes to legitimating in Australia the Howard Government's then recently accelerated dismantling of institutional support for social justice and equity.

In this context, the Kerrigans' class position takes on considerable significance. If they lack cultural capital, they nevertheless represent the small-business petit-bourgeoisie (the same 'class fraction' as the alarmingly influential racist Independent MP Pauline Hanson, and the inhabitants of *Sylvania Waters*). The material success of their tow-truck business combines with their home ownership to mark them as 'epitomising the fruition of the Australian dream.'[17] These are battlers who have made good, who are *not* victims of structural unemployment, *nor* dependent on the welfare state. As a focus of identification in a contemporary Australian film, they meshed perfectly with the anti-welfare discourses being vigorously promoted by the Howard Government in the later 1990s, and such families referenced in comedies elsewhere.[18] Not only does the working-class lifestyle of the Kerrigans enable them to be laughed at, but it also qualifies and naturalises what is actually above-average economic wealth, particularly since what it often mocked is *what the Kerrigans' decide to spend their money on*. This has two consequences. Firstly, it enables the film to exploit positively notions of the Australian 'dream', egalitarianism and the battler that cluster around the Kerrigans: as if anybody can succeed despite lifestyle (also read, economic?) adversity. Secondly, the occlusion of the material by the lifestyle/consumerist enables the film virtually to transcend class as an operative category, and thus underwrites a broadly sweeping populist worldview.[19]

Populism and the Nation

Some points about populism and its politics need to be drawn together here. The film's domestic solipsism, with its *Dad and Dave* echoes, posits that which is outside its own nuclear-familial space as potentially threatening. This collusive and suspicious address combines with the precisely unexplained, chance nature of the QC's intervention and the family's virtual transcendence of class to support a populist suspicion of politics, that is, of the real relations of power within the social formation. In their critique of Australian populism, Noel King and Tim Rowse write of television's 'address to the bothered consumer, as someone beyond politics, whose side the telecast is taking'.[20] Philip Bell, Kathe Boehringer and I have also noted of televisual (especially commercial television's) coverage of the 1980 Federal election campaign, how its constructions shrank the public sphere to its own privatised one of comforting domestic images, and how it set itself up as indifferent to *and* displacing politics.[21] In 1997, *The Castle* was able to exploit some fourteen additional years of populist media cynicism about politics.

   This populist structure of the televisual institution siding with the viewer against an other – Government/Politics/The Outside World – finds its parallel in the film's narrative, which triumphally seeks to align the viewer with the battler against government and 'big' business. At the film's end, the latter dutifully disappears for the film to celebrate the happy family. In terms of the film's address when *not* engaged in the narrative – ie. where mockery of the Kerrigans' working-class lifestyle is uppermost, and where address is designed to elicit laughter – a fascinating homology emerges. For the structure of populist thinking is almost isomorphic with that of laughter. As observed above, laughter (1) sets up an other to be ridiculed; (2) urges identification with the aggressive not-other (self) who does the laughing; and (3) disavows the aggression to preserve the ego. Populism similarly (1) sets up an other to be stigmatised or scapegoated; (2) urges identification with the aggressive not-other (self) who does the stigmatising/scapegoating; and (3) disavows the aggression to preserve the ego. Additionally, populism deploys (1) in order to disavow and displace a centrally operative form of division within the social formation – usually economic relations or 'class' as analysed by political economy, with other, less operative, forms of division which serve as decoys – Other Ethnic Group(s)/Other Nation(s) – for the former. Populism offers a sense of unity predicated on an other against which it defines itself. The populist address of *The Castle*'s laughter stigmatises the working-class lifestyle of the Kerrigans and the 'daggy' grotesque guarantees that 'nobody could really live like that'. This is the process of occlusion noted above whereby it is not another ethnic group which is othered and stigmatised, but – appropriately for the late 1990s – a lifestyle.

There are, of course, tensions between self and other which underpin the false homogeneities produced by these structures of populist narrative and laughter. The unitary fiction of the happy family ending neatly spirits away their nasty enemies, and thus any aggression involved. Similarly, the narrative moves which culminate in the triumphal outcome neatly modulate the Kerrigan family from object of laughter to agent of success, and thus spirit away any aggression involved. Structures of both narrative and laughter celebrate the spectatorial ego.

A number of accounts of the film fascinatingly reveal these self/other tensions, especially when considering the film in relation to that favourite unitary fiction, 'the nation'. Witness the following account of the film , whose discourse separates out contradictions which the film seeks to anneal:

> *The Castle* is best described as a *realistic* version of *Sylvania Waters* … while *The Castle* is pure *fantasy*, built around a foundation of Australiana which ranges from a laminex pool room dripping with trophies to a granny flat turned into a greyhound kennel, it is also *spot on* in its portrayal of aspects of the *national identity*.[22]

'To laugh at our national identity', as the article's by-line has it, is to exploit, in Sitch's words quoted in the article, 'something unique about the Australian humour. Its sense of self-depreciation [sic] is quite distinctive.' What calls itself 'self-deprecation' here is not really a national matter at all, but rather a case of one social group deprecating another within the social formation. Elsewhere, the filmmaking team expresses sensitivity to criticisms that they might be superciliously mocking the Kerrigans' lifestyle, denying 'some kind of comic attack on working-class Australia'.[23] Another review similarly invokes an essentialist fiction of the national, in this case 'cultural cringe': 'If it sounds like wall-to-wall kitsch, ripe for yuppies to lampoon, *The Castle* actually transcends satire to become a kind of tribute to the essence of our cultural cringe.'[24]

How, then, does the film construct other politics of moment? It has to be said that its likening of the Kerrigans' dispossession to that of Aborigines – 'I'm really starting to understand how the Aborigines feel', states Darryl – is neither undercut nor trivialised by the film. However, viewers' readings of such ideas may beg to differ from any preferred reading. Especially as catalysed/incited by the racist rhetoric of Pauline Hanson – Perera and Pugliese wrote of the contemporary 're-licensing of racism in Australia'[25] – the tabloid press at this time was strikingly less tolerant of black Australians than were the broadsheets. In a report on the film, a paper such as *The West Australian* apparently felt the need to reassure its readership that 'the heavy [pro-Aboriginal] socio-political stick is not wielded too menacingly in this warm […] tale.'[26] And using the label 'controversial', *The Castle*'s own Press Kit similarly distances itself from the pro-Aboriginal film, *Dead Heart* (1996), when it lists the film as one of Anne Tenney's credits. In terms of immigrant ethnicities, *The Castle* ambivalently supports *both* racist and anti-racist views: the casual racism of 'What is it with wogs and cash?', for instance, is barely countered by giving Lebanese neighbour Farouk (Costas Kilias) some fine lines: 'Here the planes drop the value [of the house]. In Beirut they drop the bombs.' The ethnicities shown are of established immigrant groups – Lebanese, Greek (Con, Tracy's husband played by Eric Bana) and another Mediterranean (the solicitor Dennis Denuto –Tiriel Mora) but significantly, and safely, not recent Asian ones of the kind railed at by Hanson. The years 1996 and 1997 in Australia saw a politically motivated mobilisation, by both the Prime Minister and Hanson, of the – historically always white Anglo – figure of the 'battler', the underdog who battles all odds to survive. (They operated as a virtual coalition as long as Howard refused to condemn her racism – he for a long time defended her on grounds of free speech – and while he 'represents himself as speaking *for* the Aussie battler, Hanson has represented herself *as* the authentic Aussie battler'.)[27] On the gender front, as noted above, *The Castle*'s family endorses a thoroughly traditional division of domestic labour.

Conclusions

The film's box-office success suggests how well its predominantly right-wing populist discourses, then, resonated in the Australia of early 1997: an anxious national formation affected by the unease generated by global economic forces – de-industrialisation, casualisation and retrenchments of labour, privatisation, the dismantling of social services – is compounded by a growing, racist unease *vis-à-vis* Asia, although none of this is imaginable from the film. One almost uncanny symptom of this anxiety is to be found in several reviews regretfully predicting *The Castle*'s lack of exportability (the markets likely envisaged would be the UK and USA)[28] This sad resurgence of cultural cringe is sadder for its echoing and reinforcing Howard's 'Little Australia' thinking.

The Castle also suggests much about the current state of the Australian audio-visual industries. *The Castle* gleefully crosses the film/television divide, hybridising film and television aesthetics and production processes more boldly and shamelessly than previous Australian films. It reaches beyond the familiar film/television convergences of television funding much film production; of television serving as principal, if not first, exhibition site for films thus funded; and the common transfers of personnel between the two media (which has led to strong televisual influences in Australian filmmaking visuals, not least in *Crocodile Dundee* (1986), which for all its grand tourist vistas, still lives by codes of televisual framing). *The Castle* exploits television's generic and aesthetic codes to a greater extent than previous Australian films. Its creative team has achieved outstanding success on television, notably with *Frontline*, on which almost all the film's crew had worked. The film casts actors known above all for their television roles; this of course hugely assisted newspaper publicity for the film. With the Press Kit listing every actor's television credits before any film credits, reviewers and other journalists were encouraged to write in television-familiar terms. *The Castle*'s enterprising aesthetic populism cleverly exploits, and seeks to redress the imbalance detailed above between the strong popularity of Australian material on television and its fitful popularity in cinemas in Australia. In this context, it is reasonable to suggest that Australia's star system is to be found on television rather than in the cinema (with due recognition allowed for the distance associated with cinematic stars and the familiarity attached to television stars or 'personalities'), and that Working Dog accordingly played on the difference. In the 1997 Australian Film Institute Awards, which. like the Oscars, reward the culturally respectable end of the production spectrum, *The Castle*, for all its manifest television influences and box-office popularity, was not overlooked. The major competition being *Kiss or Kill* (1997), *The Castle* won one award – appropriately indeed – for Original Screenplay. Working Dog is redefining 'poor cinema' in terms of television, of the avowedly popular, and of an assertive Australian populism which resonated disturbingly with the 'Little Australia' political discourses of 1997.

NOTES

1. The continuities between textual analysis and reception studies are theorised in Stephen Crofts, *Genre, Gender and Identification in Film: The Case of 'Shame'* (Melbourne: Australian Film Institute, 1993).
2. See Stephen Crofts, 'The Adventures of Barry McKenzie: Comedy, Satire and Nationhood in 1972', *Continuum*, Vol.10, No.2 (1996), pp.123–140.
3. Philip Bell, 'Television: Re-viewing Aussie Populism', in Philip Bell and Roger Bell (eds.), *Americanisation and Australia* (Sydney: University of New South Wales Press, 1998), pp.193–209.
4. All uncredited quotations on *The Castle* are taken from the film's Press Kit.
5. Bell, pp.204–209.
6. Steve Neale and Frank Krutnik, *Popular Film and Television Comedy* (London and New York: Routledge, 1990), p.149; original emphasis.
7. Tim Hunter, *Cinema Papers*, No.116 (May 1997), pp.44–46.
8. Ibid, pp.44–46.
9. *The Age* (Melbourne), 'EG' Section, 11 April 1997, p. 23, and *The Weekend Australian*, 12–13 April 1997, p.23.
10. See *The Sunday Mail* (Brisbane), 13 April 1997, pp.18–19, and *The Gold Coast Bulletin*, 12 April 1997, p.16, respectively.
11. *The Daily Telegraph* (Sydney), 22 March 1997, p.13.
12. Neale and Krutnik, p.79.
13. Ibid., p.243.
14. Mick Eaton, 'Television Situation Comedy', *Screen*, Vol.19, No.4 (Winter 1978–79) p.73.
15. See Crofts, 1996, p.37.
16. *The Gold Coast Bulletin*, (5 April 1997), p.4.
17. Kennedy, quoted in *The Canberra Times* (27 March 1997), p.16.
18. Comedies, of course, are not often socially responsible, but two less triumphalist accounts of Australian working-class life are worth recalling here. Overlaying social-realist generic elements with rape- and heist-plots respectively, *Blackrock* (1997) and *Idiot Box* (1997) construct genuinely working-class milieu, and are firmly set in Newcastle and in Sydney's Western suburbs, respectively.
19. The creative team seem to consider lifestyle alone in regularly referring to the Kerrigans as working-class, and particularly when denying 'some kind of comic attack on working class Australia.' See for example, *The Canberra Times* (27 March 1997), p.16.
20. Noel King and Tim Rowse, '"Typical Aussies": Television and Populism in Australia', *Framework*, No.22–23 (Autumn 1983), p.42.

21. Philip Bell, Kathe Boehringer and Stephen Crofts, *Programmed Politics: A Study of Australian Television* (Sydney: Sable, 1983).
22. *The Examiner* (Launceston), 6 April 1997, p.2; my emphasis.
23. *The Canberra Times*, 27 March 1997, p.17.
24. *Sydney Morning Herald*, 25 April 1997, p.20.
25. Suvendrini Perera and Joseph Pugliese, '"Racial suicide": The Re-Licensing of Racism in Australia', *Race and Class*, Vol.39, No.2 (October–December 1997), pp.1–20.
26. *The West Australian*, 19 March 1997, p.16.
27. Ibid.
28. *The Sunday Mail* (Brisbane), and *The Sunday Times* (Perth), both 13 April 1997.

11

Idiot Box:
Television, Urban Myths and Ethical Scenarios

KAY FERRES

In *Gangland: Cultural Elites and the New Generationalism*, Mark Davis offers a devastating analysis of the shrinking arena of public culture and political debate in contemporary Australia, an arena he sees as monopolised by a post-war generation with its hands firmly on the wheel of public opinion-making, and wielding its influence to keep a younger generation out of the cultural mainstream. Davis describes the ways in which this generation maintains its ascendancy in creating and brokering ideas, installing its own 'summer of love' values as the moral high ground, unwilling 'to admit that ideas can no longer pretend to cut across all times and places',[1] and lashing out at youth culture. Turning his attention to a raft of recent controversies, from the vilification of the young women complainants in the Ormond College sexual harassment case, to the pillorying of the Paxtons on the television news-magazine *A Current Affair*, Davis claims that 'it is in the highly public arena of the arts and the media that the backlash against youth culture is given its most vicious spin'.[2]

Davis draws his examples largely from print culture, from the broad-sheet press to the world of literary publishing; as he puts it, the 'areas of culture that are deemed to have "intellectual" content'.[3] This emphasis certainly helps his case, since the public institutions which support this culture – publishing houses, the mogulised media, the universities – are, in times of economic rationalism, contracting. But this emphasis also means that he cannot take account of the visual cultures – television, film, video – which draw in the 18–25-year-old demographic, and which have a recent history of contesting mainstream representation. Though Davis makes passing reference to the popular appeal of television soap operas such as *Melrose Place*, or pro-censorship panic induced by *Romper Stomper* (1992), or the films of Quentin

Tarantino, his 'insider job' written from the University of Melbourne's English Department, necessarily engages with, and to some extent reproduces, the preoccupations of the baby boomer elite he so wittily takes on. I want to take an opportunity here to discuss a film which covers some of the same ground as Davis, namely David Caesar's *Idiot Box* (1996).

Idiot Box ends with the shooting death of its urban anti-hero, Kev (Ben Mendelsohn), when police marksmen respond precipitately at a crime scene. The film explicitly pushes the buttons of contemporary urban panics: fears about listless unemployed youth, perceptions of an increase in crime and the failures of public policy in addressing these problems. This is the diagnosis of urban ills that the film works with: its focus is an urban myth of alienation expressed through a range of problematic behaviours: domestic sloth, larrikinism which edges into vandalism, and at the extreme, violence and drug addiction. But more specifically, the film targets the way the mass media is drawn into debates about these social problems, for Kev's foray into crime is set against the representation of violence in movies, television and video games, and against a concern with his habitual television-viewing. From such a perspective, *Idiot Box* examines television spectatorship as a complex cultural practice in the register of black comedy, drawing upon well-established discourses of masculinity and suburban life which hinge on the iconic 'idiot box', here understood interchangeably as the television set and the brick veneer house. Although the film documents the failure of the circuit of mass production and consumption which television and suburban living were meant to secure, it does not simply set itself up as an oppositional critique; rather it 'white-ants' the modernist project from within, disarticulating and reconfiguring academic and popular discourse about television.

The narrative turns on, and interrogates, the claim that the representation of violence on television and in movies is directly linked to an increasing incidence of violence in the community. This claim rests on an assumption that the difference between the real and the imaginary is all but erased by the vividness of the representations themselves, and that viewing is a passive but utterly absorbing practice. The opening scenes of the film, which show Kev and Mick (Jeremy Sims) watching videos, drinking and behaving badly toward Kev's protesting girlfriend, invoke this position and expose its inadequacies. These are not passive viewers, though they are habitual ones: their discussion reveals their familiarity with the conventions of crime drama, their recognition of the mistakes that undo the best-laid of criminal plans and open the way for the law to triumph, and the operations of melodrama's cross-over of action plot and emotional complication. Kev and Mick recognise the pitfalls which await the characters and actively manipulate the plot, re-making it to accommodate alternative resolutions. As viewers (but as the film insists, not as social subjects), they are in a powerful position: smarter than the robbers, armed with a knowledge of police strategy, able to outwit the authorities. These are the pleasures of spectatorship, pleasures which are extended and reworked in lounge room play. Their comic simulation of the bank heist stops short at the getaway scene: they can't supply the basic accoutrements of the bank robber, a car and an accomplice. This opening gambit sets up a proposition about the allure of representation, whilst engaging a position widely taken up in media and cultural studies (and used to counter assertions about the media's overweening influence) namely, that audiences need to be understood as actively constructing and contesting meaning, rather than as text-bound; that subject positions inscribed in the text do not set limits on the interpretation of actual viewers. The unfolding narrative tests both kinds of claim.

The comic pretence of robbing a bank is projected into real life incrementally and opportunistically, as Kev's boast that he could do better than the fictional robbers materialises less as a plan than as a series of reckless acts. The pair steal an unlikely getaway car and hoon around, then approach the local drug dealer about guns, yet the narrative is not propelled by the conventions of crime genres, nor do Kev and Mick take up recognisably criminal identities. At some level, this is still lounge room play, but with real props. As the local police sergeant later observes, Kev is 'dickhead of the week', not a crim with form. The audience witnesses performances of bravado which cement their mateship and confirm their interdependence, as Kev demonstrates and reaffirms his ascendancy, and Mick shows that he knows his place. The timeless and plotless picaresque of Mick and Kev's existence, always in the present, organised through endless repetition, resembles the daytime soap: Kev's mother characterises them as 'The Young and the Useless'. They drift from the house to the bottle shop, to the shopping mall and the Commonwealth Employment Service, spinning out their lives across the sameness of the spaces of consumption. The parallels with soap opera are clear enough, but what is missing are the familiar devices of emotional engagement, the telephones and doorbells, which are critical to soap opera's preoccupation with social relations. Kev and Mick scarcely interact with anyone at all.

Alongside these picaresque preoccupations, a second plot unfolds. A police investigation is beginning into a series of bank hold-ups. Again, the gritty glamour of the filmic crime genres is absent, displaced by the established conventions of Australian television cop shows: a pair of detectives, desultory conversation in the car and with desk officers, action largely consisting of getting in and out of cars, an ironic matching of wits in interviews with suspects and informers. In all, hardly a sign of violence or crime is evident until a hold-up is broadcast on the television news. At this point, the two plots converge, and as the two unemployed youths transform themselves into a hold-up gang, the soap opera picaresque is overwritten by the conventions of the crime genre. Kev makes the classic mistakes that Mick has described: he tells his 'missus' and 'pisses off' another 'crim'.

Television as a Promiscuous Object

The critical turning point occurs when the guns change hands. This scene turns ugly and culminates in a vicious assault, as Kev takes the guns without payment. Colin Shand (Steven Rae) turns 'dog' and informs the police. This pivotal moment is signalled by another act of violence, as Kev kicks a television set apart. The image of rage and frustration directed at the 'idiot box' is familiar enough, signifying a breakdown in the proper relations of communication. But this image is doing other work as well. As Elspeth Probyn describes the kind of work images can do, this one 'winks' at the viewer, nodding in the direction of an established meaning (in this case, that television is properly held in low esteem) but at the same time opening up other possibilities. In this case, where the film has already 'nodded' to two viewing positions – one which is confirmed in its prejudices about the 'idiot box' and another, more knowing, which cites 'active audiences' who 'negotiate meanings' – it invites us to 'follow the references mobilised by these winking images … to find ways of troubling their discursive stability'.[4] Following the references in this case involves making a different kind of connection between Kev's two violent acts, reading the television set and the guns as objects of exchange, and looking to the social contexts in which those exchanges occur.

I want to describe these exchanges as a starting point for a discussion of the wider debates about television and social relations to which *Idiot Box* refers. In doing so, I will leave the narrative aside, to concentrate on the film's interest in debates about audiences, about the place of television in discourses of modernity and about the reform of masculinity. Despite its preamble, this account is concerned less with the narrative elements of a particular film than with its representation of television and its audiences, and with the way television's place in urban social relations is discussed and understood. Its uses of the conventions of melodrama to cut across its representation of, and commentary on, those relations will be taken up again later to explore the film's engagement with modernist critiques of television and its address to its pluralised audiences. *Idiot Box* offers a commentary on urban social life which is built around a representation of its young male protagonists, Mick and Kev, as consumers of the culture of late modernity, and their lives are played out across its key suburban sites: the living room, the streets, the shopping mall and the pub. These spaces, and the practices and habits associated with them, are implicated in the production of class and gender identities. *Idiot Box* can be usefully read as one of a raft of 1990s films which address the redefinition of masculinity in contemporary contexts – for example *Strictly Ballroom* (1992), *The Sum of Us* (1994), *The Adventures of Priscilla, Queen of the Desert* (1994), *Romper Stomper* (1992) or the more recent *Thank God He Met Lizzie* (1997) and *The Road to Nhill* (1997) – and which construct ethical scenarios to accommodate the transformation of gendered social relations.

The television set which Kev destroys was offered as a gift for his mother. He buys it in the pub from a junkie, who sells it to finance her addiction. In this transaction, the set's value is linked first to its low price, and second to the prospect of further transactions with the seller. Kev recognises the junkie's desperation, just as in an earlier scene when he saw her on the shopping centre escalator, he recognised her sexual attractiveness. He does not allow her to think twice about his offer for the set, slipping the money into her pocket in a proprietorial way. But his mother rejects the present, as she rejects what she sees as Kev's resemblance to his father. His anxiety that his mother is right, that he is 'useless', is displaced by his acting on his desire to be 'fearless'. The robbery, and ultimately his death, are actions which confirm this desire, expressed in his own 'poem': 'Maximum fear, minimum time'.

The original sale of the set also sets in train the 'real' robbery: the junkie's partner is distressed not only by the loss of the set itself, but by her failure to honour a promise to stop using drugs. By removing the television set, she has taken something away from him: not just his viewing pleasure, but his sense of intimacy with her. He discusses leaving her over a game of pool with his mate. His gang hits the local bank at the same time as the amateurs turn up.

The television set functions in this series of exchanges as a promiscuous object.[5] Its status changes from commodity to gift according to its intended use, the relationship (dependent or independent) between the parties to the exchange and the context (market or domestic) in which the exchange occurs. The meanings which attach to a gift are bound up in dependent, familial relations, and the failure of an exchange can have profoundly detrimental effects on those relations. In this instance, the set loses its mystique and becomes an unexchangeable object. I want to tease out the distinction between the commodity and the gift, because television is conventionally discussed as a commodity in the circuits of production and consumption which characterise late capitalism. The specification of the kind of commodity it is has largely been left to feminist critics. Laura Mulvey,[6] and Lynn Joyrich,[7] for example, have discussed a scene in Douglas Sirk's small-town melodrama, *All That Heaven Allows* (1955), where a middle-class woman is given a television set as compensation for a decision not to make an unsuitable marriage, trading-off the active pursuit of desire for the passive pleasures of consumption. This kind of trade-off is often seen to be at work in television's address to a largely feminine audience: it represents the consolations offered to offset the housewife-viewer's confinement (the feminine viewer is almost invariably identified with the housewife) within domestic space. These analyses focus on objectification: the passive receptivity or over-identification of the feminine consumer is linked to the images of woman-as-object on the screen, the feminine identity which is constructed through, and constituted by, the active masculine look. This analysis assumes and reproduces an understanding of the organisation of gender which aligns domestic space and consumption with femininity, public space and work with masculinity. In *Idiot Box*, those relations have been reorganised: it is women who are in paid employment; the young unemployed men who have the leisure, but not the means, for consumption. Even though television viewing is no longer contained within domestic space – there are sets in shopping malls and pubs – it is the male characters who spend most time in front of the television at home. Colin Shand runs his drug deals from a garage with the set permanently on: 'The whole world in a box in the corner of the room', he marvels, ironically echoing the sales pitch of television's early promoters. Lynn Spigel has described the considerable work involved in installing the television set in American homes in the 1950s,[8] and feminist scholarship on spectatorship and consumption has paid attention to the domestic and familial contexts of viewing,[9] but generally speaking, these analyses are organised around the gendered separation of the public and private spheres of production and consumption respectively. Television is located in a capitalist system of exchange relations which offers classed and gendered positions to participants in those relations.

Idiot Box does not inscribe exchange relations in this way. The television set which fails as a gift also exists outside these spheres of legitimate economic exchange. His mother does not want it in the house, and Kev cannot resell it in the pub, because this is a space associated with the sale of stolen goods. As an object, the set is out of place in the syntax of the gift, and it does not assume the equivalence of value which underpins commercial exchange: it is out of the loop of reciprocity which operates in social and economic relations. The transactions surrounding the set serve to underline the extent to which unemployment and suburban isolation produce a population excluded from exchange relations. *Idiot Box*'s attention to youth culture is not directed to the tired clichés of the breakdown of family life; its targets are economic. The violence of Kev's destruction of the set signifies something other than a precarious psychological state or a failure to repress aggression: the failure of the social relations of production and consumption, which hinged on television's inflation of the rhetoric of 'choice', is at the centre of the filmic representation of urban malaise.

Kev and Mick repeatedly visit the bottle shop: in a parody of consumer choice, they argue but always buy the same beer, and are always short of money. Lani, the attendant, always accepts what they have and calculates the terms of the exchange. In a similar way, they meet the requirements of Social Security. In exchange for the dole, they report for assessment, and register their 'special skills': Mick as a poet, Kev as a fashion photographer. The departmental officer, unlike Lani, knows that he cannot redeem the deficit, the absent term which 'special skills' refers to – work. Mick attempts to redeem it himself, putting his identity as a poet to work in social interactions, reciting on request, troubling over what a poem is, what are its appropriate subjects. The barmaid objects to his poem, 'Hope': 'You can't have a poem about being on the dole'. But he persists with this unpromising subject, and later produces 'Hate': 'Monday's I don't mind/ They're like something could happen/Fridays I hate/They remind you nothing ever changes'.

Audiences: Making Meaning, Transferring Knowledges

Television viewing is a constant in the lives of Mick and Kev: their everyday existence moves between the couch and the bottle shop, and revolves around their consumption of beer and videos. They are neither passive viewers nor 'cultural dopes'; indeed, television viewing is one sphere of life in which they are active, and it is a habit which supports their friendship. They do, however, bring different capacities to bear on their viewing. Mick is more socially adept than Kev: he makes tea in an effort to appease Kev's mother; he makes acquaintances by participating in, and maintaining, casual exchanges; he uses talk to defuse potentially difficult situations. These are cultural competencies usually ascribed to women, but they are also the competencies which are repeatedly demonstrated in the resolution of soap opera dilemmas. Mick transposes genres from one medium to another, and transfers knowledges across different spheres of life. When he and Lani go to bed, his repertoire derives not from direct experience but from television. It has provided an education in sexual technique that he puts into practice: foreplay and oral sex; attention to his partner's pleasure before his own. The one sign of inexperience is his failure to provide a condom, remedied when he raids his brother's drawers (where he finds only one). Television plays a role in Mick's friendship with Kev, but it does not substitute for other forms of interaction in his relationship with Lani. Mick's fantasies are not spun out of television's address to its audiences. Rather, they are elicited by a bureaucracy which cannot deal with unemployment, with the failure of the circuit of high-wage productivity, mass production, and mass consumption which underpinned suburbanisation. He calls himself a poet, a claim which is not just fanciful, or simply a joke. He cultivates a poetic disposition, that is, he actively imagines and invents stories, and invites others to participate in them. He takes Lani for a walk to the freeway overpass, where they each invent a story about the cars below, his a road narrative of escape and new beginnings, hers not a narrative but an evocation of a state: she imagines a couple who decide to be 'happy'.

Tastes and viewing habits, and sexual activity, operate quite differently in Kev's relationship with his girlfriend. He refuses to takes her out and derives pleasure from denying her wishes. The dynamic of masculine dominance and feminine protest never varies. Their interactions invariably take place in front of the screen, including sexual interactions. After an inept encounter on the couch during a news broadcast, she announces her dissatisfaction very bluntly: 'I've had a piss that's lasted longer'. Kev's attention returns quickly to the screen, to a news report of a bank hold-up, which uses footage from a surveillance video recording, the images giving the illusion of presence, making the viewer a witness of 'live' action. Kev's gaze is driven by a desire to be there, in the action. Insofar as this represents a desire for unachievable power and control, his active looking is a tactic of the weak, excluded from the public spaces where desire is activated. It is also voyeuristic: in the shopping mall he surveys young women on the escalator, classifying 'spunks' and 'dogs' as their bodies move away, out of his and the camera's range. This reverses the usual representation of the voyeuristic look, which operates first through distancing and framing (the key hole, the window), and then in close-up, with the camera standing in for the subject of the look, whose gaze is often extended by an instrument, field glasses, or a telescopic sight. Kev's look does not fix its object and is quickly distracted. Just as he lacks the equipment to put his 'special skill' of fashion photography into practice, so his shopping mall perving falls short of true voyeurism. The amusement arcade, with its video games, offers the only possibility of activating desire.

Kev's sighting of the hold-up offers a moment of identification which draws the film's two plots together. The cinema audience has already seen the robbery, followed by images of a vast expanse of suburban brick and tile, crowned with a tangle of TV aerials. The image on Kev's screen completes the relay of representation which Mary Poovey describes as distinctively post-modern. Sketching a history of representation, she distinguishes a series of non-sequential stages, including the post-modern in which:

> the infinitely replicable, often electronically transmitted image always precedes one's experience of the thing itself or even renders the thing redundant, because the image is both larger than life and amenable to commodification and consumption on a global scale.[10]

This kind of representation is often taken to apply across the board in a 'media saturated' society where the visual image dominates. Yet as Poovey cautions, the transition from earlier 'modern' forms is uneven and incomplete. Panics about the media's influence often proceed from a simplistic view of the transmission of transparent images to passive viewers, and from an anxiety that the consumption of images is undiscriminating, accompanied by a removal from the 'real' and an acquired immunity to the image's material effects. Mass culture's subordination of difference to homogeneity, its presentation of itself as a series of repetitions and its organisation of desire through consumption appears, from such perspectives, to run counter to values of individuality and community. This view is articulated in the irony of *Idiot Box*'s title, and by the detectives as they drive along the freeway flanked by endless rows of brick veneer: if this is the arsehole of the universe, the police force is the toilet paper.

In its attention to viewing as the active production of meanings and identities, not limited to the range offered by a single text, and as a transposable, tactical cultural practice, *Idiot Box* discounts a simplistic reading of Kev as a television addict, as desperate for a fix as the heroin user, unable to distinguish representations from material reality. It calculates his capacity to choose among a range of potential identifications, or more accurately, the deficit or lack by which he falls short of the possibilities consumption offers. By contrasting the way he makes this deficit good with the way Mick's uses of television enable a negotiation of the micro-politics of everyday life, *Idiot Box* draws attention to the social contexts in which the struggles over meaning take place. In so doing, it does not propose a celebration of the 'resistances' enacted by active viewers, but instead offers insights about the way the discourse of choice operates in a media-saturated society and exposes its limits. As Ien Ang observes, the recognition of

audiences as active meaning-makers 'can be the starting point for a
discussion about the reach and limits of modern designs of ordered social
life, about the cultural contradictions of life in (post)modernity'.[11] This film
suggests that those starting points are not limited to a reconceptualisation of
audiences, but need to include a reassessment of the discourses and policies
which so far have reiterated those modern designs on social life, especially
the planning of urban space and the administration of youth policy. Perhaps
the problem is not young unemployed people in the outer suburbs who
watch too many videos, but an older generation of media commentators and
policymakers who look too readily to television to explain those problems.

Currently in Australia, a concern that a ratings-driven emphasis on
entertainment is incompatible with a responsibility to inform, shapes a great
deal of public discussion of television. This concern springs from a view of
mass culture's repetitions and homogeneity as the expression of a lowest
common denominator of taste, intelligence, production values and the profit
motive. The debate often falls out as an argument about public broadcasting
and commercial television, or about the concentration of media ownership.
It has lately also focused on the shift of 'current affairs' television into the
genre of 'infotainment' and the pressure on journalistic standards and ethics
as news is commodified. Jana Wendt, in her action against Channel Seven
over the issue of editorial control of the programme *Witness* and in her
Andrew Olle lecture, has taken the high moral ground on current affairs
journalism and the shaping of an informed citizenry. On the ABC, *Frontline*
has appropriated the current affairs genre and reproduced it as satire,
sometimes so seamlessly that it looks like an instance of mass cultural
repetition. *Idiot Box* engages a similar strategy, but it extends its reach
further than satire. The difference is that it uses rhetoric about television to
expose the error of blaming the media for the disintegration of the social
body, and to reintroduce a description of the economic and social contexts
in which television is installed in the cultures of late modernity.

The introduction of television in Australia in the 1950s was accompanied
by a debate whose two strands are still apparent in the oppositions invoked
by contemporary critiques. Television's potential as a means of shaping
informed citizens and building a cohesive national community is set against
its appeal to an audience whose pleasures and choices are suspect. As James
Walter has pointed out, listening to the evidence put before the Royal
Commission on Television allows us to hear that rhetoric deployed in a much
less oppositional way. The degree to which provision of television services
should be driven by non-commercial imperatives and the degree to which
they should be driven by the market was a key point of contention, but

proponents of each position made similar assumptions about audiences, whether they engaged a rhetoric about citizenship, duties and ethics, or about democracy and market freedom, choice and consumption.[12] As this debate has sifted down, and is replayed periodically in the public arena over funding of the national broadcaster or the control of media ownership, the appeal to the national interest is set against profit: the two positions – culturalist and entrepreneur – have been polarised to a greater extent than they were in the 1950s. Significantly in the present context, debate is now cast in terms of a question of taste, of high versus popular culture to an extent not evident then. A pluralised audience of niche consumers has displaced an audience of citizens. Oppositions like this are also evident in the way television has been taken up in some areas of media studies: semiological work on television genres has emphasised popular melodrama and the domestic contexts of viewing and the fashioning of gendered audiences; histories of television have taken up with the public debates about regulation of ownership and content. *Idiot Box* enjoins this debate by articulating it with a discourse about suburbia, and by (dis)locating viewing habits and contexts within a wider field of social relations. While the oppositions referred to above are still at work, they are also disarticulated and redescribed.

Masculinity Redefined

This wider field of social relations has been reproduced on television screens through a new inclusiveness of representation. Ethnic, gender and sexual diversity have been incorporated in a range of programming. In Australia as elsewhere, television in the last decade has invested heavily in the redefinition of masculinity. The increasing numbers of 'female-centred' prime-time shows began in the 1980s[13] and since then 'feminine' tastes have had an impact on plots and characterisation and the increasing visibility of masculinity as spectacle. This is most evident in imported American dramas where plots have incorporated women's own aspirations to appear in public space; the representation of active feminine desire, whether heterosexual or lesbian; and the visual display of varieties of masculinity. In particular, shows like *The X Files* and *NYPD Blue* have extended casts to include 'difference' and have made a virtue of cutting across gender stereotyping. In *The X Files*, Mulder and Scully reverse stereotypes, while Dennis Franz's Andy Sipowicz in *NYPD Blue* reworks conventional masculinity, combining some of its worst features with a redeeming struggle against them. On Australian television, shows like *Police Rescue* and *Blue Heelers* have moved in a similar direction. Gary Sweet and his male and female partners are a world away from Leonard Teale and George Mallaby, *Homicide* and *Cop Shop*. Where the characters in *Police Rescue* share confidences and struggle with emotional problems, it is difficult to imagine Teale taking a personal call at Russell Street. *Blue Heelers* is associated with the Logie-winning Lisa McCune as much as John Wood. Her character's standpoint has been critical to the way the series has taken up issues like sexual harassment and male transvestism.

At the centre of this televisual redefinition of masculinity is the concept of family. The public space of work (even police work) is infiltrated by the figures of women and familial relationships, whether these are played out by the regular cast or whether they are implicated in investigations. In one *Blue Heelers* episode, for example, the suspicious death of a respected community member is complicated by the discovery of his preference for cross-dressing, but as much of the consequent action is devoted to rehabilitating him in the eyes of his daughter as it is to finding the killer. There is a limit to this spatial rearrangement. Prime time maintains a distance from soaps in its avoidance of suburbia: this is the terrain of *Neighbours*, prime time is only passing through. In this respect, televisual discourses display the same unease with suburbia as is evident elsewhere in Australian culture.[14] While women now figure in the public spaces of prime time, and familial relations are transposed from domestic to public settings, the presence of men in the suburbs remains problematic.

Alongside this, the redefinition of masculinity in film has a different agenda. Where television draws upon its familial contexts, a number of films have focused on the body, comportment and performance. *Strictly Ballroom* and *The Adventures of Priscilla, Queen of the Desert* used the conventions of high camp to problematise the appearance of heterosexual masculinity and to emphasise its (dangerous) proximity to homosexuality. In *The Sum of Us*, Russell Crowe and Jack Thompson brought the problems of coming out closer to home. Here the strategies of representation ran in another direction: the style of homosexuality in blue singlet and Blundstone boots is a refinement of the style of Australian masculinity Jack Thompson has come to stand for. While Crowe's naturalised appearance is at the other end of the spectrum from the artifice of impersonation in *Priscilla*, it is just as contrived. In their recent appearance in *LA Confidential* (1997), (performances touted in Australia as 'Australian', rather than 'Hollywood') Crowe and Guy Pearce have reprised their heterosexual identities. Crowe's hardened, 'outside the law' cop reveals vulnerability in bed with Kim Basinger; Pearce's softly spoken, bespectacled desk officer overcomes his moral certainties to learn that policing cannot remove itself from politics and the problem of dirty hands. His virtual assault on Basinger is something to ponder.

These redefinitions of masculinity turn on the incorporation of attributes that might be designated 'feminine' and are acted out in public spaces which have been domesticated, infused with family values. These modifications produce male bodies as sexualised bodies. In *Priscilla*, the direct confrontation of a culture of masculinity is reorganised at the end through a family reunion. Russell Crowe's body in *The Sum of Us* is inscribed with signs of labour (he is a gardener), but his domestic space displays the signs of desire, images of sexualised male bodies.

By contrast, *Idiot Box* turns on conventional stereotypes and narratives of masculinity, as does the earlier *Romper Stomper*. These films examine quite different urban youth cultures and operate in very different registers, but they work over a similar problematic of mateship and loyalty, and social cohesion. In *Romper Stomper* the racist violence in inner-city Footscray is displaced by a love triangle plot in which the mateship of Hando (Russel Crowe) and Davey (Daniel Pollock) is set against the treachery of the rich girl, Gabe (Jaqueline McKenzie). Hando's craziness, underpinned by a devotion to *Mein Kampf*, is set against the mental instability – and class superiority – of the incest victim, Gabe. *Idiot Box* is also about the ways mateship can be enacted as an urban value, though the presence of women complicates the dynamic in different ways.

Mick and Kev are mates: that mateship is acted out in the dynamic of larrikinism. Kev is never happier than when he's showing his mate a 'trick' (the innocence of the term's meaning here is significant). He stirs up dogs, sets off car alarms in the pub car park, snatches the coin bucket from a charity worker in a shopping mall, performs stunts in a stolen car: the film celebrates his exhilaration in a repeated slow-motion sequence as Mendelsohn's body pivots like an athlete's. But these are the performances of masculinity deprived of a proper arena, a space of legitimisation. The materialisation of masculine identities is context-dependent, and in this film, a crucial context is missing – labour. Work spaces (except those associated with women) are not accommodated by suburban sprawl; in the film they are replaced by the CES and the endless recycling of an empty rhetoric about 'skills'. Mick makes the best he can of this. His tactics ameliorate the oppressive effects of poverty and unemployment, even if his freeway dreams will not be realised. He uses a feminised repertoire to achieve a feminised end, to make work where there is none, in conjuring poems and in smoothing out domestic life.

Conclusions

This discussion of *Idiot Box* has been an attempt to work through its engagement with television's place in social relations. It has tried to find a way though the oppositions which have come to shape and direct discussions of television; of public and private spaces of production and consumption, of an emphasis on texts and audience, on the one hand, and of technologies and systems of regulation on the other. From its installation in an assured, if anxiety-producing, place in the modern designs of an ordered national life in the 1950s, television has come to occupy a highly politicised and contested place in a reorganised public domain. A useful description of that place needs to take account not only of regulatory mechanisms and technological change surrounding television and other media, but of the shifting field of social relations and cultural practices in which its images take hold.

NOTES

1. Mark Davis, *Gangland: Cultural Elites and the New Generationalism* (Sydney: Allen & Unwin, 1997), p.xii.
2. Ibid, p.20
3. Ibid, p.ix.
4. Elspeth Probyn, 'Choosing Choice: Images of Sexuality and "Choiceoisie" in Popular Culture', in Sue Fisher and Kathy Davis (eds.), *Negotiating at the Margins: The Gendered Discourses of Power and Resistance* (New Brunswick: Rutgers University Press, 1993), p.285.
5. Nicholas Thomas, *Entangled Objects: Exchange, Material Culture and Colonialism in the Pacific* (Cambridge, MA: Harvard University Press, 1991), pp.27–30.
6. Laura Mulvey, 'Melodrama Inside and Outside the Home', in *Visual and Other Pleasures* (London: Macmillan, 1989), pp.63–77.
7. Lynn Joyrich, 'All That Television Allows: TV Melodrama, Postmodernism and Consumer Culture', in Lynn Spigel and Denise Mann (eds.), *Private Screenings: Television and the Female Consumer* (Minneapolis: University of Minnesota Press, 1992), pp.227–51.
8. Lynn Spigel, 'Installing the Television Set: Popular Discourses on Television and Domestic Space', in Lynn Spigel and Denise Mann (eds.) *Private Screenings*, pp.3–38.
9. Liesbet van Zoonen, *Feminist Media Studies* (London: Sage, 1994), p.30.
10. Mary Poovey, *Making a Social Body: British Cultural Formation 1830–1864* (Chicago: University of Chicago Press, 1995), p.185, n.14.
11. Ien Ang, 'Introduction', in *Living Room Wars: Rethinking Media Audiences for a Postmodern World* (London: Routledge, 1996), p.9.
12. James Walter, 'Citizen, Consumer, Culture: The Establishment of Television In Public Consciousness', paper delivered at the National Centre for Australian Studies (NCAS) Conference, 'Forty Years of Television', 1996, and published on the NCAS Website at http://www.arts.monashedu.au/ncas/ncashome.html. See also Walter's article, 'Controlling the Technology of Popular Culture and The Introduction of Television to Australia', *Australian Studies*, No.7 (Nov. 1993), pp.66–78.
13. Probyn, p.286.
14. Chris Healy, 'Introduction', in Sarah Ferber, Chris Healy and Chris McAuliffe (eds.), *Beasts of Suburbia: Reinterpreting Cultures in Australian Suburbs* (Melbourne: Melbourne University Press, 1994), pp.xi–xvii.

12

Ernie Dingo: Reconciliation
(A Love Story Forged Against the Odds?)

ALAN McKEE

Heartland is a 13-episode, 15-hour television mini-series starring Aboriginal actor Ernie Dingo, produced in 1994 by the Australian Broadcasting Corporation. Ross Warneke, in Melbourne's *Age* newspaper, headlined his review of the series 'Worthy Heartland Must Also Be Good Television' and worried that the programme was likely to be too 'worthy' and too informed by 'political correctness' to attract popular audiences, but stressed that *Heartland* was 'an important and worthy series'. Not before time, it puts Aborigines and some elements of their culture at centre stage. Similar doubts about the 'reach' of the show were articulated by Sue Turnbull and Rick Thompson, in a review which revealed that although they had tried to force themselves to watch the programme, they had eventually given up and (guiltily) watched an American show on another channel.[1] Both articles place *Heartland* within a strong tradition of television programmes and films representing indigeneity in Australia, but a tradition rarely commanding high ratings. Such texts are often seen to be worthy, serious, important; they demand spectatorship which is committed, socially aware and dutiful. They are not (apparently) however about entertainment or pleasure.

Aboriginal representation in Australia, indeed, Aboriginality in the public sphere more generally, is often offered for consumption in such a way; presented as duty, as burden, and as guilt. Christos Tsiolkas notes that: 'Aboriginality in Australian film has been largely defined within the documentary and the social realist genres'.[2] Indigeneity[3] in the Australian mediasphere[4] generally has been placed in genres such as these, rather than in those spaces with a less constrained commitment to entertainment. Rather than being presented as a focus for pleasure, indigeneity has been offered as something about which people should be informed, a form of civic duty.

Recent moves in the Australian public sphere have emphasised the links between indigeneity and guilt; and in very unpleasant ways. After the report in 1997 of the Human Rights and Equal Opportunity Commission into the forcible removal of indigenous children from their families, Prime Minister John Howard refused to make an apology to indigenous people (as the report recommended), on the grounds that contemporary Australians had no need to feel guilt for the acts of their ancestors. This debate was disseminated throughout the Australian public sphere, and triggered a general call from many non-indigenous Australians to be freed from the demand to feel guilt about indigenous issues.

The irony is that no such demand is being made of non-indigenous Australians. There is indeed a call to acknowledge the events of Australian history.[5] However, the conversion of this into a demand to be guilty is made not by advocates for indigenous rights in Australia, but by right-wing politicians who wish to insist that history should *not* be acknowledged (John Howard specifically came out in 1997 against what he termed 'black armband history'). The rhetorical move – by which calls for an awareness of history are made to seem like demands for guilt – is easily made in the contemporary Australian public sphere. Such an articulation seems to make sense, for indigeneity has traditionally been associated with the 'worthy', with 'duty', and thus, with guilt. Media representations continue to carry these associations: they *should* be watched, although they may not offer *pleasure* in watching.

However, it seems to me that in the case of *Heartland*, Warneke, Turnbull and Thompson are bringing these structures of interpretation to bear on a programme which simply does not require it. For *Heartland* as a mini-series – and, in particular, as a series starring Ernie Dingo – does not demand such responses. Dingo, in fact, offers a quite different form of Aboriginality in the Australian public sphere, one whose distinctiveness is well worth exploring.

Ernie Dingo is ...

Ernie Dingo is probably the best-known Aboriginal actor in Australia today. Indeed, he may well vie with athlete Cathy Freeman for the title of best known Aboriginal person in the continent. The actor's output is prodigious. At one point in mid-1994, Dingo was appearing regularly three times a week on Australian television.[6] The name and image of Ernie Dingo are synonymous with Australian television and film and are well-known currency.[7]

In contextual discourses, *Heartland* is explicitly authored as an Ernie Dingo programme:

> *Heartland* is well named. It comes from the heart. Ernie's heart. Much of it is his story. Sequences like this one, being pulled over because you're black, happened to him in real life.[8]

It is unsurprising that this would be the case as Dingo is the star of *Heartland*. And although, within film studies, auteur theory has traditionally assigned the status of author to directors, actors of television programmes and (particularly) films are often granted such a central status in contemporary discourses. As John Caughie has noted in his discussion of auteur theory, various roles might be invoked in explorations of authorship – as well as the director, these may include 'the actor, the designer'.[9] In everyday discourses of cinema, actors are often, in a common-sense way, constructed as the authors of film.[10] These attributions are unsurprising and seemingly make sense: the reading of films through their stars is a frequently explored point of view in Hollywood.[11] For Richard Dyer, the use of actors as 'auteur' figures who structure the meaning of texts is an example of the way in which the 'structured polysemy' of these films and television programmes is tied down to 'stabilise audience response'. Stars help provide the limits of interpretation, through the 'always-already-signifying nature of star images'.[12] Evidence brought to bear on a film from other texts and inter-texts in which an actor's image is formed help to limit the possible interpretations of a polysemic text.

Ernie Dingo's star image is an important part of the contemporary Australian mediasphere. In considering *Heartland*, and possible responses to it (including the guilt-wracked sense of being forced to endure something 'worthy' evinced by the reviewers mentioned above), Dingo's proclaimed status as the centre of the text must be addressed. For his image is a powerful one.

Dingo's image anchors the meaning of *Heartland* in various ways. His presence offers the text a sense of 'authenticity', a contribution which Dyer suggests is common in many 'star' images. Images are composed as much of texts purporting to represent the 'real' actor (for example, magazine interviews) as of those filmic texts in which characters are portrayed, that image comes to stand as more real than the characters in avowedly fictional texts. If the two coincide, it can be read as a validation of authenticity for the fictional character. And so, when Ernie Dingo's character refers to an aspect of Aboriginal experience; living in a country town in *Heartbreak*

High, dealing with racism in *Heartland*, the 'reality' of the celebrity guarantees the 'authentic' experience.

Beyond such general assertions however, there is a continuity to Ernie Dingo's many television appearances which suggests the outline of his celebrity image. In *Dolphin Cove, Heartland, Heartbreak High* – even, and especially, on the travel show *The Great Outdoors* which he still hosts – 'Ernie Dingo' *means* a certain kind of indigeneity.

The parameters of Dingo's celebrity image can best be suggested in a series of terms, closely imbricated: authenticity; naturalness; affability; niceness; non-aggressiveness; availability; accessibility; reconciliation; humour; common sense. In picking through the texts which contribute to this image, it becomes obvious that the 'real' Dingo revealed in contextual material is involved in a specific relationship with both Aboriginal and settler cultures; and his image signifies this relationship very strongly.

The importance of this celebrity image, and the ways it offers of interpreting the programmes in which he appears cannot be emphasised strongly enough in any attempt to understand the contemporary Australian public sphere. Indigenous issues continue to be vital to any understanding of Australia's shared domain, and national identity. The Howard government's response to the Human Rights and Equal Opportunity's Inquiry into the forcible removal of indigenous children; and the threat of a so-called 'Race election', if the Government changes the land rights 'Wik' legislation, have ensured that debates about indigenous Australians, and the ways in which Australia deals with indigeneity, remain highly visible. The contribution of Dingo's star image to the public sphere must be understood in this context.

Reconciliation

The Council for Aboriginal Reconciliation is the name given to the multi-party and cross-cultural group of Australians who responded to the Australian Parliament's invitation and offer of a unique challenge to establish a process of reconciliation. This process would help to heal the wounds of our past and build the foundations upon which the rights and affairs of indigenous Australians may be dealt with in a manner that gives respect and pride to all of us as Australians.[13]

The Council for Aboriginal Reconciliation was established by the *Council for Aboriginal Reconciliation Act 1991*, and represents the recognition by the then Labour Government of the importance of symbolic politics. As

Patrick Dodson suggested in 1994, 'Reconciliation is now firmly entrenched in the public mind and on the political agenda'. The specific practicalities of what the term might mean vary according to particular writers: but the broad sweep of the term's meaning in public discourse can be characterised as the search for: 'A united Australia which respects this land of ours, values Aboriginal and Torres Strait Islander heritage, and provides justice and equality for all'.[14] In the context of such a public climate, the importance of Dingo's image was his ability to provide a body onto which such reconciliation could be imaged; in Dingo, reconciliation could be seen.

Writing this as a historical piece, it is with an inescapable sense of loss that a paragraph such as the previous one must be written. Since the election of John Howard's coalition Liberal/National Government in 1997, the process of reconciliation has been largely refused. Funding to the Aboriginal and Torres Strait Islander Council was slashed in 1997. Indigenous people are continually constructed as 'them', against whom 'we' ordinary Australians must fight. Patrick Dodson resigned from the Reconciliation Council in 1997, unable to continue working in such a political climate.

And yet, the term remains; and Dingo remains as an important part of it, with a star image which informs those texts in which he appears, and which forms an important part of public discourse about this political thing called reconciliation.

Reconciling Cultures

As I have suggested in another article, current discourses of indigeneity invoke a suspicion that those indigenous people who have been successful in white industries such as the media are not authentically indigenous.[15] This belief relies on the understanding that indigeneity and white culture are incompatible. For an Aboriginal person to have succeeded in, or to be adept at living with, white culture, must involve being tainted by it. Dingo's star image insists that this is not the case. His claims to 'authenticity' prove particularly fascinating to television programs, and are often revisited. For example, his 'tribal name' 'Oondamaroo' is invoked in *Mulray,* and *Sixty Minutes.* He was born on 'Bullardoo cattle station',[16] and reminds us that his

> mother was a cook on the cattle station and my grandmother delivered me and my aunty was the midwife. The closest hospital was about two hours away, and it was easier to have me on the job![17]

His 'tribe' is named 'Wudjadi' and 'Dingo strives to keep his identity as a member of the Wudjadi tribe'.[18] His surname proves a constantly fascinating item. It is almost too perfect, a simulacrum of Aboriginality, again suggesting that Dingo is just playing the role of the 'blackfella'. But no, the articles insist, it is authentic:

> Dingo inherited his surname from his grandfather, Jimmy, who worked with dogs. The white people could not pronounce his Aboriginal name so they called him Jimmy with the dingoes, which eventually became Jimmy Dingo.[19]

If this were as far as Dingo's image went, it would be similar to that of many other Aboriginal actors: David Gulpilil, David Ngoombujarra and Robert Tudawali have all been the subjects of images which constructed them as being in touch with authentic Aboriginal culture. But Dingo's image is differentiated from these others. While asserting all the time his authentic indigeneity, contextual discourses simultaneously insist upon Dingo's ability to live in non-indigenous society. Indeed, perhaps the most important element in Dingo's image is his representation as a fully-functional cross-cultural personality. Partly, this ability to cope with both indigenous and non-indigenous cultures is present in the knowing distance which is often placed between Dingo and the traditional indigenous culture he is at other times taken to embody. As the *Sixty Minutes* interview makes clear, a central part of Dingo's star image, taken from his role in *Crocodile Dundee II* (1988), is 'that wink'. That wink – when Dingo says, in all seriousness, that his Aboriginal compatriot wants to eat the bad guys; and then gives the heroine a wink that only she can see, to imply that he is joking – places Dingo outside of a mythical and inarticulate Aboriginal culture. The actor's adverts for Vetta pasta, and appearance on *Mulray* – both of which denigrate bush tucker – work in a similar function. 'I wouldn't eat it', he says of the baked goanna he has just described to the host of the chat show. Comedy thus distances Dingo: he may be a representative of Aboriginal culture, but he can also step outside it, in order to view it from a white perspective.

Apart from this comic distance, Dingo's ability to live successfully across cultures is an aspect of his celebrity image which is present in much of the writing that surrounds him. For example, Stuart Freeman, the assistant director on *Heartland*, states in an interview that:

> He's a remarkable person in that he has managed to assimilate to the white man's way, but he has not moved one iota from his Aboriginal background and upbringing.[20]

Of course, this success in non-indigenous society also makes it necessary to reiterate at all times his authenticity. Sally Dingo states that:

> Dingo is not the sophisticated black guy living in a white man's world that people think. He plays the game, but he's still black as black.[21]

The cultures are constantly played off each other, in a way that is quite specific to Dingo's image:

> He is as much at home in the Aboriginal tent embassy currently occupying the site of Mrs Macquarie's chair in Sydney as he is in New York, the bush, and a film studio … He is an activist and an actor, a man who knows his Dreaming, or traditional history, and he knows white culture, be it Coca-Cola, Bollinger, or his neat black Reeboks.[22]

In short, as one journalist puts it, Dingo walks a 'tightrope … between two cultures'.[23] According to the materials which present the 'real' Ernie Dingo, he is managing to walk that tightrope most successfully. As the voice-over states in *Sixty Minutes*, 'Ernie Dingo is one of the rarest of Australian species – a black man who has succeeded in white man's society'.

Dingo's amphibious ability to survive so well across culture is neatly illustrated in his clothing. As common sense would suggest, and as Richard Dyer has written, clothes signify more than simply the ability to keep warm:

> clothes are major signifiers of power … When the West is in the ascendant, other nations dress in Western clothes; but when the relations of power shift, the leaders of non-Western nations can wear their national clothes.[24]

Bearing in mind, then, that clothes can stand metonymically for cultures, it is important that Dingo seems able to live comfortably with either. When appearing as 'himself', dressing as Ernie Dingo, he wears a variety of Western clothes, often favouring the intense formality of suit and tie (*Mulray, Sixty Minutes, Celebrity Wheel of Fortune*). Yet he also wears clothing that is coded 'Aboriginal' (*Sixty Minutes, Crocodile Dundee II*). To see him working in either of these codes of dress is not unusual.

His success in sustaining an image which retains 'Aboriginality', while making it functional within white culture, has led to Dingo's association with discourses redolent of reconciliation: 'He's looking forward to the day when white and black will stand together',[25] for example. *Sixty Minutes* refers to Dingo's desire to: 'communicate the rich heritage of Aboriginal life – to all Australians'. Similarly, on *Mulray*, when the host asks if Dingo thinks Australians are racist, Dingo replies that all Australians are racist. When Mulray, looking as though he has hit on a clever reply, asks, 'Does that include black Australians?', Dingo looks at him as though he has just missed the point, and says, 'Of course – we're Australians too'.

The image constructed for Dingo, accepted as successful within Aboriginal and settler cultures, means that as a symbol for reconciliation, he is 'a good example to both black and white', as a viewer's letter says, commenting on the *Sixty Minutes* report.[26]

Ernie Dingo is Nice

But more than this, Dingo's image promotes a particular kind of reconciliatory discourse. He is a non-aggressive figure; he is not threatening; he is available, and ordinary. In short, Ernie Dingo is *nice*. Dingo has a 'delightful, natural talent … a man at peace with himself and the environment' says Frank Arnold, director of *Waltz Through the Hills*.[27] His niceness is linked to his naturalness and his ordinariness. Ernie Dingo describes the producers of *Crocodile Dundee II* as 'just a couple of very ordinary blokes',[28] and this vocabulary seems appropriate to him.

> It is impossible to believe he aspires to the glamorous life. 'I prefer to sit around with my family, having nieces and nephews climbing all over me. I wouldn't know how to be a celebrity'.[29]

This image of ordinariness extends into an associated discourse of common sense. Lisa Amor presents Dingo's theories on improving race relations: 'His idea is that understanding could be developed by the simple exercise of Australians meeting one another'.[30]

Another potent contributing factor to Dingo's ordinariness is his *availability*. He is not a threatening figure, despite his international film success. This is in part due to the actor's constant, banal television appearances. Dingo's image is, almost literally, everyday. He is not just a film 'star'/actor. He is also a television celebrity, who appears on travel shows, on game shows, on television adverts, government announcements, documentaries, and children's programs. This last group of shows especially – appearances on *Clowning Around I* and *II*, *Waltz Through the Hills, Dolphin Cove* – contributes to the general niceness of the man's image.

Ernie Dingo was unhappy with his appearances on the comedy sketch show *Fast Forward*, finding the programme too aggressive: 'If you keep throwing shit at other people like some shows do, then sooner or later some of it is going to blow back at you'.[31] He 'doesn't see much value in being cruel and unkind'. 'There's enough animosity in the world without that crap', he says.[32] Dingo's smile also contributes to this part of his image. It is explicitly noted in the texts which construct his celebrity image – his 'infectious smile' (*Sixty Minutes*); 'a smile that takes over his face'[33] – and is much in evidence in televisual texts. In *Mulray, Sixty Minutes, The Great Outdoors* and *Wheel of Fortune*, Dingo will rarely finish a sentence without breaking into a smile and making some sort of joke. In contrast the media studies teacher he plays in *Heartbreak High* appears at first much more serious: he does not smile. However, the image of Ernie Dingo still does not allow this strange new teacher to be truly threatening; and after a series of difficulties about this character's provenance have been worked out, he does indeed begin to smile more easily, forming a camaraderie with one of the pupils. Initially rather severe, the character quickly becomes more approachable. This seems to make perfect sense. It is, after all, Ernie Dingo.

Nice Politics

Dingo's common sense and lack of aggressiveness means that politics (in the sense of traditional, party politics) has not been a central focus in the construction of his celebrity image. It is true that part of the honesty and authenticity comprising Dingo's image is his acknowledgement of the reality of racism and of the need to challenge it. But compared to Gary Foley, for example,[34] Dingo does not signify these political concerns in such a way: 'I try not to be political, but I can't get away from the fact of my Aboriginality';[35] he 'has been criticised by some sectors of the Aboriginal movement for not being militant enough'.[36] This aspect of Dingo's image is perhaps best characterised by absence: that while contextual materials present him talking about specific instances of racism, more general political anger is less present. In *Mulray*, a Saturday night variety/ entertainment show, Dingo is given the chance to address the issue of black deaths in custody. He refuses the opportunity, looking uncomfortable and refusing to be drawn. This is a typical part of his image. Again, the common sense of Dingo, his belief that racism will be overcome through the 'simple exercise of Australians meeting each other'[37] represents a non-politics, a non-racism that is a part of his image much more than is explicit commentary on land rights.

Part of Dingo's non-aggressiveness, and the fact that he can address racial prejudice in Australia without his image taking on overtones of didacticism or high-handedness, comes from his humour. This is perhaps the single most important part of Dingo's image. He is a comedian. That is how he was first known; it has been an important part of many of his acting roles; it is emphasised in most articles about him, and in all histories of his career (he is, as the *Western Daily Mail* headlines it, a 'Black Humorist'[38]). His humour interacts with all other aspects of his celebrity image, and colours every comment that Dingo makes in his own voice.

A typical example of the implementation of humour in the formation of 'Ernie Dingo' relates to the Bicentennial. Talking about an event that inspires much Aboriginal anger, Dingo voices concerns; but makes them palatable by joking rather than attacking:

> What are we doing celebrating 200 years of penal settlement? You could be hard up for a drink, that could be one excuse.[39]

His humour keeps him from being perceived as militant; it reinforces an image of him as down to earth, nice, normal. More generally, it creates a non-aggressive Aboriginality:

> Aboriginal humour is basically untapped. We laugh at nearly everything: everything is basically a laugh. We have moments of seriousness, but basically an Aboriginal lifestyle is full of humour …[40] What we [Aborigines] are all about is laughing at ourselves, and it's all we've ever done.[41]

This humorous character has particular implications for Dingo's comments which are made in a serious mode. For 'humorous' is not an antonym of 'serious' (although it may be of 'solemn'[42]), and Dingo is well equipped to talk about serious issues that relate to indigenous experience. Amor's article, 'The Dingo Manifesto', for example, presents his feelings on the Bicentennial, showing him to be perfectly capable of addressing such important issues intelligently. Dingo's image is not a solemn one. The actor can raise serious issues: but in doing this, he usually removes any sense of confrontation by simultaneously invoking humour. However, that humour need not destroy his seriousness. For instance, appearing on *Sixty Minutes*, Dingo interrogates the interviewer with a revealing catechism:

> Dingo: 'We're a multicultural country, aren't we? How do you say yes in French?'
>
> Interviewer: 'Oui'.

Dingo: 'How do you say yes in German?'

Interviewer: 'Jah'.

Dingo: 'How do you say yes in Spanish?'

Interviewer: 'Si'.

Dingo: 'How do you say yes in any one of the 3500 Aboriginal dialects of Australia?'

Interviewer: 'You've got me there'.[43]

In this exchange, Dingo makes a serious point; but in doing it as a game, and with a smile, and with timing that allows what he says to be (almost) funny, it is not presented as didactic. Rather, it is surprising; and it seems to be common sense.

Similarly, in *Mulray*, when the interviewer suddenly switches the tone of the interview to ask about black deaths in custody, the seriousness of the topic is matched by the solemnity in Mulray's tone. However, Dingo's performance rejects this. He immediately looks awkward. Leaving a noticeable gap, he looks around him, and he says that he does not know why this is the case. He rejects the attempt to make a didactic, unfunny statement, preferring to make an attempt to control the tone of the interview, to keep it generically suitable. Again, fielding another, equally well-meaning, equally concerned, equally portentous question on *Sixty Minutes*, Dingo's performance signifies discomfort. 'What is the importance of what you've done ... for your people?', asks the interviewer. Dingo looks away; laughs; says, 'That's not fair, you didn't tell me you were going to ask that one'; thinks about it; finally, makes a half joke: says that he has 'brought a bit of colour into Australian life – if you'll pardon the pun'.

In this refusal of didactic, broad political and solemn discourses, Dingo's humour is often brought into play; and his status as affable, normal, ordinary and down-to-earth is reinforced. As I suggested above, the dominant tone of Aboriginal representation in Australia has been precisely didactic, guilt-inducing, moralising and self-righteous. Some writers explicitly acknowledge the fact that this acts as a turn-off for a white viewer unwilling to face another dose of guilt. And indeed, for the reviewers of Heartland quoted at the outset of this article, it was impossible to get past such a reaction – even when the text in question does not, itself, demand it.

Dingo's *Heartland*

Returning to *Heartland*, we have an example of how the star image of
Ernie Dingo might function in relation to a particular text in which he
appears.

Heartland is an epic mini-series, centred on the character of Vincent
Burunga, a police liaison officer (Dingo). It examines his love life, his
background, his community, and a murder he investigates. It is one of the
most significant representations of Aboriginality ever produced in
Australia. In terms of sheer bulk, for example, an extra 15 hours of
television centring on an Aboriginal character is an impressive contribution
to Australian media history. The range of characters, the number of
locations, and the scope of different situations in which the central
characters find themselves all work powerfully against the force of
representativeness.[44] The facts that some episodes are written by Aborigines
(Dingo co-writes one episode) and that Aboriginal people are involved in
training for key creative positions (*The Fringe Dwellers'* Kristina Nehm is
an assistant directors on later episodes) also contribute to the importance of
the program.

As a representation of indigeneity, *Heartland* is complex. It does not
revolve around any single incident; and although there is one
hermeneutic drive which is sustained from the first to the last episodes
(investigation of a murder), it is not constantly present or foregrounded.
In such a vast text, interpretation is not a simple process. As is the case
with soap operas, it is not expected that each viewer will even have the
same experience of the text, much less provide identical readings of the
series. Generically, it is recognisable as an extended mini-series, a form
which has flourished in Australia over the past two decades.[45] And in this
massive, polyvalent text, specific aspects of the 'Dingo' image outlined
above promote particular interpretative approaches. Philippa Hawker
describes the general sweep of the series, noting, 'the difficulty the
apparently poised Vincent faces in negotiating between two cultures'.[46]
This difficulty in negotiating indigenous and non-indigenous cultures is
a recurring theme in the programme. Throughout the 13 episodes, the
presence of 'two laws' is often asserted – as, for example, in the last
episode, when a character Alf (Bob Maza) states that Ricky has been
found innocent under white law, but still faces pay back under
'blackfella' law. As the central character, a police liaison officer, Vince
must constantly try to balance these cultural demands. In situations such
as that in his hometown, when he faces pay back himself, Vince must

make sense of, and live within, what appear to be mutually exclusive demands on his sense of the law. Similarly, when the local Aboriginal community riots and attacks the police station, Vince is placed in a situation which dramatises his position: does he leave the protection of the white building and face the mob? Or is he part of that mob? Most often he seems to fully belong to neither group, rather being excluded from each by his knowledge of the other.

Heartland is also, insistently, a love story. The promotional campaign that accompanied the launch of the series presents this as in fact the most important aspect of the program. The advert shows actress Cate Blanchett (who plays the character Beth, Dingo's love interest), with her head leaning against Dingo's chest. The caption runs: 'A LOVE STORY FORGED AGAINST THE ODDS'. The romance element is foregrounded as the central element of the series. Compared to this, the murder investigation plot is relegated to a poor second place in the publicity material: a subtitle which is entirely separate from the main picture, stating 'A Murder. A Mystery'. Even then, the focus on the romance remains: 'Two Hearts Drawn Forever Closer. Two Lives Changed Forever'.[47]

It is in his relationship with Beth that the greatest difficulties in living across cultures are shown. For example, after Vince has gone back to Beth's home in Sydney and met her friends, he is uncomfortable and tries to end the relationship. After he has been involved in an incident with the police which reinforces the difficulty he will face trying to live in white culture (a policewoman pulls him over because he is Aboriginal and has a nice car), Vince and Beth have an argument:

> Vince: 'I watched you in that house. With those people. You fitted right in'.
>
> Beth: 'Yes. Like you did in Western Australia'.
>
> Vince: 'That was different – '.
>
> Beth: 'How? Look, I'm sorry if you felt left out. I'm sorry if I hurt you. I made an effort to get on with your people. So don't you go making me feel guilty for staying with my friends when you wouldn't even talk to them ...'.
>
> (*Heartland*, Episode 11)

In this program, then, the fact of living in two cultures is made to seem difficult, dangerous and dramatic. It is a violent, physical issue, an issue which involves rioting mobs and thrown stones, a possible pay back spearing. It is a fatal issue and one which has no easy resolutions. Can the Aboriginal man live in both cultures and survive?

In the series, discourses of both success and failure abound. Bob Maza, a well-known actor whose image might be characterised as one of respectability, plays Alf, an Aboriginal elder. This character criticises Vince's attempts to live across cultures, telling him on several occasions that he cannot live both white and black; that he must be true to his own black culture and roots. A strong character, one admired by others in the programme's Aboriginal communities, he insists that successful cross-cultural living is not in fact possible. But Vincent is, visibly, Ernie Dingo.

As well as being a policeman facing the difficulties of cross-cultural life on Thursday night's television, Ernie Dingo is also a happily middle-class traveller on *The Great Outdoors* on Fridays; and a friendly Aboriginal man bringing a bit of native culture to a white family on Sunday afternoons (*Dolphin Cove*). As noted above, inter-texts which address Dingo's cross-cultural 'tightrope' claim that he manages to live comfortably in white society, while remaining authentically indigenous. Dingo himself stands as living testimony to the fact that the problem Vince faces can be overcome. Can an indigenous man live across cultures? demands *Heartland*, dramatising the issue as a crisis. And simultaneously, the question posed by the narrative is answered by the celebrity image: to a watching viewer who knows Ernie Dingo, the angst of an indigenous man unable to cope with life across cultures is answered by a similar knowledge of an actor whose ability to cope in a white media while simultaneously maintaining contacts with his Aboriginal culture are widely publicised as unproblematic. This aspect of Dingo's image may well prove relevant in setting horizons on the interpretations which will be made of *Heartland*'s central problematic.

As Warneke points out, 'Among the [program's] most important facets is its romantic pairing of a black man and a white woman: I cannot recall that happening before'.[48] This is indeed the case. In the history of Australian fictional representation of indigeneity, it is true that to see an Aboriginal man with a white woman is spectacularly uncommon. In the tele-biography *Rose Against the Odds*,[49] Lionel Rose kisses his white girlfriend, but it is not a major plot point. Apart from this, examples are so scarce as to be non-existent. That forty years after the 'breakthrough' representation of indigeneity in *Jedda* (1955), this can still be the case, is an extremely telling comment on the representation of Aboriginal masculinity in Australia.

The relationship – as is the norm in romantic relationships that must remain fraught for the 13 weeks of a mini-series – proves difficult. The cultural differences between the two protagonists provide a central problem. In the last episode, these issues are still not fully resolved. Even after thirteen weeks of working at the problems of non/indigenous romance, the couple have still not managed to work out if such a relationship is in fact possible. In Episode 13, Vince refuses Beth's offer to help him out with his problems:

> Vince: 'It's men's business'.

> Beth: 'Don't hide behind that. Look, I have spent months trying to see the world your way – not to give offence, to make allowances – but it can't all be a one way street. That's not my way'.

> Vince: 'It's the only way I know'.

Some of the inter-textual advertising material, then, suggests that this central relationship is to be read seriously as a socially important representation of cultural tension.[50] But while Vince and Beth struggle on screen with their relationship – will they, won't they? will it last? can they cope with each other's cultures and different family situations? – Ernie Dingo again provides a notably relevant inter-text. He himself stands as an example of cross-cultural relationships that succeed.

Dingo's wife, Sally, is a familiar component of his more recent celebrity image; and the fact of their different cultures is often presented as relevant to an understanding of Dingo. Sally's fullest manifestation appears in *Sixty Minutes*, where she is interviewed on screen. The occasion is a Dingo family get-together. The interviewer approaches Sally and points out that 'apart from us, you're the only white person here'. The camera pans around a group of Aboriginal faces to reinforce the point. She responds, 'I hadn't even noticed that until you pointed it out just now'. The image constructed is of a happy family, one where race is irrelevant. The programme, despite being investigative journalism, does not feel any need to contradict this image with revealing footage showing that in fact Ernie and Sally's marriage does suffer from culture-clash. It is content rather to leave the image of Sally Dingo as happily integrated into the indigenous family. Yes, she says, it was a bit strange at first, but now it feels completely natural.

Sally also appears in a photograph accompanying the piece on Dingo by Linda Van Nunen, his wife's (blonde) head leaning against Dingo's chest in a position similar to that of Blanchett's in the *Heartland* advertisement. The actor's wife is also present in that text of that piece:

> they met when Sally, a former advertising manager for the Ten
> Network, gave him a lift to a charity concert she'd organised, which he
> was to compere ... Dingo says he doesn't socialise much, preferring to
> spend time with Sally. 'I depend on her a lot', he says. 'You need to
> have an escape, and my wife is my escape. We laugh a lot, and are
> educating each other, and that's the fun thing about it. I don't worry
> about where the next job's coming from. The main thing I worry about
> is making sure Sal's happy. If she's happy then I'm happy'.[51]

The *Sixty Minutes* scene of the white wife comfortable and happy with an
Aboriginal family, constructs an image of Ernie Dingo's personal life
which is open for use in making meaning of *Heartland*. In the
programme, Beth's attempts to fit into the indigenous community are
fraught with difficulties on both sides. She does not, it is made clear, fit
in. She is seen as patronising; the Aboriginal people reject her (see, for
example, the anger occasioned by her well-meaning advances at the
funeral).

However, the marriage to Sally Dingo, working as part of Dingo's
celebrity image, makes clear that Vince's (Dingo's) relationship with a
white woman in *Heartland* is not, in fact, doomed. Despite the
programme's suggestion that such a relationship will be a site of crisis,
charged with excitement and difficulty, and may indeed finally prove
irresolvable; the programme can easily be read in quite other directions
if the image of Ernie Dingo as a family man – with a banal, jolly, cross-
cultural family life – is brought to bear on the work of making meaning
from the mini-series. The experiences of Sally, as pale, delicate and as
blonde as Beth, are validated as a suitable inter-text.

Another way in which Dingo's 'real' relationship may become
involved in interpretations of Vince's romance is in the typical Dingo
lack of solemnity. In the jokes he makes about his own personal
experience of cross-cultural romance, the way in which this is played up
as a central 'issue' in the programme *Heartland*, is somewhat undercut.
While Beth and Vince have serious scenes where they try to come to
terms with cross-cultural existence, Dingo quips that: 'Yeh, it's a mixed
marriage – she's from Tasmania and I'm a mainlander'. In a magazine
interview he says:

> Sure, there are times when I wish I was white ... A good time would
> be trying to catch a cab at Kings Cross at two in the morning. Nothing

much has changed. I still push my wife Sally (who is white), out on to
the road to stop a cab ... then I slip in behind her.[52]

The happy romance that Dingo carries with him as part of his image,
'always already signifying' successful cultural crossing, is available to
those viewers who know of the 'real' Dingo in their interpretation of
Heartland.

The Burden of Representativeness

This article has not set out simply to celebrate the ways in which indigeneity
figures in the contemporary Australian public sphere. One of the problems
about Dingo's image is that he, together with Cathy Freeman, comes to
carry far too great a burden of representativeness in Australia. As the only
indigenous celebrity with such a presence on Australian television (Aaron
Pedersen has hosted the gameshow *Gladiators* and currently appears on the
ABC drama *Wildside*; Heath Bergerson has been on the soapies *Sweat* and
Breakers, but neither has such a consistent profile as Dingo), the danger is
always that Dingo comes to represent the *only* visible and acceptable form
of Aboriginality and reconciliation. Stephen Muecke in his 1992 book
Textual Spaces, ironically uses Dingo in a thought experiment to make the
point that no single public figure can adequately represent all indigenous
people:

> Let's consider some options for Ernie Dingo as he goes to work for a
> soap opera like *A Country Practice* [a hypothetical example] ... Does
> he come on as a doctor, without anyone making a fuss about his race?
> Then we are faced with the spectre of assimilation. Does he come on
> as drunk and unemployed? Then we are faced with the worse image
> of a (bad) stereotype. Was the doctor, then a positive image because it
> is a high class job? If he were a land developer or a bureaucrat, would
> that be a sell-out?[53]

The fact that Dingo is the only indigenous celebrity with such a profile must
be lamented. However, his image remains fascinating and important. In a
political climate in which reconciliation is proposed as a potential way
forward in dealing with Australian national culture, and the place of
indigeneity in that culture, the importance of Ernie Dingo must be realised;
and the possibilities he offers, for getting away from the discourses of guilt
which the Coalition government endlessly brings up, should be
acknowledged. *Heartland* is not just 'worthy', Dingo is not playing on guilt

and duty, and other ways are being offered to imagine the politics of indigeneity in the contemporary Australian media sphere.

NOTES

1. Sue Turnbull and Rick Thompson, 'It's Life Jim, But Not As We Know It', *The Melbournian*, 2 Aug. 1994, pp.31–32.
2. Christos Tsolkias, 'Upside Down You're Turnin' Me: Tracey Moffatt's *Bedevil*', in *In the Picture* (Perth), (Winter 1994), p.22.
3. While this term is not unproblematic – or particularly mellifluous – it is an accurate and useful one for this article, replacing 'Aboriginality and Torres Strait Islander identity'.
4. The term is taken from the work of John Hartley in *Popular Reality: Journalism, Modernity, Popular Culture* (London and New York: Edward Arnold, 1996).
5. See, for example, the comments of Sir Ronald Wilson, made at the 'National Media Forum', held in Perth Australia, 19–20 March 1998.
6. Starring in the ABC's detective mini-series, *Heartland*, presenting a lifestyle/travel show, *The Great Outdoors* on Channel Seven and appearing in repeats of the children's drama series *Dolphin Cove* on Channel Ten.
7. Dingo originally appeared on television as a comedian, working as a regular member of the comedy-sketch programme *Fast Forward*, (Artists Services, 1989). He appears in other children's programmes than *Dolphin Cove: A Waltz Through The Hills* (Barron Films/ABC, 1988), is a series about a brother and sister who go cross country when their mother dies, and Dingo plays the bushie who looks after them; *Clowning Around* and *Clowning Around 2* (Channel Seven, Barron Films, 1992, 1994) present him as a friend of the central (white) child, this time a boy wanting to learn circus skills; on *Dolphin Cove*, Dingo is a friend of a (non-indigenous) family. The actor has also made guest appearances in *GP*, as an aboriginal doctor confused about his cultural identity ('Special Places', ABC, 1994); *The Flying Doctors*, as an Aboriginal father caught in a cultural clash over the medicines of different races ('Breaking Down The Wall', Crawford Productions, 1990) and *Heartbreak High* (Gannon Productions for Channel Ten, 1995) as a media studies teacher and basketball coach. He has further appeared in *Relative Merits* (ABC, 1987); *The Cowra Breakout* (ABC); *No Sugar* (ABC); *The Dirtwater Dynasty* (Kennedy Miller, 1988); *Dreaming of Lords* (ABC); *Archer* (Roadshow, Coote and Carroll, 1985); *Off the Dish* (Channel Ten, 1986); *Rafferty Rules* (Channel Seven, 1990); *Joe Wilson* (Channel Seven, 1987); *The Saint in Australia* (Channel Seven, 1990); and *Dearest Enemy* (ABC, 1989). He has played roles in feature films such as *The Fringe Dwellers* (1986), *Crocodile Dundee II* (1988), *Tudawali* (1992), *Cappuccino*, (1989), *Until the End of the World* (1992), and *Blue Lightning* (1991). He appears as himself on a variety of entertainment programmes: on the *Ray Martin Show*, Dingo performs as a comic, playing a vacuum cleaner as a digeridoo; in Vetta pasta ad's he again plays a comedian, mocking bush tucker; he appears in his own special profile on *Sixty Minutes* – 'The wit and wisdom of Ernie Dingo'. He is on the 1995 Logie Awards, a range of Channel Seven promos, television coverage of the AFL football match between the West Coast Eagles and the Melbourne Demons (29 April, 1995). He has appeared on *Celebrity Wheel of Fortune*, been interviewed on *Mulray*, and chatted on *TVTV* about his work.
8. *Sixty Minutes*, Channel Nine, 12 June 1994.
9. John Caughie, *Theories of Authorship* (London: British Film Institute, 1981) p.205.
10. *Cliffhanger* (1993) is a Sylvester Stalone Film; *I Love Trouble* (1994), a Julia Roberts Film.
11. For a reading of films through their stars see Alexander Walker, *Bette Davis – a Celebration* (London: Pavillion, Michael Joseph, 1986), pp 47–48 and Charles Affron, *Star Acting: Gish, Garbo, Davis* (New York: E P Dutton, 1977), p.193.
12. Richard Dyer, *Stars* (London: British Film Institute, 1986), pp.68, 11, 144.

13. Patrick Dodson, 'Preface', in the Council for Aboriginal Reconciliation (ed.), *Walking Together: the first steps: Report of the Council for Aboriginal Reconciliation to Federal Parliament 1991–1994* (Canberra: Australian Government Printing Service, 1994), p.vii.

14. Council for Aboriginal Reconciliation (ed.), p.xi.

15. Alan McKee, 'The Aboriginal Version of Ken Done: Banal Aboriginal Identities in Australia', *Cultural Studies* Vol.11 No.2 (June 1997), pp.191–206.

16. Pat Bowring, 'Ernie Dingo: Walking Tall With Mick Dundee', *Woman's Day*, 28 March 1988, pp.62.

17. Dingo, in Lisa Amor, 'The Dingo Manifesto', *The Sun*, 23 Jan. 1988. Reproduced in *CineDossier*, No.304 (1988), p.35.

18. Ibid.

19. Janine Cohen, 'Black Humorist', *The Western Mail Magazine*, (Perth), 27–29 Nov. 1987. Reprinted in *CineDossier*, No.297 (1987), p.46; see also Bowring; Linda Van Nunen, 'The Games Ernie plays', *The Australian Magazine*, 12–13 Jan. 1991, p.25; and *Sixty Minutes*.

20. Sally Macmillian, 'Up The Magic Rock', *The Sunday Telegraph*, 13 Feb. 1994. Reproduced in *Cinedossier*, No.620 (1994), p.22.

21. Quoted in Van Nuen, p.25.

22. Berwyn Lewis, 'Ernie Dingo: A Black Proud To Be Bloody Stubborn', *The Australian*, 25 Jan. 1988. Reproduced in *CineDossier*, No.304 (1988), p.36.

23. Anon, 'Big Stars Under The Big Top', *West Australian* (Perth), 6 April 1991. Reproduced in *CineDossier*, No.472 (1991), pp.15.

24. Richard Dyer, *Heavenly Bodies: Film Stars and Society* (Basingstoke: Macmillan Education, 1986), p.91.

25. Anon, *The West Australian* (Perth), p.17.

26. *Sixty Minutes*, Channel Nine, 19 June 1994.

27. Quoted in Cohen, p.45.

28. Bowring, p.62.

29. Ibid., p.63.

30. Amor, p.35.

31. Dingo, quoted in Darren Devlyn, 'There Are Time When I Wish I Was White: Joking Aside, Ernie Dingo Reveals He Has Been A Victim Of Discrimination', *TV Week*, 5 Oct. 1991, and reproduced in *CineDossier*, No.497 (1991), p.54.

32. Anon, *The West Australian* (Perth), p.16.

33. Cohen, p.45.

34. Martin Flanagan, 'Black anger – Gary Foley'. *The Age* (Melbourne), 20 March 1993, p.5.

35. Dingo, quoted in Jodi Brough, 'Behind Ernie Dingo', *The Age Good Weekend Magazine* (Melbourne), 9 Sept. 1989, p.102.

36. Van Nunen, p.25.

37. Amor, p.35.

38. Cohen.

39. Dingo, quoted in Amor, p.35.

40. Dingo, quoted in Brough, p.102.

41. Dingo, quoted in Devlyn, p.55.

42. Jerry Palmer, *The Logic of the Absurd: On Film and Television Comedy*, (London, British Film Institute, 1987).

43. *Sixty Minutes*.

44. Alan McKee, 'Heart of the Matter', *In the Picture* (Perth), (Winter 1994), pp.13–14.

45. Stuart Cunningham, 'Textual Innovation in the Australian Historical Mini-Series', in John Tulloch and Graeme Turner (eds.), *Australian Television: Programs, Pleasures and Politics* (Sydney: Allen and Unwin, 1989), pp.39–51.

46. Philippa Hawker, 'Aboriginal Cast Coup', *The Age* (Melbourne), 23 March 1994, p.17.

47. Anon, '*Heartland*: A Love Story Forged Against the Odds: A Murder. A Mystery. Two Hearts Drawn Forever Closer. Two Lives Changed Forever', *The Age Good Weekend Magazine* (Melbourne), 19 March 1994, p.2.

48. Warneke, p.4.
49. Onset Productions, 1990.
50. Philippa Hawker, 'ABC's New Drama More Than Just Soap', *The Age* (Melbourne), 21 April 1994, p.16.
51. Van Nunen, p.25.
52. Dingo, quoted in Devlyn, p.55, Devlyn's comments.
53. Stephen Muecke, *Textual Spaces: Aboriginality and Cultural Studies* (Kensington, New South Wales: New South Wales University Press, 1992) p.12.

Australian Cinema in the 1990s: Filmography

SAMANTHA SEARLE

Feature films completed between 1990 and 1999 are listed in the filmography below. More detailed listings are produced by the Australian Film Commission, and are available through its distribution department. Invaluable reference works giving details of earlier periods of the cinema revival include Tom O'Reagan's *Australian National Cinema* (London: Routledge, 1996) and Scott Murray's *Australian Film* (London: Routledge, 1996).

d: director
p: producer
s: scriptwriter
pc: production company

1990

An Angel at My Table
d: Jane Campion
p: Bridget Ikin
s: Laura Jones
pc: Hibiscus Films Ltd

The Big Steal
d: Nadia Tass
p: Nadia Tass, David Parker, Timothy White
s: David Parker
pc: Cascade Films Pty Ltd

Blood Oath [aka Prisoner of the Sun]
d: Stephen Wallace
p: Charles Waterstreet, Denis Whitburn, Brian Williams

s: Brian Williams, Dennis Whitburn
pc: Blood Oath Productions

Bloodmoon
d: Alex Mills
p: Stanley O'Toole
s: Robert Brennan
pc: Village Roadshow (Australia) Pty Ltd

Breakaway [aka Escape from Madness]
d: Don McLennan
p: Jane Ballantyne, Don McLennan, Les Lithgow
s: Jan Sardi
pc: Breakaway Films/Ukiyo Films Australia/Smart Egg Pictures

The Crossing
d: George Ogilvie
p: Sue Seary
s: Ranald Allan
pc: Beyond International Group

Dead To The World
d: Ross Gibson
p: John Cruthers, Adrienne Parr
s: Ross Gibson
pc: Huzzah Productions Pty Ltd

Fantasy
d: Geoffrey Brown, Derek Strahan
p: Geoffrey Brown
s: Derek Strhan
pc: Combridge Pty Ltd

Father
d: John Power
p: Damien Parer, Tony Cavanaugh,
    Graham Hartley, Paul Barron
s: Tony Cavanaugh, Graham Hartley
pc: Barron Films

Harbour Beat
d: David Elfick
p: David Elfick, Irene Dobson
s: Morris Gleitzman
pc: Palm Beach Pictures

Heaven Tonight
d: Pino Amento
p: Frank Howson, Barbi Taylor
s: Frank Howson, Alister Webb
pc: Boulevard Films

Jindalee Lady
d: Brian Syron
p: Briann Kearney
s: Briann Kearney
pc: Donobri International
    Communications Pty

A Kink in the Picasso
d: Marc Gracie
p: Rosa Colosimo
s: Hugh Stuckey
pc: Rosa Colosimo Pty Ltd.

The Min-Min
d: Carl T. Woods
p: Carl T. Woods
s: Paul Holland
pc: n/a

Phobia
d: John Dingwall
p: John Mandelberg
s: John Dingwall
pc: Jadee Productions

The Prisoner of St. Petersburg
d: Ian Pringle
p: Klaus Sungen, Daniel Scharf
s: Michael Wren
pc: Daniel Scharf Productions Pty Ltd,
    Panorama Films

Raw Nerve
d: Tony Wellington
p: Michael Lynch
s: Tony Wellington
pc: Lynchpin and Tosh, Australian
    Film Commission

Return Home
d: Ray Argall
p: Christina Pozzan
s: Ray Argall
pc: Musical Films

The Returning
d: John Day
p: Patricia Downie, David Hannay
s: Arthur Baysting, John Day
pc: David Hannay Productions, Echo
    Pictures Ltd

The Sher Mountains Killing Mystery
d: Vince Martin
p: Phillip Martin
s: Denis Whitburn
pc: Avalon Film Corporation

Strangers
d: Craig Lahiff
p: Wayne Groom, Craig Lahiff
s: John Emery
pc: Genesis Films Pty Ltd

Struck by Lightning
d: Jerzy Domaradzki
p: Terry Charatsis, Trevor Farrant
s: Trevor Farrant
pc: Dark Horse Pictures

Sweethearts
d: Colin Talbot
p: Lynda House
s: Colin Talbot
pc: n/a

Till There Was You
d: John Seale
p: Jim McElroy
s: Michael Thomas
pc: Ayer Productions Pty Ltd

Wendy Cracked a Walnut
d: Michael Pattinson
p: John Edwards, Brian Rosen, Sandra Levy
s: Suzanne Hawley
pc: ABC, Classic Films

What the Moon Saw
d: Pino Amento
p: Frank Howson
s: Frank Howson
pc: Boulevard Films

1991

Aya
d: Solrun Hoass
p: Denise Patience,Solrun Hoass
s: Solrun Hoass
pc: Goshu Films Pty Ltd

Bloodlust
d: John Hewitt, Richard Wolstencroft
p: John Hewitt, Richard Wolstencroft
s: John Hewitt, Richard Wolstencroft
pc: Windhover Productions

Dangerous Game
d: Steve Hopkins
p: Judith West, Basil Appleby
s: Peter West
pc: Quantum Films, Virgo Productions

Death in Brunswick
d: John Ruane
p: Timothy White, Bryce Menzies
s: John Ruane, Boyd Oxlade

pc: Meridian Films Pty Ltd

Flirting
d: John Duigan
p: George Miller, Terry Hayes, Doug Mitchell
s: John Duigan
pc: Kennedy Miller

Golden Braid
d: Paul Cox
p: Paul Cox, Santhanu Naidu, Paul Amitzboll
s: Paul Cox, Barry Dickins
pc: Illumination Films Pty Ltd

Green Card
d: Peter Weir
p: Peter Weir, Jean Gontier
s: Peter Weir
pc: Green Card Productions

Holidays on the River Yarra
d: Leo Berkeley
p: Fiona Cochrane
s: Leo Berkeley
pc: Jungle Pictures P/L

Hunting
d: Frank Howson
p: Frank Howson, Peter Boyle
s: Frank Howson
pc: Boulevard Films

Hurricane Smith
d: Colin Budds
p: Stanely O'Toole
s: Peter Kinloch
pc: Village Roadshow Pictures

Mad Bomber in Love
d: James Bogle
p: George Mannix
s: Various
pc: Pinchgut Productions

The Magic Riddle
d: Yoram Gross
p: Yoram Gross
w: Yoram Gross

pc: Yoram Gross Films

Nirvana Street Murder
d: Aleksi Vellis
p: Fiona Cochrane
s: Aleksi Vellis
pc: n/a

Proof
d: Jocelyn Moorhouse
p: Lynda House
s: Jocelyn Moorhouse
pc: House and Moorhouse Films

Quigley [aka Quigley Down Under]
d: Simon Wincer
p: Stanley O'Toole, Alexandra Rose
s: John Hill
pc: Pathe Entertainment Inc.

Resistance
d: Paul Elliott, Jugh Keays-Byrne
p: Christina Ferguson, Pauline
    Rosenberg, Jenny Day
s: Macau Collective
pc: Phaedra Cinema

**Say a Little Prayer [aka Came Back
to Show You I Could Fly]**
d: Richard Lowenstein
p: Carol Hughes
s: Richard Lowenstein
pc: Beyond Films

Seeing Red
d: Virgina Rouse
p: Viginia Rouse, Tony Llewellyn-
    Jones
s: Roger Pulvers
pc: Seawell Films

Sweet Talker
d: Michael Jenkins
p: Ben Gannon
s: Tony Morphett
pc: Confidence Productions Pty
    Limited

Waiting
d: Jackie McKimmie

p: Ross Matthews
s: Jackie McKimmie
pc: Filmside Productions Ltd

Weekend with Kate
d: Arch Nicholson
p: Phillip Emanuel, David C J
    Douglas
s: Henry Tefay, Kee Young
pc: Phillip Emanuel

A Woman's Tale
d: Paul Cox
p: Paul Cox, Santhana Naidu
s: Paul Cox, Barry Dickins
pc: Illumination Films

1992

Alex
d: Megan Simpson Huberman
p: Phil Gerlach, Tom Parkinson
s: Ken Catran
pc: Isambard Production, Total Film &
    Television

Australian Ninja
d: Adam Ramos, Michelle Firmstone
p: Mario Difiori, Victor Sawicki
s: Adam Ramos
pc: Transworld International Pictures

Backsliding
d: Simon Target
p: Sue Wild, Basil Appleby
s: Ross Wilson, Simon Target
pc: Channel Four Films, ITEL.

Black Neon
d: James Richards, Edward John
    Stazak
p: James Richards, Edward John
    Stazak
s: James Richards, Edward John
    Stazak
pc: M C Stuart and Associates Pty

Black Robe
d: Bruce Beresford

p: Robert Lantos, Sue Milliken, Stephane Reichel
s: Brian Moore
pc: Alliance Communications Corporation, Sampson Productions Pty Ltd

Blinky Bill
d: Yoram Gross
p: Yoram Gross
s: John Palmer, Leonard Lee, Yoram Gross
pc: Yoram Gross Films Ltd

Breathing Under Water
d: Susan Murphy Dermody
p: Megan McMurchy
s: Susan Murphy Dermody
pc: Periscope Productions

Come by Chance
d: Lara Dunston
p: Lara Dunston, Terry Carter
s: Lara Dunston
pc: n/a

Cops and Robbers
d: Murray Reece
p: Tony Winley
s: Timothy Bean
pc: Total Film & Television Pty Ltd, New Zealand Film Corporation

The Cult of Death
d: Geoffrey Brown
p: Geoffrey Brown
s: Derek Strahan
pc: Cowbridge Pty Ltd

Daydream Believer
d: Kathy Mueller
p: Ben Gannon
s: Saturday Rosenberg
pc: Beyond Films Ltd., View Films Pty Ltd

Deadly
d: Esben Storm
p: Richard Moir
s: Esben Storm, Ranald Allan

pc: Deadly Productions Pty Limited

Dingo
d: Rolf de Heer
p: Marc Rosenberg, Rolf de Heer, Giorgio Draskovic
s: Marc Rosenberg
pc: Gevest Productions Pty Ltd, Australian Film Finance Corporation, AO Productions SARI, Dedra SARI, Cine Cinq SA

Fatal Bond
d: Vincent Monton
p: Phillip Avalon
s: Phillip Avalon
pc: Avalon Films (Tovefelt Productions Pty Ltd)

Fern Gully: The Last Rainforest
d: Bill Kroyer
p: Wayne Young, Peter Faiman
s: Jim Cox
pc: FAI Films, Youngheart Productions

Garbo
d: Ron Cobb
p: Hugh Rule
s: Patrick Cook, Stephen Kearney, Neill Gladwin
pc: Eclectic Films Pty Ltd

Get Away Get Away
d: Murray Fahey
p: Murray Fahey
s: Murray Fahey
pc: Total Film & Television Ltd.

Good Woman of Bangkok
d: Dennis O'Rourke
p: Dennis O'Rourke, Glenys Rowe
s: Dennis O'Rourke
pc: O'Rourke & Associates Filmmakers Pty Limited

Isabelle Eberhardt
d: Ian Pringle
p: Daniel Scharf, Jean Petit
s: Stephen Sewell

pc: Les Films Aramis, Seon Films,
Flach Films

Last Days of Chez Nous
d: Gillian Armstrong
p: Jan Chapman
s: Helen Garner
pc: Jan Chapman Productions Pty
Limited

Living Colour
d: Neal M. E. Taylor
p: Rene Nagy Jnr
s: Neal M. E. Taylor
pc: M C Stuart and Associates Pty Ltd

The Long Line
d: Aaron Stevenson
p: Aaron Stevenson, Gavin Pavey
s: Aaron Stevenson, Laurie Basten
pc: M C Stuart and Associates Pty Ltd

The Nun and the Bandit
d: Paul Cox
p: Paul Cox, Paul Ammitzboll
s: Paul Cox
pc: Illumination Films

Over the Hill
d: George Miller
p: Robert Caswell, Bernard Terry
s: Robert Caswell
pc: Village Roadshow Pictures,
Glasshouse Pictures, Over the Hill
Pty Limited

Redheads
d: Danny Vendramini
p: Richard Mason
s: Danny Vendramini
pc: Byond Films

Romper Stomper
d: Geoffrey Wright
p: Daniel Scharf, Ian Pringle
s: Geoffrey Wright
pc: Seon Films, Australian Film
Commission, Film Victoria

Secrets
d: Michael Pattinson
p: Michael Pattinson, David Arnell
s: Jan Sardi
pc: Victorian International Pictures,
Avalon-NFU Studios

**Spotswood [aka The Efficiency
Expert]**
d: Mark Joffe
p: Timothy White, Richard Brennan
s: Max Dann, Andrew Knight
pc: Meridian Films

Stan and George's New Life
d: Brian McKenzie
p: Margot McDonald
s: Brian McKenzie, Deborah Cox
pc: Lea Films Pty Ltd

Strictly Ballroom
d: Baz Luhrmann
p: Tristram Miall
s: Baz Luhrmann, Craig Pearce
pc: M&A Film Corporation

Turtle Beach
d: Stephen Wallace
p: Matt Carroll
s: Ann Turner
pc: Village Roadshow Pictures,
Regency International Pictures

Until the End of the World
d: Wim Wenders
p: Anatole Dauman, Jonathan Taplin,
Wim Wenders
s: Peter Carey, Wim Wenders
pc: Australian Film Finance
Corporation, Road Movies
Filmproduction GmbH, Argos
Films SA

The Wide Sargasso Sea
d: John Duigan
p: Jan Chapman
s: Jan Sharp, Carole Angier, John
Duigan
pc: New Line International

You Can't Push the River
d: Leslie Oliver
p: Robert Alcock
s: John Reddin, Leslie Oliver
pc: Sculpting Pictures Pty Ltd

1993

Bedevil
d: Tracey Moffatt
p: Anthony Buckley, Carol Hughes
s: Tracey Moffatt
pc: Anthony Buckley Films Pty

Blackfellas
d: James Ricketson
p: David Rapsey
s: James Ricketson
pc: Beyond Films

Dallas Doll
d: Ann Turner
p: Ross Matthews
s: Ann Turner
pc: Dallas Doll Productions

Exchange Lifeguards
d: Maurice Murphy
p: Phillip Avalon
s: Phillip Avalon
pc: Avalon Films

Fortress
d: Arch Nicholson
p: Ray menmuir
s: Everett de Roche
pc: Fortress Films Ltd

Gino
d: Jackie McKimmie
p: Ross Matthews
s: Vince Sorrenti, Larry Buttrose
pc: Filmside Productions

Greenkeeping
d: David Caesar
p: Glenys Rowe
s: David Caesar
pc: Central Park Films

Gross Misconduct
d: George Miller
p: David Hannay, Richard Sheffield-
      MacClure
s: Gerard Maguire, Lance Peters
pc: PRO Films

The Heartbreak Kid
d: Michael Jenkins
p: Ben Gannon
s: Richard Barrett, Michael Jenkins
pc: Australian Film Finance
      Corporation, View Films Pty
      Limited, Film Victoria

Hercules Returns
d: David Parker
p: Philip A. Jaroslow
s: Des Mangan
pc: Philm Production

Lorenzo's Oil
d: George Miller
p: Doug Mitchell, George Miller
s: George Miller, Nick Enright
pc: Kennedy Miller

Love in Limbo
d: David Elfick
p: David Elfick, Nina Stevenson, John
      Winter
s: John Cundill
pc: Palm Beach Pictures Pty Limited

Map of the Human Heart
d: Vincent Ward
p: Tim Bevan, Vincent Ward
s: Louis Nowra
pc: Working Title Films, Vincent Ward
      Films, Les Films Ariane, Sunrise
      Films, Map Films

No Worries
d: David Elfick
p: David Elfick, Eric Fellner
s: David Holman
pc: Palm Beach Pictures-Initial Films

The Nostradamus Kid
d: Bob Ellis

p: Terry Jennings
s: Bob Ellis
pc: Simpson, Le Mesurier Film Pty Ltd

Offspring
d: Richard Ryan
p: Phillip Emanuel
s: Richard Ryan
pc: Phillip Emmanuel Productions,
    IFM Film Associates Inc.

Open City
d: Bill Mousoulis
p: Bill Mousoulis
s: Bill Mousoulis
pc: Innersense Productions

On My Own
d: Antonio Tibaldi
p: Leo Pescarolo, Elisa Resegotti
s: Gill Dennis, Antonio Tibaldi, John
    Frizzell
pc: Ellipi Films, Alliance
    Communications Corporation, Rosa
    Colosimo Pty Ltd, Arto-pelli
    Motion Pictures Inc.

The Piano
d: Jane Campion
p: Jan Chapman
s: Jane Campion
pc: Jan Chapman Productions

Reckless Kelly
d: Yahoo Serious
p: Yahoo Serious, Warwick Ross
s: Yahoo Serious
pc: Serious Entertainment Pty Ltd

The Refracting Glasses
d: David Perry
p: John Prescott
s: David Perry
pc: n/a

Seventh Floor
d: Ian Barry
p: John Sexton
s: Suzanne Hawley, Tony Morphett
pc: Primetime, Pinnacle Pictures

Signal One: Bullet Down Under
d: Rob Stewart
p: Phillip Avalon
s: Karl Shiffman
pc: Canealian Productions, Artist View
    Entertainment

The Silver Brumby
d: John Tatoulis
p: Colin South, John Tatoulis
s: Jon Stephens, John Tatoulis, Elyne
    Mitchell
pc: Media World Features

Talk
d: Susan Lambert
p: Megan McMurchy
s: Jan Cornall
pc: Total Film & Television Pty Ltd

Tempting a Married Man
d: Adam Lynton
p: Adam Lynton
s: Adam Lynton
pc: Tears of Joy Productions

This Won't Hurt a Bit!
d: Chris Kennedy
p: Patrick Fitzgerald, Chris Kennedy
s: Chris Kennedy
pc: Oilrag Productions

Wind
d: Carroll Ballard
p: Mata Yamamoto, Tom Luddy
s: Rudy Wurlitzer, Mac Gudgeon
pc: Filmlink International, Inc. Japan
    and The Wind Production
    Committee from American
    Zoetrope

1994

**The Adventures of Priscilla, Queen of
    the Desert**
d: Stephan Elliott
p: Al Clark, Michael Hamlyn
s: Stephan Elliott
pc: Polygram Filmed Entertainment,

Australian Film Finance
Corporation

Billy's Holiday
d: Richard Wherrett
p: Tristram Miall
s: Denis Whitburn
pc: Billy's Holiday Pty Ltd

Bad Boy Bubby
d: Rolf de Heer
p: Domenico Procacci, Giorgio
     Draskovic, Rolf de Heer
s: Rolf de Heer
pc: Fandango (Rome), Bubby Pty Ltd
     (Adelaide)

Body Melt
d: Phillip Brophy
p: Rod Bishop, Daniel Scharf
s: Phillip Brophy, Rod Bishop
pc: Dumb Films, Australian Film
     Commission, Film Victoria

Broken Highway
d: Laurie McInnes
p: Richard Mason
s: Laurie McInnes
pc: Black Ray Films, Australian Film
     Commission, Queensland Film
     Development Office

Country Life
d: Michael Blakemore
p: Robin Dalton
s: Michael Blakemore
pc: Australian Film Finance
     Corporation, Dalton Films Ltd

The Custodian
d: John Dingwall
p: Adrienne Read
s: John Dingwall
pc: J. D. Productions

David O'Brien's Shotgun Wedding
d: Paul Harmon
p: David Hannay, Charles Hannah
s: David O'Brien
pc: David Hannay Productions Pty Ltd

Exile
d: Paul Cox
p: Santhana Naidu, Paul Ammitzboll,
     Paul Cox
s: Paul Cox
pc: Illumination Films

Frauds
d: Stephan Elliott
p: Andrena Finlay, Stuart Quin
s: Stephan Elliott
pc: Latent Image Productions Pty
     Limited

Hammers Over the Anvil
d: Ann Turner
p: Ben Gannon, Peter Harvey-Wright
s: Peter Hepworth, Ann Turner
pc: South Australian Film Corporation,
     Harvest Productions

Lex and Rory
d: Dean Murphy
p: Scott Andrews, Dean Murphy
s: Dean Murphy
pc: Lex and Rory Production Ltd

Lightning Jack
d: Simon Wincer
p: Paul Hogan, Greg Coote, Simon
     Wincer
s: Paul Hogan
pc: Ligtning Ridge Films Ltd, Village
     Roadshow Pictures

Lucky Break
d: Ben Lewin
p: Bob Weis, Judi Levine
s: Ben Lewin
pc: Australian Film Finance
     Corporation, Weis Films Pty
     Limited, Lewin Films Pty Limited

Mary
d: Kay Pavlou
p: Rosemary Blight
s: Kay Pavlou
pc: Australian Film Finance
     Corporation, R. B. Films Pty
     Limited, Australian Film

Commission, New South Wales
Film and Television Office

Muriel's Wedding
d: P J Hogan
p: Lynda House, Jocelyn Moorhouse
s: P J Hogan
pc: House and Moorhouse Films Pty
    Ltd

**No Escape [aka Penal Colony, aka
Escape from Absalom]**
d: Martin Campbell
p: Gale Ann Hurd
s: Michael Gaylin, Joel Gross
pc: Allied Filmmakers

Police Rescue
d: Michael Carson
p: John Edwards, Sandra Levy
s: Debra Oswald
pc: Southern Star Entertainment Pty
    Ltd

The Roly Poly Man
d: Bill Young
p: Peter Green
s: Kym Goldsworthy
pc: Rough Nut Productions Pty Ltd

Sirens
d: John Duigan
p: Sue Milliken, Sarah Radclyffe
s: John Duigan
pc: Australian Film Finance
    Corporation, WMG Film GmbH,
    British Screen Finance Ltd, Samson
    Productions Ltd, Sarah Radclyffe
    Productions-Sirens Ltd

Spider and Rose
d: Bill Bennett
p: Lyn McCarthy, Graeme
    Tubbenhauer
s: Bill Bennett
pc: Dendy Films Pty Limited

The Sum of Us
d: Kevin Dowling and Geoff Burton
p: Hal McElroy

s: David Stevens
pc: Southern Star Entertainment Pty
    Ltd

Traps
d: Pauline Chan
p: Jim McElroy
s: Robert Carter, Pauline Chan
pc: Ayer Productions Limited

1995

All Men Are Liars
d: Gerard Lee
p: John Maynard
s: Gerard Lee
pc: Arenafilm

Angel Baby
d: Michael Rymer
p: Timothy White, Jonathan
    Shteinman
s: Michael Rymer
pc: Astral Films

Back of Beyond
d: Michael Robertson
p: John Sexton
s: Paul Leadon, Rick J. Sawyer, Anne
    Brooksbank
pc: Back of Beyond Films

Dad and Dave: On Our Selection
d: George Whaley
p: Anthony Buckley
s: George Whaley
pc: Anthony Buckley Productions

Epsilon
d: Rolf de Heer
p: Domenico Procacci, Rolf de Heer
s: Rolf de Heer
pc: Digital Arts, Fandango, Psilon Pty,
    The Australian Film Finance
    Corporation

Hotel Sorrento
d: Richard Franklin
p: Richard Franklin

s: Richard Franklin, Peter Fitzpatrick
pc: Bayside Pictures

Metal Skin
d: Geoffrey Wright
p: Daniel Scharf
s: Geoffrey Wright
pc: Daniel Scharf Productions

Say a Little Prayer
d: Richard Lowenstein
p: Carol Hughes
s: Richard Lowenstein
pc: Flying Films

Shine
d: Scott Hicks
p: Jane Scott
s: Jan Sardi
pc: Momentum Films

Talk
d: Susan Lambert
p: Megan McMurchy
s: Jan Cornall
pc: Suitcase Films, Australian Film
     Commission

That Eye the Sky
d: John Ruane
p: Peter Beilby
s: John Ruane, Jim Barton
pc: Entertainment Media

Vancant Posession
d: Margot Nash
p: John Winter
s: Margot Nash
pc: Wintertime Films

1996

Cosi
d: Mark Joffe
p: Richard Brennan
s: Louis Nowra
pc: Smiley Films

Hotel de Love
d: Craig Roseberg
p: David Parker, Michael Lake
s: Craig Rosenberg
pc: Village Roadshow Pictures

Dating the Enemy
d: Megan Simpson Huberman
p: Sue Milliken
s: Megan Simpson Huberman
pc: Dating the Enemy Pty Ltd

David Williamson's Brilliant Lies
d: Richard Franklin
p: Richard Franklin, Sue Farrelly
s: Peter Fitzpatrick, Richard Franklin
pc: Bayside Pictures

Dead Heart
d: Nick Parsons
p: Bryan Brown
s: Nick Parsons
pc: Dead Heart Productions

Floating Life
d: Clara Law
p: Bridgit Ikin
s: Eddie Ling-Ching Fong
pc: Hibiscius Films

Idiot Box
d: David Caesar
p: Glenys Rowe
s: David Caesar
pc: Central Park Films, The Australian
     Film Finance Corporation

Lillian's Story
d: Jerzy Domaradsky
p: Marion Macgowan
s: Steve Wright
pc: CML Production Pty Ltd

Love and other Catastrophes
d: Emma-Kate Croghan
p: Stavros Efthymiou
s: Yael Bergman, Emma-Kate
     Croghan, Helen Bandis
pc: Screwball Five Pty Ltd

Love Serenade
d: Shirley Barrett
p: Jan Chapman
s: Shirley Barret
pc: Jan Chapman Productions

Lust and Revenge
d: Paul Cox
p: Jane Ballantyne, Paul Cox
s: Shirley Barret
pc: Illumination Films

Mr Reliable
d: Nadia Tass
p: Jim Mc Elroy, Terry hayes, Michael
     Hamlyn
s: Don Catchlove, Terry Hayes
pc: Hayes McElroy, Specific Films

The Quiet Room
d: Rolf de Heer
p: Rolf de Heer, Giuseppe Pedersoli
s: Rolf de Heer
pc: Vertigo Productions

To Have and Have Not
d: John Hillcoat
p: Denise Patience
s: Gene Conkie
pc: Small Man Productions

Turning April
d: Geoffrey Bennett
p: Laell McCall, Heather Ogilvie
s: James W. Nichol
pc: Small Man Productions

Zone 39
d: John Tatoulis
p: John Tatoulis
s: Deborah Parsons
pc: Media World Features

1997

The Big Red
d: Stephen Elliot
p: Finola Dwyer
s: Michael Thomas

pc: Scala Productions

Blackrock
d: Steve Vidler
p: David Elfick
s: Nick Enright
pc: Beyond Films

The Castle
d: Rob Stich
p: Debra Choate
s: Santo Cilauro, Tom Gleisner, Jane
     Kennedy, Rob Stich
pc: Working Dog

Dark City
d: Alex Proyas
p: Andrew Mason
s: Alex Proyas, Lem Dobbs, David
     Goyer
pc: Dark City Productions

Diane & Me
d: David Parker
p: Matt Carroll
s: Matt Ford
pc: Matt Carroll Films

Doing Time for Patsy Cline
d: Chris Kennedy
p: John Winter
s: Chris Kennedy
pc: Oil Rag Films

Dust Off the Wings
d: Lee Rodgers
p: Lee Rodgers, Ward Stephens
s: Lee Rodgers, Ward Stephens
pc: Bombshell Films

Fistful of Flies
d: Monica Pellizzari
p: Julia Overton
s: Monica Pellizzari
pc: Long Black Productions

Heaven's Burning
d: Craig Lahiff
p: Al Clarke, Helen Leake
s: Louis Nowra

pc: Duo Art Productions

Joey
d: Ian Barry
p: Michael Lake
s: Stuart Beattie
pc: Village Roadshow Pictures

Kiss or Kill
d: Bill Bennett
p: Bill Bennett, Jennifer Bennet
s: Bill Bennett
pc: Bill Bennett Productions

The Last Bus Home
d: Johnny Gogan
p: Paul Donovan
s: Johnny Gogan
pc: Goutte d'Or Distribution

Love in Ambush
d: Carl Schltz
p: Jean Pierre Ramsey
s: Loupe Durand, Davide Ambrose,
    Christine Miller, John Howlett,
    Tom Hegarty
pc: Pro Films

Paradise Road
d: Bruce Beresford
p: Greg Coote, Sue Milliken
s: Bruce Beresford
pc: Village Roadshow Pictures

Paws
d: Karl Zwicky
p: Andrena Finlay, Vicki Watson
s: Harry Cripps, Karl Zwicky
pc: Latent Image Productions

River Street
d: Tony Mahood
p: Lynda House
s: Phillip Ryall
pc: House & Moorhouse

The Road to Nhill
d: Sue Brooks
p: Sue Maslen
s: Alison Tilson

pc: Gecko Films

Sound of One Hand Clapping
d: Richard Flanagan
p: Rolf de Heer
s: Richard Flanagan
pc: Artist Services

Thank God He Met Lizzie
d: Cherie Nowlan
p: Jonathon Shteinman
s: Alexandra Long
pc: Stamen Films

True Love and Chaos
d: Stavros Andonis Efthymiou
p: Ann Darrouzet
s: Stavros Andonis Efthymiou
pc: Westside Films

Under the Lighthouse Dancing
d: Graeme Rattigan
p: David Giles
s: David Giles, Graeme Rattigan
pc: Silver Turtle Films

The Well
d: Samantha Lang
p: Sandra Levy
s: Laura Jones
pc: NSWFTV Office/Southern Star
     Xanadu/AFFC

1998

Aberration
d: Tim Boxell
p: Scott Lew, Chris Brown, Ian
    Ousley
s: Scott Lew, Darrin Oura
pc: Grundby Films

All the Way
d: Marque Owen
p: Marque Owen
s: Marque Owen
pc: Beyond Films

Babe: Pig in the City
d: George Miller
p: Barbara Gibbs
s: George Miller, Judy Morris, Mark Lamprell
pc: Kennedy Miller Productions

The Beggar's Opera Cafe
d: Vicky Fisher
p: Katina Bowell
s: Vicki Fisher
pc: The Beggars Opera Cafe

Cat's Tales
d: Ralph Lawrence Marsden
p: David Fraser, Mark Freeman
s: Ralph Lawrence Marsden
pc: Screencraft Productions

Channelling Baby
d: Christine Parker
p: Caterina De Nave
s: Christine Parker
pc: Oceania Parker Ltd., New Zealand Film Commission

The Craic
d: Ted Emery
p: Alan Finney, David Foster, Marc Gracie, Stephen Luby
s: Jimeoin
pc: Foster Gracie

Damien
d: Paul Cox
p: Andy Howard, Grietje Lammertyn, Tarsicius Vanhuysse
s: John Briley, Hilde Eynikel
pc: ERA Films

Dead End
d: Iren Koster
p: Bill Lewski, Tracey Silvers
s: Iren Koster
pc: Showcase Entertainment

Dear Claudia
d: Chris Cudlipp
p: Jim Mc Elroy, Des Power
s: Chris Cudlipp
pc: DC Films Limited

Demons in my Head
d: Neil Johnson
p: Grant Hoi
s: Neil Johnson
pc: Empire Motion Pictures

Dreamtime Alice
d: Cherie Nowlan
p: Cherie Nowlan, Cate Blanchett
s: Mandy Sayer
pc: n/a

Erskineville Kings
d: Alan White
p: John Swaffield
s: Alan White, Anik Chooney
pc: @ radical media

Eye of the Beholder
d: Stephen Eliot
p: Manon Bougie, Al Clark
s: Stephen Eliot, Marc Behm
pc: Village Roadshow Productions, FilmlineInternational Inc, Ambridge Film Partnership, Behaviour Worldwide, Eye of the Beholder Ltd, Hit and Run Productions

Feeling Sexy
d: Davida Alan
p: Chris Noonan, Tracey Robertson, Glenys Rowe
s: Davida Alan
pc: Binnabura Film Company Pty Ltd

Fifteen Amore
d: Maurice Murphy
p: Maurice Murphy, Brooke Wilson
s: Maurice Murphy
pc: MTMX Movies

Fresh Air
d: Neil Mansfield
p: Rosemary Blight
s: Neil Mansfield
pc: R.B. Films

Head On
d: Ana Kokkinos
p: Jane Scott
s: Andrew Bovell, Mira Robertson, Ana Kokinos
pc: Great Scott productions

Hurrah
d: Frank Shields
p: Julie Marlow, John Wolstenholme
s: John Wolstenholme, Frank Shields
pc: Hurrah Productions Pty Ltd

I'll Make You Happy
d: Athina Tsoulis
p: Liz Stevens
s: Athina Tsoulis
pc: Ample Films

In The Winter Dark
d: James Bogle
p: Rosemary Blight
s: TimWinton, James Bogle, Peter Rasmussen
pc: R.B. Films

James
d: Lynda Heys
p: Sharon Kruger, Ross Matthews
s: Stuart Beattie
pc: Blackwood Films

Lawn Dogs
d: John Duigan
p: Ron Daniels, Amy.J. Kaufmann, David Rubin
s: Naomi Wallace
pc: Toledo Pictures

Liquid Bridge
d: Phil Avalon
p: Brian Williams, Phillip Avalon
s: Pim Hendrix
pc: Avalon Films

Matrix
d: Larry Wachowsky, Andy Wachowsky
p: Bill Pope

s: Larry Wachowsky, Andy Wachowsky
pc: Village Roadshow Productions, Groucho II Film Partnership, Silver Pictures

The Missing
d: Manuel Alberti
p: Geoffrey Hall
s: Manuel Alberti
pc: Roadshow

The Monkey's Mask
d: Samantha Lang
p: Robert Connolly, John Maynard
s: Anne Kennedy
pc: Arenafilm Pty Ltd

Mr Accident
d: Yahoo Series
p: Warwick Ross, Yahoo Serious
s: David Roach, Yahoo Serious
pc: Goldwyn Films

Muggers
d: Dean Murphy
p: Chris Craib, Nigel Odell, David Redman, Gary Smith, Gareth Wiley, John Wostenholme
s: Dean Murphy
pc: REP Distribution

Occasional Course Language
d: Brad Hayward
p: Michael Lake, Joel Pearlman, Trish Piper
s: Brad Hayward
pc: Very Chancy Material Pty Limited

Paperback Hero
d: Antony Bowman
p: Lance W Reynolds, Dani Rodgers, John Winter
s: Antony Bowman
pc: Polygram Filmed Entertainment

Passion
d: Peter Duncan
p: Matt Carroll
s: John Bird, George Goldsworthy

pc: Beyond Films, Hollywood Partners,
The Australian Film Finance
Corporation, The Movie Network
(TMN)

Praise
d: John Curran
p: Martha Coleman
s: Andrew McGahan
pc: Emcee Films

Reflections
d: Geoffrey Brown
p: Cathy Brown
s: Terry O'Connor
pc: Combridge International

The Ridge
d: Janet McLeod
p: Angela Borelli
s: Janet Mc Leod
pc: Two-Up Films Pty Ltd

Sample People
d: Clinton Smith
p: Emile Sherman, Jonathon
Shteinman, Barton Smith
s: Clinton Smith, Peter Buckmaster
pc: Living Motion Pictures

Saving Grace
d: Costa Botes
p: Larry Parr
s: Duncan Sarkies
pc: Kahukura Films, New Zealand
Film Commission

Snowdrop
d: Julie Money
p: Michael Cook
s: Jeff Truman, Trevor Shearston
pc: Adelphi Films

Somewhere in the Darkness
d: Paul Fenech
p: Paul Fenech, Brendan Fletcher,
David Webster
s: Brendan Fletcher, Paul Fenech
pc: Livewire Films

Spank
d: Ernie Clark
p: David Lightfoot, Rolf de Heer
s: David Farrel, David Lightfoot
pc: Ultra Films

Strange Planet
d: Emma-Kate Croghan
p: Bruno Charlesworth, Stavros
Kazantzidis, Anastasia Sideris
s: Ann Turner, Stavros Kazantzidas
pc: Premium Movie Partnership,
Showtime Australia, Strange
Planet, New South Wales Film &
Television Office, The Australian
Film Finance Corporation

Two Hands
d: Gregor Jordan
p: Marian Macgowan
s: Gregor Jordan
pc: Beyond Films, CML Films,
Meridian Films, The Australian
Film Finance Corporation

Via Satellite
d: Anthony McCarten
p: Phillipa Campbell
s: Anthony McCarten
pc: Satellite Films, Portman
Productions

Waste
d: Tony de Pasquale
p: Tony de Pasquale, Geoffrey Cooper
s: Jeff Afiouni, Greg Afiouni, Tony
De Pasquale
pc: de Pasquale Productions

When Love Comes Along
d: Garth Maxwell
p: Jonathon Dowling, Michael Fautl
s: Garth Maxwell, Rex Pilgrim
pc: MF Films

Wild Blue
d: Garth Maxwell
p: L. Grant Bradley
s: Dale G. Bradley
pc: Daybreak Pictures

A Wreck A Tangle
d: Scott Paterson
p: Nicki Roller
s: John O'Brien
pc: Rectango Pty Ltd

1999

Bored Olives
d: Belinda Chayko
p: Bruce Redman
s: Stephen Davis
pc: Red Movies Pty. Ltd

Change of Heart
d: Rod Hay
p: Murray Fahey, Rod Hay
s: Coral Drouyn, Murray Fahey
pc: A Change of Heart Film Production Pty

Cubby House
d: Murray Fahey
p: Chris Brown, David Hannay
s: Ian Coughlan
pc: Beyond Films

Dogwatch
d: Laurie McInnes
p: Richard Brennan
s: Laurie Mc Innes
pc: Black Ray Films Pty Ltd

Drover's Boy
d: Chris Langman
p: Andrew Steuart
s: Nerys Evans
pc: Spandau Productions

From the Outside
d: Andrew Dominik
p: Michele Bennett
s: Andrew Dominik
pc: Pariah Films Pty Ltd

He Died with a Felafel in his Hand
d: Richard Lowenstein
p: Andrew McPhail, Helen Panckhurst, Domenico Procacci
s: Richard Lowenstein, John Birmingham
pc: Notorious Films Pty. Ltd

Hildegarde
d: Di Drew
p: Heather Ogilvie, David Hannay
s: Gabrielle Prendergast
pc: A Duck Film

Holy Smoke
d: Jane Campion
p: Jan Chapman
s: Anna Campion, Jane Campion
pc: Miramax Films

In a Savage Land
d: Bill Bennet
p: Jennifer Bennet, Bill Bennet
s: Bill Bennet,Jennifer Cluff
pc: Hollywood Partners, The Australian Film Finance Corporation

Komodo
d: Michael Lantieri
p: Tony Ludwig, Alan Riche
s: Hans Bauer, Craig Mitchell
pc: ScanboxAsia Pacific Ltd.

Komodo – The Living Terror
d: Michael Lantieri
p: Tony Ludwig, Alan Riche
s: Hans Bauer, Craig Mitchell
pc: ScanboxAsia Pacific Ltd.

Looking for Alibrandi
d: Kate Woods
p: Robyn Kershaw
s: Melina Marchetta
pc: Beyond Distribution

Me Myself I
d: Pip Karmel
p: Fabien Liron, Andrena Finlay
s: Pip Karmel
pc: Gaumont, Les Films du Loup

My Mother Frank
d: Mark Lamprell

p: John Winter
s: Mark Lamprell
pc: Beyond Films, The Australian Film
    Finance Corporation

Pitch Black
d: David Twohy
p: Tom Engelman, Tony Winley
s: Jim Wheat, Ken Wheat
pc: Intrepid Pictures

Selkie
d: Donald Crombie
p: Jane Ballantyne, Robert George
s: Rob George
pc: Bluestone Pictures Pty Ltd

Siam Sunset
d: John Poulson
p: Al Clark
s: Max Dann, Andrew Knight
pc: Channel Four Films, Showtime
    Australia, Artist Services, New
    South Wales Film & Television
    Office, The Australian Film
    Finance Corporation, South
    Australian Film Corporation

Soft Fruit
d: Christina Andreef
p: Helen Bowden

s: Christina Andreef
pc: Soft Fruit

Something Different Tomorrow
d: Jason McFayden, Shannon Swan
p: n/a
s: Jason McFayden, Shannon Swan
pc: n/a

Strange Fits of Passion
d: Elise McCredie
p: Lucy Mc Laren
s: Elise Mc Credie
pc: Arena, Film Victoria, Meridian
    Films, American Broadcasting
    Company (ABC)

Unconditional Love
d: P J Hogan
p: Jocelyn Moorhouse
s: P J Hogan, Jocelyn Moorhouse
pc: Avery Pix

What Becomes of the Broken Hearted
d: Ian Mune
p: Bill Gavin
s: Alan Duff
pc: New Zealand Film Commission,
    South Pacific Pictures, Polygram
    Filmed Entertainment

Australian Cinema in the 1990s:
A Select Bibliography

LINDA SMITH

Excellent bibliographies covering the development of Australian Cinema until the late 1980s have been published in recent years; the works listed below are included to suggest something of the range of work now underway around the subsequent cinema. For a comprehensive survey of the pre-existing literature see Brian Reis, *Australian Film: A Bibliography* (London and Washington: Mansell Publishing, 1997).

a) Books and Anthologies:

Australian Council of Government Film Libraries/National Film and Sound Archive, *Focus on Reel Australia* (Canberra: Australian Council of Government Film Libraries, 1990).

Australian Film Commission, *Analysis of The Performance of Australian Films Since 1980: A Paper for The House of Representatives Standing Committee on Recreation and the Arts Inquiry into the Performance of Australian Film* ['The Moving Pictures Enquiry'] (Sydney: Australian Film Commission, 1991).

Australian Film Commission, *Low Means Low: The Collected Papers from the Low Budget Features Seminar* (Woolloomooloo: Australian Film Institute Publications, 1996).

Chris Berry, *A Bit on the Side: East – West Topographies of Desire* (Sydney: EM Press, 1994).

Al Clark, *The Lavender Bus: How A Hit Movie Was Made and Sold* (Sydney: Currency Press, 1999).

Felcity Collins, *The Films of Gillian Armstrong* (St Kilda: Australian Teachers of Media, 1999).

Eva Cox and Sharon Laura, *What Do I Wear for a Hurricane? Women in the Film,*

Television and Radio Industry (North Sydney: Australian Film Commission, 1992).

Rebecca Coyle (ed.), *Screen Scores: Studies in Contemporary Australian Film Music* (Sydney: Australian Film, Television and Radio School, 1998).

Stuart Cunningham, *Framing Culture: Criticism and Policy in Australia* (North Sydney, NSW: Allen & Unwin, 1992).

Stuart Cunningham and Graeme Turner (eds.), *The Media in Australia: Industries, Texts, Audiences* (Sydney: Allen & Unwin, 1993).

Rosemary Curtis and Cathy Gray, *Get The Picture: Essential Data on Australian Film, Television and the New Media* [fourth edition] (Sydney: Australian Film Commission, 1996).

Jonathan Dawson and Bruce Molloy (eds.), *Queensland Images in Film and Television* (University of Queensland Press: Brisbane, 1990).

John Frow and Meaghan Morris (eds.), *Australian Cultural Studies: A Reader* (St. Leonards, NSW: Allen & Unwin, 1993).

Ross Harley (ed.), *New Media Technologies* (Sydney: Australian Film, Television and Radio School, Australian Film Commission, 1993).

Roslynn Haynes, *Seeking The Centre: The Australian Desert in Literature, Art and Film* (Cambridge: Cambridge University Press, 1998).

Andrew Jakubowicz *et al.*, *Racism, Ethnicity and the Media* (St Leonards, NSW: Allen & Unwin, 1994).

Karen Jennings, *Sites of Difference: Cinematic Representation of Aboriginality and Gender* (Melbourne: Australian Film Institute, 1993).

Ross Jones, *Cut! Protection of Australia's Film and Television Industries* (NSW: The Centre for Independent Studies, 1991).

Franz Kuna and Graeme Turner, *Studying Australian Culture: An Introductory Reader* (Hamburg: Verlag Dr. Kovac, 1994).

Marcia Langton, *'Well I Heard It On the Radio and I Saw It on The Television': An Essay For The Australian Film Commission on the Politics and Aesthetics of Film-making By and About Aboriginal People and Things*, (Sydney: Australian Film Commission, 1993).

Adrian Martin, *Phantasms: The Dreams and Desires at the Heart of Our Popular Cinema* (Melbourne: McPhee Gribble, 1994).

Mark McAuliffe, *Mad Max in Search of the Goddess: Australian Masculinity in Crisis* (Melbourne: La Trobe University, 1995).

Brian McFarlane and Geoff Mayer, *New Australian Cinema: Sources and Parallels in American and British Films* (Victoria: Cambridge University Press, 1992).

Hugh McKay, *Reinventing Australia: The Mind and Mood of Australia in 1990* (Sydney: Angus & Robertson, 1993).

Toby Miller, *The Well-Tempered Self: Citizenship, Culture and the Postmodern Subject* (Baltimore and London: The John Hopkins University Press, 1993).

Simon Molloy and Barry Burgan, *The Economics of Film and Television in Australia* (Sydney: Australian Film Commission, 1993).

Albert Moran (ed.), *Film Policy: An Australian Reader* (Brisbane: Griffith University, 1994).

Rachel Moss, *Mapping Spaces: Feminism, Identification and Cinema* (Adelaide: University of South Australia, 1994).

Stephen Muecke, *Textual Spaces: Aboriginality and Cultural Studies* (Sydney: University of New South Wales Press, 1992).

Scott Murray (ed.), *Australian Cinema* (Sydney: Allen & Unwin, 1994).

Scott Murray (ed.), *Australian Film 1978–1992: A Survey of Theatrical Features* (Melbourne: Oxford University Press/Australian Film Commission/Cinema Papers, 1993).

Hamid Naficy and Teshome H. Gabriel (eds.), *Otherness and the Media: The Ethnography of the Imagined and the Imaged* (Langhorne, Penn: Harwood Academic Publishers, 1993).

Gael Newton and Tracey Moffatt, *Tracey Moffatt: Fever Pitch* (Armidale, NSW: Piper Press, 1995).

Tom O'Reagan, *Australian National Cinema* (London: Routledge, 1996).

Neil Rattigan, *Images of Australia* (Dallas: SMU Press, 1991).

Mary Anne Reid, *Long Shots to Favourites: Australian Cinema Successes in the 90s* (Sydney: Australian Film Commission, 1993).

Jocelyn Robson and Beverley Zalcock, *Girls' Own Stories: Australian and New Zealand Women's Films* (London: Scarlet Press, 1997).

James Sabine (ed.), *A Century of Australian Cinema* (Port Melbourne, Victoria: William Heinemann Australia, Mandarin Australia, 1995).

David Stratton, *The Advocado Plantation: Boom and Bust in the Australian Film Industry* (Sydney: Pan Macmillan, 1990).

Graeme Turner, *Making It National: Nationalism and Australian Popular Culture* (St. Leonards, NSW: Allen & Unwin, 1994).

Graeme Turner (ed.), *Nation, Culture, Text: Australian Culture and Media Studies* (London: Routledge, 1993).

Graeme Turner, *National Fictions: Literature, Film and the Construction of Australian Narrative* [second edition] (St. Leonards, Allen & Unwin, 1993).

J.C. Wisdom-Hill, *The Impact of New Media Technology on Women in Film, TV, Video and Related Media Industries* (Adelaide: Women in Film & Television, 1995).

b) Articles and Book Chapters

Chris Barry, 'Heterogeneity as Identity', *Metro*, No.91 (Spring 1992), pp.48–51.

Helen Barlow, 'The Australian Film Finance Corporation', *Cinema Papers*, No.84 (Aug. 1991), pp.34–39.

Chris Berry, 'Not Necessarily the Sum of Us: Australian Not-So-Queer Cinema', *Metro*, No.101 (Spring 1995), pp.12–16.

Katherine Biber, '"Turned Out Real Nice After All", Death and Masculinity in Australian Cinema', in Katherine Biber, Tom Sear and Dave Trudinger (eds.), *Playing The Man: New Approaches To Masculinity* (Annandale, NSW: Pluto Press, 1999), pp.27–38.

Alison Butler, 'New Film Histories and the Politics of Location', *Screen*, Vol.33, No.4 (Winter 1992), pp.413–26.

Ashley Carruthers, 'Substantial Ways of Reading Cultural Difference in the Mainstream Australian Media', *Media Information Australia*, No.77 (Aug. 1995), pp.86–93.

Siew Keng Chau, 'A Half-Opened Door: Australian Perspectives on Asia', *Cinemaya* (Autumn–Winter 1992), pp.17–18.

Ian Craven, 'Cinema, Postcolonialism and Australian Suburbia', *Australian Studies*, No.9 (Nov. 1995), pp.45–69.

Freda Frieberg, 'Lost in Oz? Jews in The Australian Cinema', *Continuum*, Vol.8, No.2 (1994), pp.196–205.

Serge Grunberg, 'Australia, from the Desert to Hollywood', *Metro*, No.100 (Summer 1994), pp.27–31.

Sneja Gunew, 'Arts for a Multicultural Australia: Redefining the Culture' in S. Gunew and F. Rizvi (eds.), *Culture, Difference and the Arts* (St Leonards: Allen & Unwin, 1994), pp.1–12.

Robert Horton, 'Dancing The Light Down Under', *Film Comment*, Vol.29, No.1 (Jan.–Feb. 1993), pp.6–7.

Mary Kalantzis, 'Ethnicity Meets Gender Meets Class in Australia', in S. Watson (ed.), *Playing the State* (Sydney: Allen & Unwin, 1990), pp.39–59.

Harlan Kennedy, 'New Wizards of Oz', *Film Comment*, Vol.25, No.5 (Oct. 1989), pp.18–26.

Carol Laseur, 'beDevil: Colonial Images, Aboriginal Memories', *Span*, Vol.37 (Dec. 1993), pp.76–88.

Andrew Lattas, 'Aborigines and Contemporary Australian Nationalism: Primordiality and The Cultural Politics of Otherness', in Julie Marcus (ed.), *Writing Australian Culture, Social Analysis*, Vol.27 (1990), pp.50–69.

Rose Lucas, 'Round the Block: Back to the Suburb in *Return Home*', in Sarah Ferber *et al.* (eds.), *Beasts of Suburbia: Reinterpreting Culture in Australian Suburbs* (Melbourne: Melbourne University Press, 1994), pp.111–26.

Catharine Lumby, 'Music and Camp: Popular Music Performance in *Priscilla* and *Muriel's Wedding*', in Rebecca Coyle (ed.), *Screen Scores: Studies in Contemporary Australian Film Music* (Sydney: Australian Film, Television and Radio School, 1998).

Sue Maslin, 'A Boy's Own Story', *Metro*, No.91 (Spring 1992), pp.30–33.

Adrian Martin, 'Ghosts … of a National Cinema', *Cinema Papers* (April 1994), pp.14–15.

Adrian Martin, 'More than Muriel', *Sight and Sound*, Vol.5, No.6 (June 1995), pp.30–32.

Toby Miller, 'Screening Cultural Studies', *Continuum*, Vol.7, No.2 (1994), pp.11–45.

John Morris, 'The Australian Film Finance Corporation: A Reply', *Cinema Papers*, No.85 (Nov. 1991), pp.28–31.

Stephen Muecke, 'Narrative and Intervention in Aboriginal Film-making and Policy', *Continuum*, Vol.8, No.2 (1994), pp.248–58.

Tony Safford, 'Two or Three Things I Know About Australian Cinema', *Media Information Australia*, No.76 (May 1995), pp.27–9.

William Safran, 'Diasporas in Modern Society: Myths of Homeland and Return', *Diaspora*, Vol.1, No.1 (1991), pp.83–99.

John Slavin, 'The Films of Jane Campion', *Metro*, No.95 (Spring 1993), pp.28–30.

Jon Stratton and Ien Ang, 'Multicultural Imagined Communities: Cultural Difference and National Identity in Australia and the USA', *Continuum,* Vol.8, No.2 (1994), pp.124–58.

Jon Stratton, 'National Identity, Film and the Narrativisation of Multiculturalism and "Asians"', in *Race Daze: Australia in Identity Crisis* (Sydney: Pluto Press, 1998), pp.136–68.

Graeme Turner, 'The End of the National Project? Australian Cinema in the 1990s', in Wimal Dissanayake (ed.) *Questions of Nationhood and History in Asian Cinema* (Bloomington: Indiana University Press, 1994) pp.202–16.

Graeme Turner, 'Whatever Happened to National Identity?', *Metro,* No.100 (Summer 1994), pp.32–35.

Meret Valtweis, 'Success Is In The Air: *Strictly Ballroom*'s Soundtrack', *Perfect Beat: The Journal of Research Into Contemporary Music and Popular Culture,* Vol.1, No.3 (July 1993), pp.38–49.

Notes on Contributors

Tara Brabazon is a lecturer in the School of Media, Communication and Culture at Murdoch University. She has published numerous articles in the areas of sport, cultural historiography, popular music, film and television studies and fashion. She is currently writing a book entitled *Tracking the Jack: Rediscovering Britain in the Antipodes.*

Philip Butterss teaches in the English Department at the University of Adelaide. He is co-editor (with Elizabeth Webby) of *The Penguin Book of Australian Ballads* (Penguin, 1993), and editor of *Southwords: Essays on South Australian Writing* (Wakefield Press, 1995). He is currently working on a study of masculinity in contemporary Australian cinema.

David Callahan teaches at the University of Aveiro, Portugal, and is a member of the Executive Committee of the European Australian Studies Association. He has published articles on Australian subjects in several journals, most recently on Janette Turner Hospital in *Ariel*. He is currently writing a book on post-national literature and film.

Ian Craven teaches Film and Television Studies at the University of Glasgow, and is an editor of *Australian Studies*. He has contributed articles on Australian topics to many journals, and edited *Australian Popular Culture* (Cambridge University Press, 1994). He is currently preparing a study of the South Australian Film Corporation.

Stephen Crofts is Director of the Centre for Film, Television and Media Studies at the University of Auckland. His publications include *Identification, Gender and Genre: The Case of Shame* (Australian Film Institute, 1993) and (with Kate Beoehringer and Philip Bell), *Programmed Politics: A Study of Australian Television* (Sable, 1983). His newly completed study of Australian cinema will be published shortly by Oxford University Press.

Kay Ferres is Senior Lecturer in the School of Humanities at Griffith University, Brisbane. She is the editor of *A Time To Write: Australian Women Writers 1890–1930* (Penguin, 1993), and is currently completing *Curious Pleasures*, a book about gender and representation co-authored with Jane Crisp and Gillian Swanson (to be published by Routledge). *An Articulate Country: Re-inventing Australian Citizenship*, co-authored with Denise Meredyth, will be published by the University of Queensland Press later this year.

Liz Ferrier is based in the English Department at the University of Queensland. She is the author of numerous articles on Australian Literature, spatial theory and media studies, and is currently editing a collection of essays concerned with relationships between sexuality and space. She is currently a section editor (Arts) for the *Routledge International Encyclopaedia of Women's Studies*, to be published early in the new millennium.

Lisa French teaches Media Arts at Deakin University, Victoria. Her particular research interests include Australian film and feminist filmmaking. She has a background in cultural administration, and has been Director of the ATOM Awards to Short Educational Films and Television (1988–90), and Director of the St Kilda Film Festival (1991–93). She is currently a board member of The Australian Film Institute (AFI), and The Melbourne International Film Festival (MIFF), and is also the Managing Editor of *Practice: A Journal of Visual, Performing and Media Arts*.

Ben Goldsmith recently completed his doctoral thesis at the University of Queensland. His research involved a comparative analysis of the industrial, institutional and critical determinants of literary production in Australia in the 1930s, and of film production in the 1970s. He is a Queensland correspondent for the journal *Overland*, producing a regular column on film, an editorial assistant on the *Journal of Australian Studies*, and assistant editor of the *Australian Studies Bulletin*. He is currently working as a research assistant at the Australian Key Centre for Cultural and Media Policy at Griffith University.

Leah McGirr recently gained her MLitt in Cultural Studies from Central Queensland University, Queensland.

Alan McKee is based in the Department of Media Studies at Edith Cowan University, Perth. He has contributed numerous articles to academic journals both in the UK and Australia, and is an editor of *Continuum*. He is currently Secretary of the Cultural Studies Association of Australia.

Emily Rustin is a postgraduate student in the John Logie Baird Centre at the University of Glasgow, Scotland.

Samantha Searle recently completed her MA at the University of Queensland, and is reviews editor of *Australian Studies*. She has contributed articles to journals both in Europe and Australia.

Nigel Spence has edited *A Northward Flitting: The Colonial Travels of the Hon. Albert Norton* (Centre for Australian Language and Literature Studies, 1998), and co-edited (with Leonie Rutherford and Megan Roughley) *The Collected Poetry of Louisa Lawson* (Centre for Australian Language and Literature Studies, 1996). His current research interests are in the field of Children's Literature and Australian Cultural and Literary History.

Index

Books of Related Interest

Business Institutions and Behaviour in Australia

David Merrett, *University of Melbourne*

This volume breaks new ground in the historical study of Australian business institutions and practices. It places the rise of big business in Australia in a comparative context through a study of its 100 largest firms in the first six and a half decades of the twentieth century. Unlike many of the wealthy economies of the northern hemisphere, Australia's lists of the 100 largest firms were dominated up to World War II by those from the resource and service industries. The high levels of foreign direct investment in the resources and manufacturing industries is also highlighted. Other chapters employ modern theories of the firm to explore business behaviour in more depth than has been the case in previous writings in Australian business history. This collection presents important new research findings and signals new directions for future research.

168 pages 2000
0 7146 4994 5 cloth
0 7146 8055 9 paper
A special issue of the journal Business History

Sport in Australasian Society
Past and Present

J A Mangan, *University of Strathclyde* and
John Nauright, *Charles Sturt University* (Eds)

This volume examines the emergence of sporting cultures in two of the world's most prolific nations based on per capita international performance. This is the first book to discuss the historical development of sport in both Australia and New Zealand. These two countries both have a long history of involvement in international sport through their history as members of the British Empire and Commonwealth and the Olympic movement. Australia and New Zealand inherited the games-playing traditions of the English public schools but quickly developed their own distinct sporting cultures. In this collection leading and emerging scholars explore the establishment of the games ethic in Australasian private schools and the emergence of Australasian physical cultures based in schools, on sports fields, in the stands and at the beach.

376 pages illus
0 7146 5060 9 cloth
0 7146 8112 1 paper
Sport in the Global Society No 18

FRANK CASS PUBLISHERS
Newbury House, 900 Eastern Avenue, Ilford, Essex, IG2 7HH
Tel: +44 (0)20 8599 8866 Fax: +44 (0)20 8599 0984 E-mail: info@frankcass.com
NORTH AMERICA
5824 NE Hassalo Street, Portland, OR 97213 3644, USA
Tel: 800 944 6190 Fax: 503 280 8832 E-mail: cass@isbs.com
Website: www.frankcass.com

Fairbridge: Empire and Child Migration

Geoffrey Sherington, *University of Sydney* and
Chris Jeffery, *Researcher for the State Archives and The Freemantle Arts Centre Press*

In the half-century after 1913 approximately 5,000 children were sent from Britain to Australia, Canada and Rhodesia under the auspices of the Child Emigration Society, established by the South African-born Kingsley Fairbridge in 1909. The Fairbridge Society's 'child emigration' scheme became the best known and most celebrated of the twentieth-century juvenile migration schemes from Britain to the Imperial Dominions.

This study investigates the motives for the establishment of the Fairbridge child migration scheme, examines its history in Australia and Canada, and outlines the experiences of many of the former child migrants. The book is based upon extensive research in the PRO and government archives in Australia and Canada as well as archives of the Fairbridge Society in England, Western Australia and New South Wales, plus surviving records of the Society in British Columbia and on interviews with former Fairbridge children. This detailed and scholarly examination places such a significant scheme as Fairbridge's clearly in its historical context. Oral history, interviews and photographs complement the documentary research.

304 pages 28 photographs 1998
0 7130 0206 9 cloth
0 7130 4036 X paper
Woburn Press

The Australian Security Intelligence Organization
An Unofficial History

Frank Cain, *University of New South Wales*

304 pages illus 1994
0 7146 3477 8 cloth
0 7146 4124 3 paper
Studies in Intelligence Series

FRANK CASS PUBLISHERS
Newbury House, 900 Eastern Avenue, Ilford, Essex, IG2 7HH
Tel: +44 (0)20 8599 8866 Fax: +44 (0)20 8599 0984 E-mail: info@frankcass.com
NORTH AMERICA
5824 NE Hassalo Street, Portland, OR 97213 3644, USA
Tel: 800 944 6190 Fax: 503 280 8832 E-mail: cass@isbs.com
Website: www.frankcass.com